NORTH TO NORWAY

Europe, South to North, by Motorbike

NORTH TO NORWAY

Europe, South to North, by Motorbike

Stephen Oliver

TREGARTH
—— PRESS ——

NORTH TO NORWAY

A Tregarth Press book
First published in Great Britain in 2025

Tregarth Press
Abermaw, Great Britain

Cover design by Nicola Bartholomew
ISBN: 978-1-916843-01-1

For Mum, Brenda Oliver, from whom I learned to love languages

Travel makes one modest. You see what a tiny place
you occupy in the world.

Gustave Flaubert

CONTENTS

Part One
TO TARIFA

If I wanted to go to there I wouldn't
start from here

Map data © 2024 Google Inst Geog Nacional

1

Across the Bay of Biscay

Portsmouth to Santander

A knot of nervous excitement tightened in my stomach as I drew up to the queue that had formed on the other side of the check-in at Portsmouth ferry terminal, ready to hand over my passport to the pretty ticket officer. She went through my paperwork, studied my passport, handed over the ticket for my cabin and a sticker for the bike, and—with a winning smile—waved me on.

'Have a great time in Spain. Ride safely now.'

I fumbled with my gloves and, having only managed to stuff my damp palm into one mitt, ended up riding off with the other dangling from my mouth like a retriever with a dead bird. I joined the long line of bikes on the quayside where the rumble of modified exhausts filled the air, competing with the cackle of seagulls lining the fence. The queue snaked eventually to the security sheds ("No photography or mobile phones") where intimidating border officers were quizzing everyone.

'Have you got any guns, knives or other offensive weapons on your person or on the bike?' asked a tall, swarthy man whose face seemed incapable of cracking a smile.

'No,' I answered truthfully. But I thought for a moment and realised I had a Swiss army penknife buried deep in my toolkit. He'd already lost interest and waved me on, so I stayed stumm.

I wondered how the campervanners lining up behind us would deal with this question. What clandestine contraband lurked within their homes-on-wheels? Perhaps they'd have their cutlery confiscated.

On the other side of security I found myself in the centre of a wasps' nest of Vespas. Festooned with stickers and luggage strapped onto every panel of bodywork, the little scooters resembled overgrown insects buzzing with activity. GoPro cameras sprouted from handlebars like curious antennae, ready to capture every twist and turn of their journey. These riders, several heading two-up for a week-long jaunt, seemed unfazed by the long haul ahead. I admired their pluck, and wondered how their nimble little machines would fare compared to the power and comfort of my Honda motorbike.

They had a long way to go, heading to Guimarães in Portugal for the European Vespa Days event where 6,800 of the little wasps from thirty different countries were expected to gather. I talked to one of the *Vespisti* who had come down that day from Yorkshire.

'I used to have one of these,' I said, pointing to his duck-egg blue scooter. 'I bought it off a friend who'd had a stroke and couldn't ride anymore. He could only make right-hand turns, as his balance went if he tried to go the other way.'

'That'd be a problem aw reet,' he replied.

'It had sat unused in his garage for years. Each fuel line was gummed up and it stuttered at anything more than forty miles an hour,' I added.

'Aye, they like to be used... I do thousands of miles a year on mine,' he said enthusiastically.

The Vespa had been my way back into riding after a long break. I'd always felt vulnerable perched on top of its bouncy seat, legs gripping thin air. The fact that it would only go faster than forty downhill with a tailwind made it an even more exposed ride. I couldn't begin to imagine tackling the distances these Vespa riders were doing, especially two-up and laden with kit for a week.

I recalled the day I turned up at Derbyshire Police HQ in Ripley to start my BikeSafe course. The copper on the barrier came out from his portakabin, clipboard in hand.

'You must be Mr Oliver. Welcome.'

As he'd not seen my number plate I was puzzled as to how he knew who I was.

'Easy,' he said. 'You're the only one on a scooter.'

He snickered to himself, clearly anticipating the sarcastic fun the other riders on their Harleys, Fireblades and Ninjas were going to have with me.

On board the recently launched ship *Galicia* I shackled down the Honda. There was the usual deck cacophony of clanging metal, frenetic unpacking of panniers, securing of bikes to the car deck floor, inaudible deck announcements and the thunderous roar of lorry engines echoing through the huge space, mixed in with the heady cocktail of oil and exhaust fumes. My gloved palms were clammy; this wasn't the place to make a mistake. There'd be plenty of people around to help pick up the bike if I dropped it on a patch of oil, but oh the shame of it. The deck was well lit and for once on a ferry there was room to move around. Usually it's a tight squeeze between bikes, helmet in one hand and luggage in the other, banging into sticky-out bits of machinery and people. The Brittany Ferries *gilets jaunes* were helpful. I specially wanted to protect the bike's saddle during the long and sometimes choppy crossing of the Bay of Biscay.

'*Il y a un coussin pour votre selle dans le coin.*'

I grabbed a deep squishy foam rubber mat from a pile in the corner and lashed down the Honda under it.

I shoved the bike one more time. It held fast. Satisfied, I made my way with the jostling crowd to a snug cabin, my home for the next day at sea.

I'd been dreaming about this trip for months. My winter had been spent hunched over maps and guidebooks, reading about places to visit and delving into the history and culture of where I might perhaps find myself once the warmer days came.

Tempting though it was to set off with a fixed plan, especially having devoted those hours to research, I wanted to be more creative this year, to cast aside rigid schedules, embrace the flow and go where the whim took me. Those pandemic months of not being able to travel anywhere much further than the bottom of the garden had awakened a deeper need within me, a wanderlust which ordinary journeying wouldn't satisfy. I was freed from the shackles of work and I wanted new experiences. If I trusted in serendipity, maybe more unexpected exploits might happen?

My resolve to have no set plan was, of course, partly theoretical. I'd not ended up on the ship on this day and route by accident. It didn't book itself, nor had the Mallorca-bound ferry I had arranged for later in the month, once I'd made it to Tarifa. Still, with four sea crossings bookending my Iberian travels to the Balearics this year, the rest was up to me. I decided to enlist the help of strangers to decide my routes. Each evening, wherever I ended up, I'd put several different place-names on pieces of paper, a daily set of alternative waypoints, and ask someone else to make the choice for me.

A few rules, though. I like a rule or two.

Firstly, each route would be no more than roughly six or seven hours in the saddle—a decent day's riding. It's always tempting to press on but if I'd wanted to get there quickly, I'd have flown with my wife Judith from East Midlands Airport. This would be a trip to relish. Besides, long rides in the heat day after day are taxing. I've learned that a couple of hundred miles a day is ample.

Secondly, I wanted to explore new places, so I'd avoid locations I already knew.

Thirdly, if the map showed a green box ("worth visiting") around a town or city it qualified for automatic inclusion.

Lastly, an inviolable rule, I had to visit Tarifa, the most southerly point of mainland Europe from where I would begin my journey north and explore the limits of the continent. It's the longest possible journey in a single direction in Europe, and I wanted to fully experience the contrasts between the hot semi-desert Spanish south and the frozen tundra inside the Arctic Circle at North Cape, Norway.

Ideally, I'd have started my ride from Spain, and maybe taken the short hop over the Med from Mallorca before turning north at Tarifa. I keep the bike in England, though, so I had to go south before turning round. Arse about face, I know.

The search engine claimed that the most direct Tarifa–Nordkapp route was 5,534 kilometres. In reality it's longer. No one in their right mind, other than a hardcore long-distance rider, would want to do it in the two days eleven hours (tolls) or two days nineteen hours (no tolls) that the mapping indicates.

The year before, returning to Portsmouth from Spain in the early evening, I'd been talking to a biker from Glasgow as we waited to disembark. I assumed he was overnighting somewhere on his way up to Scotland.

'Ach, I'll not bother stopping; I want to see how long I can keep going before I fall asleep on the handlebars.'

I wasn't entirely sure if he was joking.

I like to challenge myself and it seemed to me that a long-distance ride was a great way to ease myself into a retirement that didn't involve pipe and slippers. Some people do these long journeys in a single intense stretch, some spin them out over weeks or months. I was going to do it in relaxed fashion over the course of two years. Why rush a good thing?

Once I'd thrown my kit into my cabin, changed out of the hot and heavy biker gear and freshened up, it was out to the bar with a pile of maps, a guidebook, pen and paper. (A tip for you if you're about to take the ferry trip to Spain: the Commodore C-Club Lounge is a pleasant place to while away the long hours of the crossing. The drinks are on tap and there's a neverending buffet.)

There was a gentle murmur of conversation as I walked into the lounge which was tastefully decorated with reproduction paintings, including a Velázquez print, sculptures, and some elegant modern furniture. It hardly felt like a ferry, more like an upmarket hotel. I carefully balanced my tray of Beaujolais and Roquefort, tomatoes and crusty French bread and navigated to a spare seat that looked out over the bow. I put my rucksack with maps and guidebooks on the seat next to me. A seagull appeared to hover over the deck, kept aloft by the wind that blew up from the prow. It stayed there for minutes, grabbing a free ride far out into the English Channel, before suddenly darting off as a wave broke hard and splashed over the glass.

'Is this chair free?'

I recognised a South African accent.

I looked up to find a short, slightly rotund man in his late sixties, his gait slightly awkward, a limp making him lurch towards me.

'Norman,' he introduced himself, settling in with a groan.

'From Cape Town and, er, Gillingham.'

'I'll clear the decks for you,' I replied, removing my rucksack from the chair to give him more room.

I spread the maps out on the table and started to think of alternative routes south from Santander. I could go south towards Segovia, east towards Bilbao and the Basque Country, west into Asturias and the dairy countryside of Oviedo or head for the churches and cathedral of León. I was totting up the distances between the little marker posts, doing a mental calculation of time in the saddle.

Every option was open to me. I felt freer now, happier. In the past, I'd have known exactly where I was going. My satnav would have been programmed, accommodation booked and the bulging folder of maps, hotel bookings, places of interests and press cuttings all ready. My nervousness at letting go of a supporting itinerary had disappeared. For a moment I sat back in the chair, put the map down and closed my eyes contentedly.

'Where are you going?' asked Norman.

'Honestly? I don't know yet,' I replied. 'I'm letting fate decide.'

He raised an eyebrow from behind his thick glasses. I noticed his stubbly beard and pitted skin. He was, it turned out, a biker too. It didn't take long to find common ground, especially since he owned a blue Honda NC750 DCT, identical to one I'd sold earlier that year. *Quelle coïncidence.* He was taking his car to Spain on this occasion, touring Galicia and northern Portugal.

'Spring this year I was on the North Coast 500,' he said, rubbing his right arm.

I knew it well. I had ridden Scotland's fabled route in 2021.

'You know the Tomintoul to Cockbridge road in the Cairngorms then?'

'The one that's always the first to get cut off in snow,' I replied.

He looked pensive and nodded. 'Yeah, that's the one. Had an off there. A bad one.'

'There must have been some snow on the road. One minute I was enjoying the scenery and the next I'm waking up in an ambulance.'

'Concussion, broken shoulder, arm, hip.'

'No clue what happened. Bike ended up tangled in a wire fence, deep in the heather. They found me in a ditch; not a watery one, thank God.'

His voice hinted at genuine relief.

'How do you feel about riding now?' I asked.

'Still love it, despite everything. Well, you just do, dontcha?'

His craggy face seemed to soften as he spoke.

'I've done some tough rides in my time—the veldt, North Africa, stuff in the Outback. First real spill happened in Scotland. Ironic, eh? Had to replace the big BMW, that's why I got my automatic bike. Can't squeeze a clutch lever properly now. Can't hunch over the bars for long stretches either. Makes everything creak.'

He groaned, a dry sound that hinted at the battles his body had waged.

'But you'll get back to touring, I guess?'

'Certainly hope so. Right now, Steve, I envy you more than words can say. I can hardly wait to be back on a ferry with my bike again. Like you.'

A warm, contemplative smile flickered across his face.

'Come on then, where are you going tomorrow?' his mood visibly lifting.

'It's a toss-up between these three routes.'

I explained to him my lottery system. I scribbled Basque Country, Segovia and Oviedo on three scraps of paper, scrunched them up and popped them in my now empty wine glass. Norman thus had the dubious responsibility of choosing my first destination.

'It's a novel way to go.'

Before he made his choice he smiled then eased himself out of the chair and hobbled off to get himself another beer.

While he was at the bar, bending down to extract a cold Heineken from the all-you-can-drink fridge, I was suddenly struck with doubt. What if this random method of travelling meant I would have to miss things I wanted to see, places I should visit that I'd read about in my winter hibernation? The Guggenheim in Bilbao was on my bucket list, as was the infamous Civil War town of Guernica, movingly immortalised by Picasso. Would a direct route south make me bypass those?

I overthought things, as usual. Choosing a path meant rejecting others, but who's to say which is best? The joy of a motorcycle is going wherever, whenever. Or as the Spanish say, *El camino es siempre mejor que la posada* (The road is always better than the inn).

Norman reappeared with beer in hand and, thoughtfully, another red wine for me.

'Seeing as you're using your wine glass to decide your near future, I thought I'd bring you another. In case you want to have second thoughts. *In vino veritas* and all that.'

I handed Norman the glass with the chits in it. He made a theatrical gesture with his hands, shaking them as if to relieve tension. Two stubby fingers pulled out a slightly wine-stained piece of paper.

'You are going to...' he paused. 'Segovia! Well, good luck, bru. Stay shiny side up and enjoy it, every moment now.'

He soon buried himself in a book and left me to realise once again how lucky I was to be making this trip.

The crossing from Pompey takes twenty-four hours, and it's easy to settle into the relaxed atmosphere on board. I soon felt the effects of the wine and headed off to my bijou cabin for a doze. It was inboard (i.e. cheaper) so sans porthole, but at least I was far away from the pet deck. The ferry is a great way for second-home owners to bring their dogs to Spain for a long summer at their villas but noisy if you're unfortunate enough to be billeted close to the canine companions.

Cross-legged on my bunk I opened the map again. My fingers traced a path from Santander to Segovia—a detour from the most direct route to Tarifa, but much more direct than staying up north in the Basque region. A win, in my view. The obvious route went through Burgos, a major stop on the Camino de Santiago, and Aranda de Duero, the heart of the Ribera del Duero wine region.

Before long the ship's gentle sway and the engines' deep hum carried me off to a deep and slightly vino-fueled doze from which I later woke to find the maps randomly scattered over the floor, which seemed fittingly prophetic.

Since the ferry's passage felt steady, I took advantage of the calm seas and headed for the shower's hot blast to wake myself up. Freshly scrubbed, I donned a new black tee-shirt emblazoned with the "Honda Wanderlust" logo, advertising my motorcycling blog.

Stepping onto the deck, a stiff wind buffeted me. The white cauliflower clouds of the English Channel had vanished, replaced by an expanse of grey nimbus over the Bay of Biscay. A small group huddled near the railings, their attention fixed on a young woman in a dark blue polo shirt emblazoned with a killer whale. Natasha, a drama student as I later learned, was passionately describing ORCA's efforts in whale and dolphin conservation, a collaborative project involving the ferry company and other organisations.

'This is a prime feeding ground for cetaceans... dolphins, porpoises and whales,' she explained.

'Krill and plankton swirl up from the deep in the Bay of Biscay. It's like an all-you-can-eat buffet for these magnificent creatures.'

We scanned the white-capped waves, the choppy water making it difficult to spot anything. Natasha, armed with a hefty pair of binoculars, continued her patient vigil. While the rest of us, chilled by the wind, contemplated retreating indoors for warmth and maybe a beer, Natasha remained glued to the spot. She was dedicated to her cause.

'Hope you see something soon,' I said.

'Oh, thanks. I do, most times,' she replied, without breaking off to look at me. 'Usually when it's me and the sea and everyone else has gone.'

I held onto the railings for a last scan of the sea as a large wave buffeted the ship. Nothing to see. Natasha's binoculars were still pointing seawards as I hauled open the heavy deck door.

It was far too early to go to bed, especially after my snooze, so I headed back to the tranquility of the lounge. On my way I passed several groups of motorcyclists in the bar. Of course, they'd long taken off their leathers and the crash helmets were tucked away in cabins, but there's a manner that identifies them, a certain male confidence, a slightly road-worn appearance, maybe a little unkempt, a preponderance of facial hair and some mullets too. The branded clothing—Triumph, BMW, Royal Enfield—were the clinchers.

The boisterous laughter echoing from the bar drew my attention, their camaraderie evident even from afar. I hesitated, a familiar anxiety creeping in. Should I venture in, introduce myself, try to join their fellowship? I imagined their dismissive glances, their closed circle, my intrusion unwelcome. It was a ridiculous fear, a childish insecurity that lingered despite years of confident travel and countless encounters with strangers. Yet, there it was, the same shyness that used to grip me as a kid, the fear of being an outsider, the awkwardness of not belonging. I walked on, seeking the sanctuary of the lounge. What did it even mean to be a real biker and be accepted into the tribe? I didn't have the answer, but the question lingered, a deeper echo of that childhood unease. Next time, I resolved, I wouldn't let that fear hold me back.

In the Commodore's cosy embrace once more I settled into a corner beneath a flickering display of the ship's location and occasional orca sightings. A slightly comical pop art statuette based on the enigmatic painting *Las Meninas* by Velázquez stood guard over the now empty buffet. As I jotted notes, Australian accents filled the air. A couple took the chairs next to mine. They looked rather conservative and stern. In my imagination I placed them as captains of their golf club. They were not dressed for casual travel, as most of us were. She wore a smart white blouse and expensive looking skirt; he had brogues on and a tie. I smiled and nodded a wordless greeting to them and stuck my head back into my notes.

'Wandered far, Mr Wanderlust?' My tee-shirt was more visible than I'd thought.

I introduced myself.

Denny and Frank, from Brisbane, owned a classic Morgan. They were giving it a 'good run' to their Almeria home. The car was kept garaged with friends in London when they returned to Australia.

'I was a stockbroker in the City. We bought the house in Spain years ago and even though we've retired back to Oz, every few months we return to Europe. Mind you, Brexit means we can't spend as long in Spain as we used to.'

I nodded sympathetically.

'Do you always bring your car over?' I asked.

'No, we've a banger we keep in Almeria, but I reckoned it was time to give the old girl a good thrashing.'

Denny leant over, slapping his thigh and grinning. 'He means the Morgan.'

'We used to tour everywhere in it. It's thirty years old. We've a wicker basket on the back for luggage and some handy spares,' he laughed.

'Besides which it doesn't go too fast these days,' added Denny, 'which may be a good thing.'

'Hah!' winked Frank. 'The last time we were over I got fined by *Trafico* €125 for going no more than five kph over the limit. Our old Spanish banger has a rather muddy number plate now. Keep forgetting to clean it. You know what I mean?'

Frank and Denny exchanged knowing glances. Who'd have thought it? My golf club captains were a pair of sly old foxes. I asked which country they liked the most—apart from Spain, of course.

'Norway. Beautiful,' said Denny. 'Wonderful scenery and great roads. The people are so friendly, though they think we're American. I'd love to go back someday, but it's even more bloody expensive now.'

'Next year I've big plans for Norway,' I declared.

They hadn't ventured as far north as where I was setting my sights but wished me luck. The mention of Norway stirred something within me and I began to wish I'd started saving up earlier.

Our conversation flowed effortlessly, meandering through politics, life in Australia, and their voyages across the globe. Frank's tie loosened as the evening wore on, and that ever-open bar came in handy, lubricating our lively discussion. I felt slightly ashamed that I'd let unconscious bias creep in and rushed to (false) judgment. They were delightful, different and lively, not what I'd expected. I felt guilty for not keeping an open mind, which surely is what travel should be about. With a goodbye wave and a loud *Adios, amigo,*' they disappeared into the night, leaving me to ponder the unexpected connection we'd forged. It was a reminder that travel often surprises, challenging our assumptions and opening our eyes to the richness of human experience. If we let it.

2

Segovia–Guadalupe–Cordoba

Santander to Segovia

O nce I escaped the fume-filled confines of the car deck on the *Galicia*, I breathed a deep lungful of fresh air the instant my tyres hit the tarmac of the dockside in Santander. It was a bright, sunny Cantabrian day. My satnav told me one direction and the road signs another. Frustration mounted as I found myself going round in circles. Other better prepared motorcyclists made a more rapid departure, riders sticking out a leg in greeting as they roared off. Burgos was my waypoint en route to Segovia, leading into the mountains and away from the busy dual carriageway.

I was in no rush so I stopped at a roadside caravan for coffee and some greasy churros, a pitstop to gather my thoughts. The aluminium chair and sticky table, on which I laid out my map, were already warming in the heat of the day.

The Mirador de Cabañia promised spectacular views of the Cantabrian Mountains so off I headed.

I rode through the charming village of Alceda, its Galician-style houses with oriel windows overlooked elaborate balconies covered in flowers. I found myself on a street named Avenida Generalissimo Franco. The dictator's birthplace was in nearby Ferrol. Most places in Spain have eliminated references to Franco, but he clings on here.

As the road climbed ever higher, up to 1,000 metres above sea level, snow poles appeared and the buildings became more rugged, no longer white-washed but stone-built, with heavy rocks placed on the tiled roofs to stop the harsh winds parting them from the walls. The air turned sparklingly crisp and clear, and I brought the cumbersome Honda to a gentle halt on the perilously gravelly parking area by the mirador signboard that named the distant peaks. The view back towards the coast was dramatic, a small patch of sea glinting through a gap in the jagged hills.

I glimpsed a weathered sign: *"Piramide de los Italianos"*. A rusty wire fence, easily breached, led me across a rough field and up a mound. Spain's only pyramid loomed before me; an unsettling monument built with Francoist slave labour. Two rusty crosses were etched out of its concrete façade, decaying tributes to fallen Italian soldiers from the Spanish Civil War. Empty, eerie, the mausoleum awaited its misguided demolition under the *Ley de Memoria Democrática,* the Democratic Memory Law. I resolved to track down more Civil War sites, if only I could find them. Spain's divided history is spoken of in hushed tones, even now.

The road snaked over the 1,011-metre Escudo Pass, revealing the distant blue expanse of Embalse del Ebro, one of Spain's largest reservoirs. I descended to the water that lapped at the roadside. The lake brimmed with life, small sailing boats heeling over in the breeze. Beyond the reservoir tarmac stretched before me, becoming a pencil-thin line that shimmered into infinity. My bike was the only vehicle on this lonely, awesome stretch.

The road was cracked and patched with time and sun. I rode carefully, hugging the faded white centre line, where safety lay. Telegraph poles flashed past as the temperature gauge climbed to 29° C. Sweat trickled down my back. It was barely believable that winters here demand eight-foot snow poles, which now joined the telegraph poles along the verge.

This parched landscape, dotted with scrubby bushes and stunted trees, resembled a *dehesa*, the dry pastures of Extremadura further south. The high plains stretched towards a distant escarpment. The road still pencilled towards it but was joined by a pinprick of light in the distance that grew rapidly into four motorcycles. A flash of friendly waves and they were gone. Solitude enveloped me once more.

The end of the plain approached. The road entered a gully, beyond which was a small cliff, covered in trees. A metal roadside barrier appeared, a flashing light on the chevrons warning me of impending danger. The chequered markings lay battered and squashed flat against the rocks. There were no skid marks. Clearly some unfortunate soul had failed to make the turn. Another sharp bend came quickly after, followed by an abrupt hairpin. I was now on the *escalada* (ladder), which led down into the Ebro River canyon and on towards Burgos. I took pleasure in riding the twisties again after the long straight, wiggling on the saddle to loosen my joints and to better make the turns.

Burgos loomed on the horizon, its outskirts an uninspiring sprawl of hulking industrial estates and boxy apartment blocks that gradually gave way to affluent neighbourhoods. An odd sight ahead forced me to squeeze hard on the brakes. Dominating the middle of a roundabout was a large iguanodon the size of two double-decker buses. Artistic roundabouts were not uncommon in Spain, but this was a masterpiece. I tried to imagine the lively council meeting where this behemoth was created.

'Jorge,' I pictured a councillor booming, 'listen. Let's put a huge dinosaur in the middle of that new roundabout, it's guaranteed to stop joyriders going over it.'

Smiling at the glorious absurdity of it I pulled over and took some photographs for my dinosaur-obsessed grandson.

My way into Burgos was blocked by a posse of police cars and red and white barriers. People were everywhere, linking arms and laughing. Though a Wednesday afternoon, everyone wore costumes, some in fancy dress, some in traditional outfits. Parking, usually a breeze, became a game of musical scooters in the chaos. I wedged myself and the bike backwards between two dust-covered relics outside a bustling bar. Stifling heat pressed down from the sky, the walls, the road. I shed my helmet and slung my jacket over my shoulder.

'It is the Festival of San Pedro and San Pablo,' chirped a girl in a smart blue blazer and white trousers, a flag held proudly in her hand.

'*Muy grande y muy importante,*' she added, lest I fail to appreciate the celebration's significance.

I squeezed my way through the crowds, a near-impenetrable mass of inhabitants and visitors. This being Spain, of course, their annual fiesta was a week-long extravaganza. *Los españoles* love fiestas: religion meets history meets party town. Giant mannequins of kings, queens, knights, Sancho Panza and his donkey led by bands in traditional garb, paraded through the main square and the adjoining streets. It was a riot of noise and colour and joy. Balloons bobbed overhead, floral displays and ticker tape danced in the breeze. It was as though the whole city had been shaken up and its cork had just popped. It fizzed with excitement.

'This is our first fiesta for two years,' an attractive blonde with a red neckerchief and low-cut tee-shirt told me.

Curiously, she had a large penguin badge on her left breast, as did her gaggle of friends.

'Yes,' said another. 'The pandemic cancelled it. Now we really celebrate.'

They both jiggled their chests at me and sashayed on through the crowds, penguin badges twinkling in the sunlight. I was enjoying the atmosphere and its flirtatious participants. I found a wall to lean on and enjoyed the floorshow for a bit longer. The bars were chokka, so a cooling drink was out of the question. I weaved my way out of the crowds and back to the bike, leaving them to their well-deserved celebrations, which I suspected were about to get messy.

As I accelerated away from Burgos, leaving the festive fun behind, the landscape morphed into a string of shanty villages, their roadside buildings a desolate mix of emptiness and decay. Faded *Meubles* signs hung askew on furniture warehouses like forlorn sentinels amidst the rural emptiness. I passed an old flour mill, the painted stucco walls peeling great chunks onto the baked earth and its rotten windows gaping limply with no sign of activity or life. This was a sign of how sparsely populated Spain truly is. Its population density is a mere third that of the UK, yet its landmass is twice as large. As in Britain, young people gravitate towards the bustling cities of Madrid, Barcelona and Valencia, leaving poorer regions like Castile and León to earn their nickname *La España vacía* (Emptied Spain).

A flash of movement caught my eye, a pair of storks roosting atop two mobile phone masts, their nests both creative and pragmatic. One, seemingly unfazed by my presence, loped off gracefully into the sky, our paths converging for a moment before it glided away towards a distant field. A short while later, a dust cloud erupted on the horizon, a swirling vortex obscuring the road ahead. As I neared the maelstrom, the culprit emerged: a tiny Fiat 500 bouncing along a farm track, its wheels churning the bone-dry earth. I coughed as dust seeped inside my helmet.

This was rugged country *por excelencia*.

Where Burgos had been lively, Aranda de Duero, the heart of the region's renowned wine production, was sleepy. I took a seat under a parasol. It was early afternoon and several locals in the Bar La Goleta had nodded off in the heat. One of them slipped gently off his stool onto the floor. He was a wrinkled old man in a scruffy check shirt and filthy sandals, as though he'd recently come into town off the fields. His mates, equally rustic, glanced over to where he lay, sprawled on the tiles, and decided to leave him to doze off his vino. They returned to their ritual lunchtime dominoes. La Goleta (schooner, in English) featured much maritime memorabilia, though the nearest sea was a good morning's ride away.

Large piled plates of tooth-breaking *torreznos*, giant pork scratchings which dwarf our Black Country versions, dotted the bar. Resisting temptation, I downed a restorative coffee and *bocadillo de jamón*.

In Spanish I asked the proprietor for the Wi-Fi code.

'*Torreznos*,' he smiled, pointing to the curly golden pile of fried pigskin.

'No, I meant what's your Wi-Fi password, please?' I repeated, fearing my Spanish was worse than I thought.

'*Es esso*,' (it's that).

Should have guessed. "Scratchings" was the password. He raised a quizzical eyebrow at me and harrumphed.

With my iPhone connected, I opened the Paradors website. Run by the Spanish government, they're a collection of nearly 100 characterful hotels housed in historic buildings—castles, monasteries, even an old hospital. They showcase local cuisine, art and culture, offering an intimate way to experience the regions.

An overnight stay in the Segovia parador was my initial aim. With a click, my hopes were dashed. No room at that particular inn. Maybe my ad hoc travel philosophy was doomed to early failure? Not to be beaten, however, I tracked down a parador eleven kilometres away: *Real Sitio de San Ildefonso*. Tucked away high in the Sierra de Guadarrama, it was in an even more intriguing location and part of the Royal Palace of La Granja, built by Carlos III. A room was mine with the press of a button. How wonderful, this tech.

Aranda was full of bodegas and surrounded by vineyards. Enticing though the prospect of a little wine tasting was, I had a sacrosanct rule on the bike: no ride and imbibe. No space presented itself in which to stuff a bottle, not even a tiny one, so while Señor still snoozed on the floor and the dominoes clacked, I headed out of town before I could be tempted.

I had moved but a short way, crossing a bridge over the river, when a scrubby piece of brownfield caught my eye. Upon it was a semi-derelict long, low building with arched windows set high up on the walls which bore the painted words "*Campo de prisoneros del Franquismo* 1937–1939". This needed no translation. It was a concentration camp, one of several hundred erected during the Civil War. In 2013 four mass graves with 129 bodies were uncovered, apparently executed by Nationalist forces. Some estimates hold that there are still over 120,000 victims of the war lying in ditches and other unmarked graves. Franco's forgotten victims.

I walked pensively over to the building. No museum or even an information board. Nothing, *nada*. As with the *piramide* earlier in the day, it is still rare in Spain to find official recognition of such historical places. The 1977 *Pacto del Olvido* (Pact of Forgetting) helped restore democracy to Spain after Franco's death. But it also meant that wounds still fester, unresolved injustices haunting successive generations, denying victims their dignity. It perplexed me why so little effort had been made to preserve the past and to contextualise the Civil War for future generations.

I carefully picked my way over the broken bricks and glass that littered the concrete floor of the camp, strewn with empty bottles, litter and used syringes. It was at least light inside. Had it been dark I would have gone no further. The malevolent air that seemed to seep out of its very bricks reminded me of *Valle de Cuelgamuros* (The Valley of the Fallen) outside Madrid that I had visited some years before. In this huge stone basilica and memorial Franco lay for forty-four years. Not only was it one of the most austere and sinister places I'd ever seen but it was catnip to a large group of ageing Francoists. They had waved their black and red Falangist flags in my face and chanted '*Cara al Sol*' (Facing the Sun), the former unofficial anthem of nationalist Spain, as I had ridden my bike through its portal. It was one of the creepiest experiences I've ever had in Spain, ghosts of a dictator still echoing today.

I gunned the bike away from Aranda as soon as the speed limits allowed, happy to leave it behind. After the joy of Burgos, it seemed an oddly unsettling place.

At Cuellar I diverted off the main road to Segovia onto a narrow B-road that wound its way through wide stands of pine trees on one side of the road and vines on the other. I came across Peñafiel, a small town dominated by a Gothic castle exactly as you would imagine a child would draw—crenellated golden stone walls and round towers from which princesses might declare their love to princes wielding swords on the battlements below. I wanted a closer look and rode the winding road to the main gate. Built in the fifteenth century, Peñafiel castle oddly contrived to look almost modern. It was a far cry from the crumbling castles of ancient Britain.

I walked up to the ticket office. The woman on duty was less than friendly.

'*Non*. You cannot visit on your own. Only in a group, with guide. The wine tasting is included.'

Since the next group tour was an hour later I carried on to the refreshingly different Coca Castle, a short detour away on a deserted road. It was the kind of quiet and arrow-straight stretch where one might be tempted to see what the bike was capable of, speed-wise. My courage ran out well before the speedometer hit the stops, but still forty miles passed remarkably quickly.

Photos couldn't capture the sheer audacity of Coca Castle. It is a ruddy brown fortress plunged into a dry moat—a Lego model built for giants, massive yet somehow graceful. No one was around, so I eased the bike past the temporary bullring set up in the grounds and parked by the main entrance. Its Mudéjar brickwork and Moorish design with Gothic architecture offered an unusual backdrop for a selfie.

The towers of the fortress grew outwards as they soared higher. It could have been an enormous cake mould turned upside down. It was quite unlike anything I'd seen before or since. Far off the tourist track, it had an ad hoc approach to entry. A sign on the gate said there might be a guided tour or then again, possibly not. Entry was a few euros, if you'd like to stump up—no problem if not. The open rooms were empty, apart from the armoury, which was rammed with weaponry, yet devoid of attendants.

By now I was parched as the heat of the day was at its fiercest. My throat was sandpaper, raw from dust and the day's heat. I could barely croak out my drink order at the charmingly basic Bar El Rinconcito, its red plastic chairs and tables arranged under a pair of stout trees overhanging its front terrace.

I fancied a cold, soft beverage, so I asked the dumpy barmaid, whose head barely reached above the bar top for a Coca-Cola. It seemed appropriate, given the eponymous castle.

'Aquí vendemos solo Pepsi,' came the answer from somewhere below decks.

They only sold the competition. Chilled condensation beading the glass, the treasonous brown elixir slipped down deliciously.

Although the road to Real Sitio de San Ildefonso was temptingly straight and fast, I was taking it easy now and pootled along under a cloudless sky, gathering fewer insects to join the mass grave that had already formed in squished layers over the windshield and my visor.

It had been a long day. I was relieved to pull up in front of the splendid parador, a palatial building built from light grey stone and with a butterfly-yellow rendered façade.

I found a handy parking spot right by the main entrance and went through the laborious ritual of locking it securely with a monster chain through the rear wheel and secured a sturdy disc lock on the front brakes. I hauled my heavy panniers off and, struggling to lug my clobber, staggered into the mercifully air-conditioned lobby. There appeared to be no reception, which was odd. I dropped the gear to the floor and went in search of help. Eventually, a dark-suited girl with a corporate name badge appeared from a side door. She saw my dumped pile of gear, frowned and shook her head.

'This is not the hotel. This is the *Centro de Conferencias*. The parador is round the corner and down the street. You can park there, not here. It's about 500 metres away,' she added. Her expression betrayed not the slightest sympathy for my plight.

I snarkily suggested to her that a large sign might be a useful addition to the outside of the building. There was one, she replied, I'd just walked past it.

Chastised, I reversed everything I'd done only minutes before, cursing under my breath, and went once more in search of my bed for the night, resolving next time to pay signage more attention.

The accommodation didn't disappoint; it was an ancient and magnificent building, much of it made with bricks that looked like leftovers from Coca Castle. I wandered out to have a look at the Royal Palace of La Granja, a short walk away. It was late in the evening so I could only stroll through the beautiful gardens, the last light turning the palace façade a warm gold. Tomorrow, I'd be gone before they unlocked the gates.

For tonight, though, I needed to eat. I'd covered 436 kilometres, a good start. I had left Cantabria and the coast. I was heading into the rural heart of Spain, growing in confidence, enjoying the ride and my own company. I went in search of food and that long-awaited bottle of vino tinto.

Segovia to Guadalupe

They say an army marches on its stomach. Bikers bike on it, too. I'd slept like a dormouse (*dormí como un lirón*, as they say, quaintly, in Spanish). I felt refreshed. And still ravenous. I wolfed down the hotel's legendary *desayuno*: fruit and yogurt, pastries and delicious *ponche Segoviano,* a sponge cake with cream filling covered with marzipan. My trouser belt would be even tighter than usual if I also explored the hotel's hot food offerings.

I normally liked to start a ride before the sun gets up too much. Today, though, it was a relaxed start. I was going to meet a fellow biker in Ávila, south of Segovia, for lunch. I didn't know Noel personally, but we both knew Neil, a great mutual friend. Neil and I had been at university together. He now lived in Paraguay, but Noel was Madrid-based, had heard of my trip and wanted to meet up.

But first, I rode to see the sensational Roman aqueduct, Segovia's most famous monument which dominates the city centre. I pulled up underneath the two-tiered aqueduct, with its 166 soaring granite arches, not a single one held together with mortar. I craned my neck to see this ancient construction. It was truly impressive, and I climbed up to get a closer look. Each step up those hundred feet was a furnace. By the time I reached the ancient water channel, sweat was streaming down my face.

There were few tourists here, and certainly no other UK registration plates to be seen. It felt a privilege to be in this part of Spain, so historic and original. In the Second World War this was neutral territory; Spain did not suffer the bombing and destruction that obliterated so many other parts of Europe.

The Honda zipped through Segovia with the freedom only a bike can offer—down narrow alleys, past the cathedral, and through a bustling market square laden with brightly coloured fruits and vegetables, olives, spices and chorizos. The cops didn't even blink as I rode on the pavement. Another fairy tale castle, the Alcázar, loomed as I escaped the city. But I was done with castles for now, and that rendezvous with Noel in Ávila awaited. Time to get cracking.

An hour's ride or so later Ávila's magnificent walls rose like something from a timeworn storybook—a Spanish Carcassonne, yet blissfully free of tourist hordes. I was happily sitting surrounded by statues in the quiet sunny square by the cathedral when through the stone wall gate strode a tall be-leathered guy, with grey hair and beard, in his sixties but looking ten years younger, carrying a black crash helmet. This had to be Noel, and he clearly realised he got the right bloke.

'Stephen, I presume. Neil has told me a lot about you,' he said, smiling broadly.

Knowing Neil's sense of humour, I wasn't sure this would have been good. Noel's English was completely fluent. He was Argentinian, from Buenos Aires, with an Austrian father and an EU passport. It didn't take long to find more common ground than our mutual mate, whom he'd known for years, ever since they were both working in banking in South America.

Over a delicious *chuletón*, a veal chop dish, served with white beans, *torreznos* and mashed potatoes, I found an easy connection with Noel. We were at the same stage in our lives, after following different career paths, but faced similar challenges. We discussed how Brexit was changing plans for people, including Neil, who wanted to live in Portugal now that he was retired. We spoke of our families, our own plans for life after retirement and, of course, motorcycling. Noel's lips broke into a wide smile.

'My aunt—bless her soul, she never married. She was quite a character. Well, she had a scooter back in Argentina when I was a kid. Let me have a go when I was, oh, about eleven. That's when it started, y'know? A spinster aunt got me hooked. I've had loads of bikes over the years. My wife and I, we tour over Europe, South America... *estupendo*.'

'Ever done a tour in Britain?' I asked.

'Not on the bike, no. It's on my—what's the phrase—bucket list.'

'Well, you'll have to come over. Scotland, Wales, Ireland, all simply brilliant riding and way cooler than this.'

The shade had vanished quicker than our fizzy waters and we were now both beginning to boil in our heavy protective trousers.

We settled the bill. It was a remarkably reasonable €50 for the two of us.

'Come on, let's take a look at this Kawasaki Ninja of yours.'

We were walking back to our bikes when I suddenly remembered my biking lottery. I explained it to Noel, who was tickled at the idea of deciding my next destination for me. We spread out the map on his saddle, his fingers jabbing at various places in turn.

'You could go to Madrid, where I'm heading. Or to Cáceres.'

'Both great places to go on the bike, but I've visited both in 2018,' I interjected.

'How about Guadalupe, perhaps?'

'Okay, Guadalupe it is, then,' I decided.

'There's a wonderful monastery and those mountain roads are great,' he added enthusiastically.

Noel rode off over the cobbles, waving as he left. It had been an enjoyable meeting. I'd made a new riding buddy, got an offer of a stay in Madrid and hatched a tentative plan to ride together in Ireland the following year.

Following lunch with Noel I took a true connoisseur's route that snaked its way through not one, but two mountain ranges. The *Sierra de Gredos* and the *Sierra de Guadalupe* unfolded in a dramatic panorama. This was a land of rich abundance—emerald forests of eucalyptus swaying in the breeze, orchards bursting with apple blossoms, and carpets of silver-green olive groves stretching towards the horizon. Even the rocks whispered stories of the Earth's ancient past. The newly created Geopark of Villuercas-Ibores-Jara bore the hallmarks of lavish funding. New information boards sponsored by a chorus of organisations were full of facts. No faded, peeling signage here.

New tarmac flowed like lava through the valleys, its siren call tempting me speedily through each bend. The engine purred contentedly as I carved through switchbacks, the cough-lozenge scent of eucalyptus filling the air. I stopped to decipher the signs about the rather lovely *acarospora oxytona* lichens that brightened the rocks like splashes of yellowy paint. The shady valley light made the scene even more atmospheric.

I needed to stretch my legs and fill the nearly empty tank. A short stop at a Repsol garage on the outskirts of the pottery town of Talavera de la Reina and the bike was full of fuel once more. The spirited riding was costly. I rode off past massive fincas or country mansions built high on little hillocks, fronted by huge cypress trees.

A good 300 head of cattle, a mooing, dusty mass rumbled slowly alongside the road's rough grassy banks, the surface lethally scattered with mud and cow shit. I braked, gently, very gently. Up into the hills again and my ride turned sinuous, putting my skills to the test, each tight bend demanding utter focus. As the afternoon sun slanted across the road, the switchbacks flickered their hypnotic chiaroscuro, light into shadow into light. It was a lot of fun.

Tiredness, after a second long day on the road, crept insidiously upon me. The small mountain village of

Guadalupe came into view, its imposing monastery sitting high on the hill next to the parador, which I later discovered was full. These magnificent buildings dwarfed the pretty houses and stone-slabbed square with its lovely old central fountain, the heart of the village's bars and restaurants. A hill-cool breeze carried the scent of woodsmoke and freshly baked bread, an enticing welcome.

I booked into the simple Hostal Alfonso XI, around the corner and down a side street off the main square. I was glad to have landed in this delightful village and I was going to make the most of it. I chucked my gear into the room and headed out to stretch my stiff legs.

The parador was another gorgeous Mudéjar building that dated back to the 14th century and was once a school and hospital that used to be part of the Royal Monastery next door. I walked in through the main gate into a cool, cloistered courtyard full of ponds and fountains, orange and lemon trees, a haven of tranquility bathed in the subtle, classy lighting of the late evening. The past whispered secrets from every corner. Whitewashed walls, elegant arches, and a roof that looked like a checkerboard fresh out of a fairytale. The place oozed opulent hospitality.

What a great place it would have been to stay, I thought to myself. I showed my parador passport (yes, there is such a thing and I had collected many stamps in it over the years). The young receptionist generously stamped my little brown book, despite my being a visitor not a guest. Points mean discounts.

'There's a room free tomorrow night,' she suggested.

I shook my head regretfully.

'I'm on a road trip and the road keeps calling.'

But I was sorely tempted. It was another choice I'd made, not to spend more than a night anywhere. Too much to see, too little time.

After exploring the monastery I strolled past the restaurants and bars in Plaza Santa Maria but there were few people or cars around. I usually eat in a different place from where I stay but my hostal was buzzing. A football match was showing on the bar TV and the noise drifted outside. I headed to a street table with my maps and ordered a beer and a big ham roll.

I was sitting watching the swifts circling the monastery roof when my phone rang. It was Phil, a skiing nut, good friend and a leading magistrate up north. We cut to the chase.

'We're thinking about booking Morzine next year,' he said. 'When are you free?'

I checked my calendar and rattled off some weeks. It felt odd to be planning for snow when the pavements could have fried an egg.

'What's that racket?' he asked.

'The football and the local birds.'

There was a perplexed pause.

'Are you abroad? Mixing with the locals again?'

'Extremadura. Middle of Spain, on my motorbike trip.'

I filled him in on the journey, relieved to speak English for a change. My self-taught Spanish was halting, as were my rusty German and French these days.

'Phil, a favour. I need you to play judge for a moment,' I asked.

'What's the trouble? Upset the cops?' He probably thought I had a speeding ticket.

'No. Not yet, anyway. Do I ride to Seville, Córdoba or Granada tomorrow?'

'No idea. Any preference?'

'Do you let your defendants choose their jails?' We laughed.

'Okay, I sentence you to Córdoba,' he declared.

Jail might have been quieter that night. The post-football revelry raged on, even after I retreated to my basic, cell-like room (at €40, what can you expect?). The din was still continuing well past midnight. I'd finally drifted off when soon afterwards wicked indigestion woke me. I tossed and turned until, by dawn, I'd had enough and decided to escape early. I needed milk, yogurt, anything soothing that the nearby mini mercado could offer.

Córdoba

I paid the *cuenta* at the Alfonso XI. Outside, the market was waking. Vans spilled forth colourful produce, chickens squawked, cheeses and chorizos glistened, ready to sweat in the coming heat. The police were already on duty. One, spotting my UK plates, approached. A fellow biker, he peppered me with friendly questions about my route and how easy I found riding on the *lado equivocado del camino* (the wrong side of the road).

Suited up, I departed at half past eight, the officer saluting me out, even lifting for me the plastic barrier that sectioned off the market square where I was parked. Classy. Let's hope all my police encounters are this pleasant, I thought, as the Honda rumbled out of town.

It was the coolest part of the day, I was alert, and what was best, my stomach had settled down. Córdoba was due south on a winding road through the rest of the Geopark, so I had to get back into the swing of it quickly, shifting my weight about on the saddle, leaning into the delicious curves, judging the exact line through the bends. With no traffic about, it was exhilarating riding, better than any car could offer, except maybe on a racetrack. The bends teased themselves out into a die-straight road, and the landscape opened up. It was a great flat area of *dehesa*, brown grass, brown rocks, and splashes of green from the thousands of scrubby holm oak trees with pigs foraging beneath them. An abandoned power station, its huge concrete blocks visible for miles, broke the distant horizon, while a faint haze softened the outlines of distant rolling hills.

I stopped for coffee in Valdecaballeros, its whitewashed houses a taste of Andalucía to come. The square was festooned with giant dreamcatchers that cast dappled shade.

'For your village fiesta?' I asked the girl serving my cortado.

'No, these make us happy year-round, so we keep them up. We like to dream in Valdecaballeros,' she smiled.

Here, life might lack the airs and graces of the big cities but seemed to be focused on simple joys. Maybe this was a lesson in life, like the one I'd learned from my friend, Chris, who'd suffered a stroke in early middle age and subsequently sold me his Vespa. He led a simpler life now. He'd recovered completely and found happiness in a minimalist life surrounded by a few treasured possessions, spending time peacefully in his garden overlooking the rolling Cotswold hills.

As I rode out of town, I passed villagers doing their daily exercises on the outdoor gym equipment, seesaws, bikes and pull-up bars cemented into the pavement. One old lady, her grin revealing a single tooth, paused her exercises to wave at me. I was warming to this friendly place.

Soon I was motoring alongside a reservoir, its shockingly low water level stood out distinctly against the rocky shore. A dark line tens of metres above the grey-blue water showed where the surface should have been. The verge was just a few feet away, and the edge fell precipitously with no barrier to stop a deadly drop.

This was one of four connected reservoirs, an inland sea, with natural beaches and places to swim, as well as providing vital water to city populations far away. *La Siberia Biosphere Reserve* is a haven for birds, from eagles to vultures, according to the viewpoint info boards. No sooner had I stepped back from reading when I saw it: a Spanish imperial eagle, gliding gently in a wide arc above, its two-metre wingspan keeping it aloft on the thermals rising from the car park. Suddenly it darted away over the water, with a lazy flap of its wings. A special moment. For a while, I watched this magnificent bird patrol the sky, then returned to my bike with a contented sigh and steered back to the tarmac. I turned, hoping someone else had seen it too, but I was alone. It saddened me not to be able to share the moment.

The scorching Extremaduran sun made La Siberia feel a world away from its Russian namesake. By midmorning it was already past thirty degrees. I weaved along the reservoir's edge, captivated by a tiny, conical volcano that formed a miniature island in the glassy expanse. New EU-funded bridges stretched across the water, monumental modern infrastructure in a deserted landscape. With no other soul in sight, I seized the opportunity for a photo of my bike parked commandingly in the middle of the road, framed by the reservoir.

The scorching sun baked the landscape in all directions. Endless solar arrays, like giant silver sunflowers, pivoted to capture the light. This was a land of thirteen-hour summer days and almost constant sun. Suddenly a barrage of impacts rattled my bike and clattered my trousers. Fearing a shredded tyre, I slowed, only to find the front of my bike a locust cemetery. It wasn't the heat that was killing the crops in the barren fields, it was these ravenous swarms.

By noon the mercury approached forty as I rolled into Cabeza del Buey, a sleepy railway town. The train from here to Madrid was a seven-hour crawl; only the long-distance high-speed rail project, slated for 2030, promised a faster connection. I'd seen the distant works near Talavera. Cabeza was unexpectedly charming, its main street lined with bars. I parked in precious shade and collapsed into the nearest café-bar. Sweat poured off me. The 4 Ases was a simple spot with heavenly air-conditioning. As tapas, tomato salad, and an icy 0% Amstel beer was brought to my table, I noticed I was the centre of curious attention. A friendly, stubbly-faced man in a green shirt approached. Behind him, his bustling family filled the bar. Sadly, his name escaped me amidst the bar chatter.

'Where are you headed?' he asked. 'Córdoba? You'll pass my town: Hinojosa del Duque. Eight chapels, a cathedral...' The man's pride in his town was clear, a reminder of Spain's deep religious roots.

We talked work.

'*Soy herrero*,' he said. '*Hago puertas de hierro forjado.*'

He was a blacksmith, making the wrought-iron gates I'd admired, is what I think he said.

'*Mi abuelo también era hervidor*,' I replied.

A quizzical smile. Maybe I'd misunderstood him. He scurried off to rejoin his hungry family, who were tucking into their tapas.

My grandfather was also a smithy (*herrero*). Except that I'd turned him into a kettle (*hervidor*), as I found out later when I dug out my dictionary.

My lunch break was bliss, but the grips were scorching upon my return. The dashboard read a blistering 42°. I'd never ridden in such brutal temperatures. Vents open, it felt like riding into a blast furnace. Abandoned factories, relics of a different era, whizzed by like a Mad Max landscape. A nuclear power station, cast aside in favour of cleaner solar power, dominated the landscape for miles.

Then came the N432. This modern highway should have been smooth, but the melting tarmac made the bike squirm. An SUV crept close to my rear wheel, only a metre or two away, in a terrifying game of chicken, no matter how quickly I rode. A junction, and I suddenly swerved off the highway, heart pounding as I watched him vanish into the distance. Finally, a reprieve from this asphalt duel.

An hour later, relief washed over me as I ascended the long drive to the imposing white parador in Córdoba. Imperiously situated on a hill, it offered sweeping views of the city. Booking it online during last night's insomnia had been a wise move. I made a beeline for the pool where a cooling dip was the only thing standing between me and heatstroke. Clad in nothing other than skimpy budgie smugglers (bike, weight-saving, definitely not for posing), flip-flops, and a slightly threadbare Honda tee-shirt, I skipped down for a dip. A big, kidney-shaped pool, shady grassy area, bar and some great views over the city. Book and beer. Jackpot.

My dinner decision had already been made. With a fabulous menu on offer in the restaurant, I was dining in tonight. Exploring Córdoba could wait until tomorrow. Besides, I had some washing to do. My limited luggage wouldn't suffice for the whole trip so regular sink laundry was part of my daily ritual. That camping sink plug I'd bought before leaving was coming in handy.

A few dozen lengths of the pool stretched my tired limbs and gave me an excuse for toasting afterwards on the sun lounger, so by the time I had togged up for dinner in my only decent pair of shorts and shirt, I was glowing and hungry. On the pretty terrace overlooking the extensive gardens, pool and the city in the distance, I enjoyed *mazamorra* (cold almond soup with olives) and *raba de toro* (oxtail, red wine and vegetable stew), washed down with a Ribera del Duero red. There was a little space left for dessert and I was tempted by pastel córdobés, a flaky puff pastry filled with angel hair jam.

Soon I was feeling stuffed, as I told the waiter who asked if I'd also like some cheese: '*Soy lleno, gracias. Solo la cuenta por favor.*'

I settled the bill and wandered into the gardens, the lights of the city twinkling in the clear night air. Heady scents of jasmine and wisteria wafted around, coming in waves on the gentle breeze. Quite a day, I thought, contentedly. I tucked the moments away in my memory bank. They'd do nicely for a bleak winter's day sometime in the future.

Mezquita

The next day I headed off early into the city to beat both the crowds and the heat. I didn't fancy walking around wearing my heavy gear, so I left my kit with the concierge and rode in shorts and a shirt, thus breaking one of my cardinal safety rules. Sometimes you must take a calculated risk. It felt utterly liberating, even for the short ride into the city, where nobody was wearing protective kit on their bikes or scooters, other than obligatory helmets.

I headed off to a bar for coffee. Spanish guitar music drifted out of the arched doorway. I found myself downwind of a couple of wrinkled old guys who were chain-smoking industrial strength cigarettes. Everyone around me seemed to smoke. It was like being in the middle of a forest fire. I gulped down my cortado, its robust bitter flavours biting my throat.

At ten, the Mezquita opened its magnificent doors, and I was at the front of the queue. The *Mezquita-Catedral de Córdoba*, known by its ecclesiastical name of *Catedral de Nuestra Señora de la Asunción* is regarded as one of Spain's greatest treasures—and that's saying something in a country that can boast so many extraordinary architectural jewels. I've seen some fabulous buildings, including the Alhambra in Granada and Seville's Alcázar but the Mezquita blew me away. It's a massive, complex structure, a former mosque and present-day cathedral. I walked through the magnificent doors to be confronted by an apparently endless series of delicate arches supported on slender pillars, which made the roof seem to float. Hundreds of pastel-hued arches stretched away into the distance, as though I were in a chamber of mirrors, each one reflected into infinity.

Despite the crowds I was immersed in an immense space of hushed calm, only the soft patter of footsteps and a gentle murmuring were audible. I walked between the columns, admiring the restrained detailing, not really understanding the nuances of its religious significance but totally struck by the soaring imagination on display.

In the centre I came across the Christian cathedral, uniquely built within the mosque. In its own much more ornate way, it too was extraordinary, but somehow its Catholic pomp left me much less moved. I'm not religious and yet the mosque spoke to me in a way the cathedral did not. I sauntered round, engrossed in my thoughts for an hour or so before I emerged blinking into the sunlight of the Patio de los Naranjos with its rows of orange trees and cypresses. I would have been happy with my trip if the Mezquita had been the only place I visited, so sublime was it.

I headed along the Jewish quarter's narrow streets full of the excitable chatter of tourists and locals alike, lined with whitewashed houses, their gaily coloured window boxes crammed with flowers. Bijou bars and restaurants, chalkboard menus propped outside on artists' easels, pressed in from every side.

In the Plaza del Potro I stumbled upon the fountain and inn immortalized in *Don Quixote*. It made me wonder: in my entire brewing career, had I ever encountered a pub as famous as this one? Likely not, though I'd certainly known my share of 'dens of iniquity','as Cervantes himself described this very posada.

My next stop was the magnificent Roman bridge across the River Guadalquivir, past the railings with their inevitable collection of padlocks. As I arrived, I saw an arresting sight at the end of the bridge. A vivacious dark-haired bride, in white dress and tiara, accompanied by a woman photographer and another older woman, who I guessed to be her mother. I watched from a discreet distance as the photographer shot some pictures on the bridge.

As they walked past me afterward, I said *'Felicidades'* (congratulations) to the bride.

She threw her head back and laughed.

'I am modelling the dress for a wedding website, but *gracias de todos modos.*'

She threw me a kiss, as she tottered away on high heels for her next pose.

I would have loved to spend more time in Córdoba; I felt I'd only scratched its surface. I returned to the hotel to load up. The concierge, whose pungent after-shave permeated his little office, handed me my bags. I needed a destination for today. Which were the best paradors a day's travel away, I asked. I'll take his first suggestion, I decided. He paused, a hand still on my bag, put his thumb and forefinger to his mouth in contemplation.

'Many choices. Arcos is very charm. Ronda... has best views. Maybe Cádiz, you know, very old city. Near Jerez... you like sherry? Sevilla, that is lovely—'

I began to regret asking the question. He was going to reel off an entire list.

'*Gracias, señor,*' I interrupted.

'*Sé a dónde voy. Arcos.*'

I knew where I wanted to go. The receptionist had it sorted by the time I had packed the bike. Her freshly printed booking confirmation was in my hand. Arcos awaited, no detour required on the road towards my goal of Tarifa. I still had five days until the Mallorca-bound ferry at Dénia, the second of my pre-booked crossings. Easy-peasy.

On the road again and the mercury was climbing to uncomfortable levels in the high thirties. Even with the slipstream of the bike I seemed to be riding into a cooker on full blast. The afternoon sun beat down mercilessly as I pulled over to check the GPS. A good many kilometres still separated me from Arcos, so with a pang of regret I carried on past the turn-off for the Castillo de Almodóvar. The chance to see the filming location for *Game of Thrones* was tempting, but the lure of Arcos was stronger.

With a twist of the throttle, I veered off the main road. The hum of traffic faded as the bike purred contentedly through more olive groves, the trees planted in serried ranks in endless fields, interrupted only by the odd finca or glinting tin roof. The olive trees gave way to fields of cereal, arid in the July heat, rocks scattered among the stubbly crops. Not for nothing was this place known as the '*Sartén* [frying pan] *de Andalucía*'. Ahead, a cluster of buildings rose from the dusty plain, a beacon in the shimmering heat. "Marchena", the sign declared.

3

Marchena–Arcos–Tarifa–Ronda

The Bar Najocamon was a typical unassuming locals' bar. No different from thousands like it dotted across Spain: simple white plastic tables and chairs outside on a shady veranda. Office workers, farmhands and shopgirls were in a hubbub of conversation. It's busy so it must be good, I thought. I parked nearby to keep an eye on my bike, glad to avoid the growing hassle of securing my gear at every stop.

I snagged a shady seat, ordered an aqua and unzipped my jacket. There was a buzz, not from the chattering crowds, but from a bee, a large and vicious one, a free-riding stowaway from my ride. It stung me, hard, on the chest before buzzing off.

'Bastard,' I uttered, which drew some glances from nearby.

My water arrived with a generous tumbler of ice. Hoicking up my shirt, I tipped the entire contents over myself to soothe the pain, drawing a startled look from the slender, auburn-haired waitress. She fetched another bottle and thrust it at me.

'¡Inglés loco!' she muttered, gesturing in my direction with a dismissive flick of her hair.

Yet more glances from nearby.

The sting had faded to a dull throb by the time the plate held the last crumbs of my lunch. The bill came to single figures, a far cry from city prices. I recalled the old days when you could have a three-course meal for 200–300 pesetas, a couple of quid. And often with wine thrown in for free.

Back on the bike, my jacket zipped up tight against attack bees despite the swelter, I kicked up the stand and set off toward Arcos de la Frontera. A lazy afternoon ride, ninety kilometres or so.

Moments later, less than a few hundred metres down the road, I eased off the throttle for a mini roundabout. I looked right... clear. I rolled on through... and then halfway round, the bike vanished from beneath me. Without warning, all grip vanished.

One moment the sun was on my face and all was well. The next, there was a clattering of scraping metal and shattering plastic as my world flipped sideways. I couldn't process the sensations of falling, of no longer being in control. I wondered how much it was going to hurt. Curious, really, how time slows down when the unexpected happens. I didn't feel any impact with the ground, just a sense of speed as the road got unnaturally close to my left flank.

Time warped, each agonising second stretching into eternity. Then impact. A bone-jarring crunch, sliding helplessly along the rubbery, greasy tarmac, my helmet an inch above the road. Then the searing hot violence of friction against my leather-clad limbs as the road grabbed me to a halt. As I stopped, sprawled in the middle of the roundabout, the bike floated away from me and crashed into the kerb some way off.

What the fuck just happened?

I lay on the road, panting with the adrenaline rush. How had I done that? I don't make mistakes. I can't make mistakes. I'm on my own. I've never done that, why here, why now?

These questions and a profound feeling of disappointment and anger at myself arrived in a tumbling rush.

I eased onto my hands and knees and then hauled myself into a sitting position. As I turned round I expected to see a car's number plate at eye level heading towards me. There was none. No traffic to squash me, thank God. I sat for a few seconds, trying to gather some sense of whether I was intact. I waited for the pain to pierce the anæsthetic haze of shock.

A battered car suddenly rounded the corner. It stopped a short distance from me, brakes squealing. I gingerly staggered to my feet. I could walk, which was a good sign. Slowly I limped off the road onto the verge and sat down again. My heart thumped like a war drum, my breaths coming raggedly. A girl, no more than twenty, slightly built and concerned-looking, got out and came over. I tried to speak, but nothing came out of my mouth. My tongue stuck to my palate with dryness. I still had my visor down, so she couldn't see my goldfish expression.

The bike was still half in the road, on its side, so I had to move it. It's a heavy beast, especially with a load of luggage. I tried to pick it up, but a sharp pain in my left side made me wince. The girl and I were no match for it. A few seconds later she flagged down another car. A young man emerged. He and the girl seemed to know each other, and she gestured with her open arms as if to say *I don't know what to do*. His biceps bulged as he effortlessly raised the bike that had defied me moments ago. He deftly placed it on the side stand, parked it neatly on the verge, and ensured it wasn't pouring petrol anywhere.

By now I was able to speak but the adrenaline coursing through my veins did little for my Spanish as I garbled '*Gracias*' to my two Samaritans. A few moments later they were gone and the police arrived. By now I was standing up straight and clutching my arm to my chest. Two bearded cops, one taller than the other, emerged from their car, faces etched with concern. They were Policia Local, both in their thirties, I guessed, probably not used to many Brits mucking about in this Spanish hinterland.

'Were those other cars involved in your crash?' asked the first cop.

'*Non, solo yo,*' I answered. Just me.

Maybe he thought they'd caused it and scarpered.

They rapidly established that I hadn't thrown a pillion passenger off into the scrub nearby. Once they were satisfied that I wasn't drunk or drugged up, and that I was mostly intact, they joined me in a grim survey of the damage. Together we looked over the sorry state of my previously pristine pride and joy. The Honda now sulked, scuffed and distinctly worse for wear, with various panels cracked, some lights skewwhiff but still apparently in working order. One of the officers started the motor and twiddled the handlebars.

'How old is this bike?' the taller one asked, his English flawless.

'New. Only a few months old.' A flicker of surprise flashed in his eyes. 'Unlucky you then. Looks like a Spanish car now, you know. Dented.' He laughed. I didn't see the joke.

We inspected the roundabout. I showed them where I'd gone down. Long silvery lines from the foot peg traced my accident into the tarmac. The smaller policeman slid on the surface, one foot in front of the other, as I used to on icy playgrounds.

'*Muy deslizando. Problamente un derrame de combustible,*' he declared.

The slick rubber surface was coated with the discharged diesel fuel of thousands of lorries from the nearby industrial estate.

I had had no chance.

'Do you want to make a claim against the *ajuntamento* [local council]?', said the tall cop, pulling out his notebook.

I thought for a moment. I imagined weeks of correspondence and hassle, a chunk of my summer spent hunched over a laptop, phone calls and costs and then ultimately a big '*NON*' from a faceless bureaucrat who had never slid prone over a greasy small-town roundabout in the heat, wondering if they, their bike and their road trip were well and truly fucked.

'No,' I said, sighing. 'I'll sort it out with my insurance company.'

'Okay. So where are you headed?'

'Mallorca.'

He whistled low. 'Long ride ahead. Take it more slowly, yeah?'

I wanted to comment about the council's lamentable lack of road maintenance but I bit it back. I didn't know the Spanish word for lamentable. The cops were still writing notes when an ambulance turned up, blues and twos announcing its presence.

I was being treated to the full Saturday afternoon service. In this small Andalucían town, I imagined such incidents were a welcome change from the usual weekend wedding fights and drunken fiestas.

'How are you feeling?' asked the young, bearded ambulanceman kindly, in Spanish.

What is it with facial hair in these hot climes? He invited me into the stifling interior of his ambulance. God, it's hot in here. I began to feel a little dizzy.

He had a few glistening beads of sweat on his forehead, the temperature was in the high 30s, and smell of cleaning fluid was overpowering.

He wore a white uniform, pens lined up in his breast pocket and rubber gloves at the ready.

'*Te duele alguna parte?*' (Do you hurt anywhere?)

I began to feel dizzier and sat down. My ribs were beginning to hurt now.

'*Me duele un poco aquí,*' I replied.

I gingerly pointed where my phone had done its best to rearrange my ribs. The phone was fine, my chest apparently not. He had a good poke about and checked the other bits of me that might be storing up agony.

'You are lucky. You have only broken a rib, maybe two. Lungs sound clear. Your heart rate is a little fast and blood pressure high. Nothing else seems broken. You feel okay to carry on?'

'Should I get an X-ray?'

'The hospital is closed now. Nothing they can do for ribs anyway. Be careful. It'll hurt for a few weeks. Try not to laugh or cough. And no sex.'

I laughed. Ouch.

As I eased myself out of the ambulance's stifling embrace, the heat of the sun felt like a slap. A stab of pain made me wince. I heard the ambulance door slam, a harsh finality to it. Is this where the road trip hits the buffers? How will I manage with these busted ribs?

The policemen were still waiting in the shade of a carob tree. They gave me their details, a report already scribbled down. I scanned it, hoping my Spanish was good enough to understand if my insurance company would give me problems later.

Meanwhile, they'd checked over the bike. One of them, a fellow biker, spoke up.

'I own a Yamaha. I dream of riding to England someday, like you've come here. Look, your fork... leaking oil.'

I bent over... arghh, bad move. My ribs screamed in protest. The fork looked fine to me, but I promised to watch it. He eyed me, one eyebrow raised. A silent fitness test, I reckoned.

Thing was, none of us truly knew if the bashed-up Honda would run in a straight line or wobble down the road like a drunk at a disco. They offered me an escort out of town to check the bike's roadworthiness and, I suspected, make sure I didn't keel over again and give them more paperwork.

On the edge of town, they overtook, an arm pointing right at the next T-junction. I waved thanks, pain flaring as I lifted my hand. They peeled off, and by the time I reached the junction, I'd clean forgotten where they'd pointed. So, naturally, I turned left, straight back into town. I passed the restaurant, the waitress even busier now. A few turns later, I came across my nemesis again—the slippery roundabout. I slowed to a crawl, going as straight as I could, backside clenched tight enough to crack a walnut.

I passed the police car again, returning to base. I swore I saw them shaking their heads as I rode on.

Get my act together. Quick. I found a disused garage and stopped under the shade of its decaying forecourt, a stray cat strolling over to investigate my boots.

I dug around in the panniers to find some painkillers. Gulping down the biggest possible dose with tepid water I started to shake a little. I was still in a state of mild shock. My heart was beating like a misfiring motor. Damn. My atrial fibrillation (AFib) was back.

An abandoned plastic chair lay on its side by a fuel pump. I picked it up carefully and sat down for a rest, my eyelids drooping despite the discomfort. I needed a siesta.

I woke sweating and thirsty from a slumber that felt like an hour but was no more than ten minutes. The cat lay sprawled at my feet. My ticker had settled down a bit but events in Marchena had evidently triggered an episode of AFib, a condition which makes my heart beat irregularly. I had been taking medication for it for a few years. It's unpleasant; I feel like a fish is flapping away in my chest and I have the sensation of a lump in my throat and my temples ache. Caffeine, chocolate and too much booze are triggers. Oh, and stress. Especially stress.

I tried to pull myself together. I was not going to let this setback affect me. I was a good rider. Shit happens. You've a trip to do. This is supposed to be fun. Stop feeling sorry for yourself.

I hauled myself onto the battered bike. But every bump, every pothole, sent a fiery jolt through my chest. I was stuffed with painkillers, the max dose before a lazy wooziness set in. As I rode away from Marchena, my nerves rattled, I felt a tinge of shame along with the throbbing pain. Lucky, I reminded myself. It could've been much worse. But the 'what ifs' buzzed in my ears like angry mosquitos: a car behind me, higher speed, a pedestrian... I was annoyed, too, at the state of the road. I knew it wasn't my fault, but I'd crashed, nonetheless.

I forced myself to think positively even though the old biker cliche was echoing in my head: there are two kinds of biker, those who've crashed and those who will. Well, that rite of passage was done. I was still here, the bike still ran, scuffed but functional even though bits dangled where they shouldn't. My plan of tackling those twisty mountain roads dissolved into nothing. At Utrera, I abandoned the scenic route for the straight road to Arcos. I needed time to process the crash, whatever that meant.

Now each roundabout was a trial, crossed at a snail's pace. Ridiculous, unsustainable. I scolded myself, locked in an internal debate. This was bad luck, nothing more. I wasn't reckless. The road was the trap. My logical brain knew this wouldn't happen twice, yet my gut clenched with fear it might.

My mind suddenly filled with an accident I had seven years earlier. The closest I'd ever come to death. I had crashed a single-seat light aircraft into the ground from a hundred feet. I had stalled the wing on take-off, a classic pilot error, the type that usually end badly. The plane had plummeted in a couple of seconds headlong into the grass runway.

The ground crew thought I was dead when they ran over to the scene. I should have been, but for a stroke of luck. I was saved only by the fuselage which rolled, crumpled and absorbed the impact. The plane was a wreck. I had walked away with a bruised ego, sore backside and a stiff neck.

It was after that my AFib started, which I guess was not surprising.

It took me a while to get back into the cockpit, but eventually I had regained my confidence and even gone on to be an instructor, having learned a hard lesson. Needless to say, I also had to pass a series of medicals. The memory steeled me. This was simply a setback which I would overcome.

I became conscious of the iron grip of tension in my muscles and white-knuckling the grips. Time to loosen up. I pulled over. There was no traffic, so no witnesses watched my super-gentle shakedown session, flinching every time my ribs complained. Motorcycling and tension were not good bedfellows. I felt the flow state again and returned to the road.

A large roundabout approached and I scanned its surface with the intensity of a bomb disposal expert. Seemed okay. Taking a deep breath—well, more of a shallow one; deep breaths hurt like hell, as I soon discovered, along with coughing and laughing—I leaned into a smooth left turn, countersteering precisely. The bike purred beneath me, and a sliver of confidence returned. Maybe this trip wouldn't (unlike like my little plane) be a complete write-off.

By the time I reached Arcos ("Gateway to the *Pueblos Blancos* [White Villages] of Cádiz") I was feeling much calmer and at ease, both with myself and the battered bike. I rode up the steeply cobbled street and stood on the foot pegs to prevent the vibration jabbing into my ribs as I rode into a large, shady square surrounded by orange trees. I tucked my bike into a corner and parked up. The old hotel, close to the heart of the old town, was decorated with trelliswork and traditional *azulejos* (painted tiles) and precariously situated on the edge of a steep cliff overlooking a river gorge and the endless Andalucían plain beyond. A large convent stood next door.

I craved a different kind of sanctuary: my room.

Carrying the bags was a torture-fest and of course the room was upstairs, with no lift, and at the far end of a corridor. The Juliet balcony offered a glimpse of my bashed bike, parked in a quiet corner of the Plaza del Cabildo. I showered, inspected my bruised chest, and changed into sandals, shorts and a shirt. I rested. The bike could wait until tomorrow. I needed to take my mind off things so went off to explore the old quarter.

Whitewashed houses spilled down ancient, cobbled lanes, a maze of history. I stumbled upon a small square where a group of performers in vivid traditional dress were singing and acting a playlet. The young crowd cheered and applauded enthusiastically when the singers finished and began to move onto the next busy venue.

I settled into a small red wooden chair on the thronged street outside the Taberna Jóvenes Flamencos, its lively atmosphere thick with the buzz of conversation punctuated by the odd raucous note of a two-stroke scooter rasping past. Bread, olives, goat's cheese salad... a monastic dinner. Beers followed, cool and sharp against the fading ache. Whether I should mix *cerveza* with the strong painkillers I doubted, but I was hurting less; tonight, I didn't care.

Dark had enveloped the town by the time I plodded back to the hotel. The terrace bar overlooked the steep cliff. It was a dizzying plunge from the railings to a plain dotted with the distant glistening diamonds of small settlements. On the horizon was a shimmer of deep gold which faded into inky hues, where the sun had set.

I contemplated what I should do now. Today had been tough. Part of me wanted to head off straight to Dénia to get an earlier ferry to Mallorca as soon as possible. But that would mean missing Tarifa, the southernmost point and my goal for this first trip. That felt like defeat. I was determined to make it. I had gone as far west as I really wished to go. Much further and I would be in Portugal. Over a decaf, the map spread before me, I studied the routes. The random nature of my route so far, that had been fun, was a welcome spontaneous change from a tightly scripted schedule. But— and it may have been a reaction to the accident—I felt I needed to take command again. It was almost a physical urge. I invoked rule five. I was in charge. Tomorrow we, the bike and I, would go to where Europe ends and Africa begins, to see Morocco across the Strait of Gibraltar from Tarifa and then to the Rock itself. I pretended to be confident, kidding myself. In reality, I'd got a bad case of the collywobbles.

Tarifa

The insistent clanging of the convent chapel bell every hour until midnight meant sleep came late. Examining the bike before my delayed breakfast, it looked superficially okay. Closer inspection revealed the damage: a new pannier, mirror, side wing, various lower fairing panels and a fog light were needed at the very least. Cursing my lack of cable ties to secure the dangling bits, I cobbled together a repair with some half-dried superglue and duct tape. Hopefully, it would hold until Mallorca for a proper fix. As I gingerly knelt on the cobblestones, a whoosh split the air, followed by another. Rising to my feet, I peered over the stone balustrade that separated the square from the cliff.

Below, an iridescent green canopy bloomed rapidly into a hot air balloon. Phoenix-like it had risen from out of sight beneath the square. I watched mesmerised as it ascended towards the basilica roof on the opposite side of the plaza. A single question gripped people watching with me: would it clear the obstacle? With a long jet of flame reaching skyward, the basket lurched over the high tiles before swooping away over the old town. Two more brightly coloured balloons, still hovering over the gorge, climbed higher as they approached the buildings. Perhaps, like us, they thought the green one had a close call.

After patching up the bike, I loaded up my bags in several trips, avoiding the discomfort of a single haul. A policeman patrolled the square, checking license plates, ITV (MOT) certificates on windscreens and parking receipts. He passed by, tickets in hand, as I secured my pillion bag. With a nod, he eyed the scrapes on the bike, furrowing his brow in mock sympathy before moving on. Dents and scratches were a rite of passage for Spanish cars; damage wasn't unusual, even on new vehicles. I decided to see the Honda's bashes as badges of honour, a souvenir of its travels.

A few minutes later, the policeman returned, his patrol complete. He enquired about my journey, my origin and destination. A biker himself, like many Spanish officers, when off-duty Señor Jiménez rode a Ducati. Its signature red paint scheme had been a frequent sight on the trip so far. I recounted the mishap in Marchena, praising the helpfulness of his colleagues. He then knelt on the dusty ground to examine the damage.

'*Un momento,*' he said, and opened his bike's pannier.

He rummaged around and emerged with a wad of cable ties.

'Here,' he offered, 'take what you need.' He grinned, swung onto his cop-Yamaha, and waved goodbye, disappearing to fine a few more unsuspecting motorists with parking tickets. A moment of kindness I appreciated a lot.

I was still sore as I climbed aboard the beaten-up bike but my heart was back to its normal rhythm and—despite the noisy church bells—I felt refreshed and ready for another day's adventure, hopefully one less traumatic than yesterday.

From Arcos I made quick stops in Jerez de la Frontera, Spain's sherry capital, and Cádiz. While Jerez held out the promise of a future visit to do some bodega tours, Cádiz was more of a mixed bag. On a narrow isthmus, towering cranes and naval ships hinted at its industrial side, borne out by a whiff of oil in the air. Yet despite its reputation as a drug trafficking hub, this ancient city, allegedly the oldest in

Western Europe, preened with baroque beauty and sheltered one of Spain's grandest cathedrals.

I rode past leafy parks along the congested seafront, the Costa de la Luz a stone's throw away across the grass, then wove through the old town's narrow streets. Eventually I emerged onto a dual carriageway, which led across an impressive suspension bridge back to the mainland and my next stop: Tarifa. Opting for a scenic coastal route, I meandered past sleepy resort towns when, near Barbate, the sign "Trafalgar" jolted me into the past. This was the site of Nelson's last battle, in 1805, the place where he met his end. Cape Trafalgar's lighthouse stood proud on a sandy outcrop, a tempting spot to picture the naval clash that took thousands of lives. Sadly the road to the lighthouse was barred, forcing me to settle for a sandy lay-by.

An old man in a faded shirt sat under an umbrella collecting a few euros from drivers simply for pointing them to a spot to park. He had pinched eyes and deep wrinkles in his nut-brown forehead. He seemed to have a good system going, but no one minded. I tossed a coin into his tin.

'It's a long way to the *faro, hombre.* You'll roast in those clothes. *Muy calor.*'

He mimicked sweat dripping off his forehead.

I asked about the distance, my ribs still tender. He gestured toward the dunes. 'Two kilometres, no proper path.'

And besides the lighthouse?

'*Nada*... we Spaniards and the French, we lost that battle. Why should we remember it?'

A fair enough question. I ventured onto the beach, the distant lighthouse a slender white beacon.

'I'll look after your things if you want to leave them here,' he offered.

I wasn't sure I could trust him. I didn't fancy a long walk anyway, so strolled to the beach nearby. This would be as close as I'd get. Gazing at the breakers, I tried to evoke the chaos, the courage of battle... but the calm sea didn't help. As

I returned, the old man nodded, the hint of a smile crossing his face. Later, I discovered plans for a visitor's centre here were scrapped for environmental reasons. So much for concrete history—this slice of British victory remains a place for the imagination.

The strong scent of seaweed hung in the air. Across sunflower fields on the inland hills, hundreds of wind turbines whirred in the constant breeze, a hallmark of this region and appropriate for the "Wind sports capital of Europe" as the Tarifa town sign declared. I'd reached the southern limit of Europe, navigating the minor coast road from Trafalgar that snaked along the shore, sand drifting from the dunes over the road making the surface treacherous.

Because the town is at the narrowest point of the Strait of Gibraltar, where the Mediterranean Sea and the Atlantic Ocean meet, strong winds are forced through the gap. Thermals winds from the heated land masses add to the wind's strength and the result is one of the windiest places in Europe.

The long road into town was lined with shops overflowing with garishly coloured surfboards. Dark wetsuits dangled from racks like macabre puppets, while carefree youngsters milled about, sipping coffee or beer in surfer–dude bars as the sea bobbed with cool windsurfers and kite surfers. The average age must have been twenty. I felt rather old.

Turning right at the Puerta de Jerez, the old town gate, I passed the castle and WW2 bunkers overlooking the strait. I eased my way through the holiday traffic, past the 10th century Castle of Guzman El Bueno and towards the beach. Bustling families streamed towards the sands. The road itself petered out, replaced by sand drifts. I squeezed the bike between two VW campervans plastered with surfing stickers, their roof racks adorned with drying wetsuits flapping in the wind.

There was no fanfare or impressive sign announcing the fact that I stood at the southernmost point of mainland Europe accessible by vehicle. The short remaining stretch would be on foot. With the Atlantic Ocean on my right, Mediterranean on my left, I walked across the causeway to the old guard tower by the locked, rusty gate. Across these austere gates lay the Isla de las Palomas, a former military site and refugee prison, now a wildlife reserve.

I could not actually set foot on the physical southernmost point, but really who cares about a few hundred metres or so. The gates marked my southern journey's end. From now on it would be northwards.

Sharing my minor disappointment with a Swedish family, we bemoaned the missed opportunity at this ultimate spot, a mecca for travellers from over Europe. I wondered what Nordkapp would be like. The Swedes had the answer.

'We were in Nordkapp last year,' said the man in a wide-brimmed hat and Hawaiian shirt.

'It was much better. It had a big visitor's centre, and you can walk right to the end where there is the big world statue. The Norwegians know how to make money because it is expensive to go in. Here it's free, at least,' he smiled.

His pretty wife, who was pushing a buggy with a small blonde child in it, added that they'd met several people who'd cycled the whole trip from Tarifa to Nordkapp, an impressive feat of endurance. We swapped photos by the gates, then I headed back along the causeway, past the giant Instagrammable Atlantic and Med signs. Less than nine miles away across the Strait of Gibraltar lay Morocco, shimmering in the heat haze. Ferries ploughed through the busy waters, criss-crossing with countless other ships. Another continent, another world, so tantalisingly close.

A beachside *chiringuito* promised a cool drink and a sandwich. It is northward all the way up from here, I mused, reflecting on reaching this southernmost tip of Europe. 36° latitude... an achievement, crash or no crash.

At least 5,500 kilometres (3,500 miles) stretched from here to Nordkapp. The Iberian journey up to now was the appetiser but I was delighted to have made it this far and relished the rest of the trip.

Over an ice-cold lemonade, a bocadillo and a strong cortado coffee I pondered on what drove me to push to these out of the way places.

I had spent twenty-five years climbing all 283 Munros in Scotland, that is, mountains over 3,000 feet. I loved ticking them off one by one, but it was more than simply an exercise in collecting hills. I craved the excitement of discovering new places, of dealing with the weather, the logistical challenges as well as the sheer physical fitness I needed to summit these tough peaks. As my knees have got creakier, my need for mountaineering is being replaced by other pursuits; I realised that long-distance motorbike tours fulfil an unconscious ambition to keep moving and push myself as long as I'm able.

I have, too, a sense of time slipping away. In addition to my heart problems, I've a number of other medical issues, like many guys in their sixties: worn-out joints, an eye and hearing problems, prostate and associated misfiring componentry. Finding insurance cover is becoming more problematic and I know that at some point this adventuring may have to stop. I want to stave off that day as long as I can.

What's more, I've a number of mates who never got the chance to do this kind of stuff. Mates for whom it's now too late.

I looked round for a waiter so I could pay the bill and spotted on the back wall of the beach café a rustic blue sign hanging from a nail. In slightly faded lettering it read:

"*Vive la vida como si fueras a morir mañana. Aprende como si fueras a vivir siempre.*"

(Live life as if you were to die tomorrow. Learn as if you were to live forever.)

It summed up my thoughts. That life-affirming message shook me out of my philosophical reverie along with the caffeine that was by now working its magic.

Back on the bike after lunch, I left the crowds and seaside vibe of Tarifa behind. From here I'd be heading east with the sea on my right. It was time for Gibraltar. I had no idea what to expect. The ten-mile ride was along a busy road, over a marshy isthmus, which was a scene not unlike The Wash or Morecambe Bay with reeds swaying and tidal pools shimmering. The Rock loomed ahead, only immediately to vanish in the heat haze. It was the strangest sensation, like a mirage, a trick of the eye... yet it was real, and getting closer. An enormous container ship anchored in the bay dwarfed the sailboats and ferries traversing the strait, one of the world's busiest shipping lanes.

The border crossing teemed with cars. Brexit hasn't helped. I filtered carefully down the middle of two lanes, wary of a vehicle door suddenly opening on me. That move likely saved me an hour. Soon I was at the checkpoint, passport stamped, out of the Schengen Zone and back on British soil.

Accelerating away from the border cabin, a bright orange windsock caught my eye. An Airbus 320 sat shockingly close on the tarmac. I was motorcycling across the international airport's runway, control tower looming ahead. I had visions of being buzzed by an incoming aircraft, so picked up the pace to safety on the other side. Gibraltar was a densely packed place, full of oddities and naval history, which created a weird shift from Spain. I stuck my crash helmet on top of a red Victorian postbox for a photograph. Here bobbies patrolled in traditional British police uniform. I rode around the centre, past the British bars and shops. Local lads on scooters oozing bravado weaved through the narrow streets, their wheels flirting with slides on the bends.

Reaching Europa Point near a mosque, I spotted two Japanese girls. I asked if they'd mind snapping a picture of me with the imposing 426-metre Rock as a backdrop. They giggled politely at my offer to return the favour and struck a whole series of playful poses, complete with the classic peace sign. Odd place, Gib.

Back through the border and stamped into Schengen again, my route took me along the coast through the exclusive resorts of Sotogrande and Estepona, with their manicured golf courses and multimillion-euro developments.

But my sights were set higher, on a legendary motorcycling route that snaked through the mountains: the A397 from San Pedro de Alcantara to Ronda. I'd often seen pictures of this spectacular road in motorbike magazines, which should be no surprise as many new bikes are launched to the press here.

The banked, sweeping corners and a surface that promised to stick like Velcro—or so I hoped—promised a dream ride. Off I went. My confidence rose with every bend, impressed by the grip from the tyres and the Honda's handling. The NT1100, though not a classic sportbike, held its own. The tarmac felt almost like a racetrack, and the mountains echoed with the sound of other bikers enjoying themselves, some scraping their pegs through the twisties. I wasn't quite that aggressive, but I still managed to keep many of the faster cars and bikes at bay, though an occasional boy racer would blow by in a blur.

On the other side of the road a simple café called Venta el Madrono came into view. The famous gathering place for bikers and cyclists used to be a roadworker's cottage but was now adorned with biker photos and memorabilia. I pulled over for a refreshing ice cream and to savour the superb views over the mountains and back down to the coast.

The car park was proof of the international appeal of this route. Bikes from France, Germany, Italy and even Croatia shared the space; I was the only British representative in the concours. Happy to have flown the flag, I continued along the exciting contours of the Rio Seco. A large bend marked the transition from reddish volcanic rock to the white limestone of the Sierra Blanca. After crossing a high plain, the road straightened and began the spectacular descent towards Ronda, my stop for the night.

My parador room had a balcony which directly overlooked the Puente Nuevo, which spectacularly straddled the gorge of El Tajo. It might have been new by name, but it was built in 1793 and spanned the two sides of the town above the Guadalevin River. Above the huge central arch was a small chamber and a door over the precipitous drop. It had a grim history, as during the Civil War both sides used it as a torture chamber and victims were hurled out of the window onto the rocks 120 metres below.

It was hard to imagine such brutality as I watched the dusky shadows gradually subdue the sunset's golden rays upon the beautiful stonework of the bridge. I sipped a glass of red wine thoughtfully, leaning on the balcony railings above the same, deadly drop.

4

Sierra Nevada–Costa del Sol– Tabernas

Ronda to Nerja

After dinner last night I had set out to find the bullring which originally inspired Hemingway to write *Death in the Afternoon*. The town took to the American author, and he became its favourite adopted son, illustrated by the monuments to him that pop up in different places. It was a romantic place, one of the jewels of Andalucía, even if bullfighting was not your thing. The bullring was locked for the evening, so I had to content myself with walking around the outside, admiring a huge statue of a heroic bull that resisted the matador's *estoque* (sword) for a record length of time. That bull had some bollocks, and they were—literally—on show, dangling beneath the statue like footballs.

When morning came I had to summon up some balls myself to handle a necessary, if dreaded, task: dealing with my insurance company. I rang the number on my policy. It was a lengthy call. Shortly afterwards, I got a call from a loss adjuster who wanted to see the bike. I told him I was in Spain if he didn't mind flying out. He laughed, politely declined the offer and we fixed a date for when I was back in Derbyshire to come to assess the damage.

'I'll try to crash somewhere more convenient next time,' I said, immediately regretting it.

'Ride safely.'

Insurance sorted, I decided to cut myself some slack by having an easy day so booked accommodation not too far away at Nerja. It was almost in the right direction along the Costa del Sol, towards the eventual ferry at Dénia. I headed out of town into the Serranía de Ronda, a junior version of the neighbouring Sierra Nevada. My chest was sorer than yesterday, and I still had a few weeks of discomfort to look forward to. I spoke to a work colleague who'd broken his ribs while skiing.

'Six weeks it took, six weeks,' was his happy forecast.

My route took me through Ardales, and the *Desfiladero de los Gaitanes,* a massive gorge where the narrow *Caminito del Rey* (King's Path) clings precariously to the walls 300 metres above the water. Much of the lofty walkway consisted of wooden duckboards grafted onto the cliffside, held on with thin strands of wire and some planks hewn into the rockface. I walked a tentative stretch, mandatory safety helmet strapped tightly under my chin. A sweaty day became even sweatier. The path was busy with people navigating their steps like tightrope walkers. Some were evidently petrified, others brazenly peering over the railings in search of the rare wild cats, genets and mongooses that called this royal place home. There were plenty of goats and a few tawny vultures wafting about in the updraughts, but the more exotic residents remained out of sight that day. The gorge far below, the gentle jade waters that threaded through the narrow limestone cleft and the rickety wooden walkways that crossed it filled me with joy. This, though, was not a place for anyone suffering from vertigo, so that was a pleasure I'd be unable to share with my wife; her fear of heights is legendary.

Even though that part of Andalucía was not far from the sand- and sun-worshipping coast, there were few tourists among the lesser-known White Villages. These were places worth hunting for, like mountain truffles. I rode through Álorá, its castle perched on top of a breast-like hill. People stared at me from house doorways, men gawped from outside bars and small children peered out of shop fronts as I pootled through, my visor up in the searing heat. A woman, deeply wrinkled and dark-skinned, her hair tied back roughly in a tight bun and wearing a floral housecoat, swept dust off her front step with a besom broom worn to an angle from years of chores. Stray dogs ran out at my passing, barking fiercely, sometimes from several directions at once. My heart beat faster. One of those canine terrorists under the front wheel would be bad news and I kept a wary eye on the mangy mutts in the mirror until, bored, they gave up the dangerous doggy dodgems.

In my distraction the TomTom led me down a narrow track with a badly broken surface that suddenly dropped ever more steeply down a convex slope. Too narrow a road to turn round on, I was committed now. The slope must have been a descent of one in three or more, even steeper than an infamous road in Wales which I'd ridden once and yet which scared me rigid. This accidental road, with its poor surface, was even worse and there was no way back. Did the hounds chase me there on purpose, like a lamb over a cliff? I picked a careful line through the potholes and rubble, hanging back on the pillion to keep the centre of gravity away from the front wheel. The ABS chattered as the tyres scrabbled for grip. Fortunately it wasn't a long descent and I squeezed through a gap where a wrecked car had come to grief against a wall.

The road returned to something close to level and I breathed a sigh of relief, like arriving at the foot of a black ski run, intact but cowed. A few minutes later the now decent tarmac passed a large finca, imperious on a man-made hillock of earth, with row after row of palm trees to act as guards to the house. Large birds swooped overhead, each pass taking them lower until they were almost assaulting me with anger. It was a private place up in those defended hills and I sensed it wished to be left in quiet existence away from the secular world of the Costa below.

An hour later, I pulled up in Torremolinos, buzzing with holidaymakers, ice creams, sunloungers and questionable tee-shirts—the popular Spain of countless brochures and summer escapism. It was another, very different face of Andalucía but probably the one it's best known for. My stop was brief. A cool drink, an ice cream, and a makeshift repair for my shredded riding trousers, a visible reminder of my accident. The rip in the left knee had worsened, but some handy duct tape kept the leg intact. It wasn't stylish, but protection mattered more. A short stop in the town satisfied my curiosity. It was a busy place, a classic Spanish costa resort grown out of any recognition from its modest days as a small fishing village in the 1950s and one which is the summer holiday dreams for millions. I was staggered at the amount of high-rise development going on. Torremolinos is a money magnet.

Equally wealthy, but with a greater sense of history was Málaga, my next stop. City centre parking was a nightmare. After circling a big square several times, a moped-sized space materialised before the cathedral. Several bikers eyed it, but with a surge of un-British decisiveness (a car helpfully blocked them), I claimed it. *Olé.*

Jacket slung over my shoulder, I inhaled the intoxicating blend of aromas wafting from *turrón* (toothsome Spanish nougat; a dentist's delight) shops and windows overflowing with Ibérico hams and a thousand varieties of chorizo.

Málaga is a lovely city in its own right and merits a day or two's exploration before heading off to the Costa. The marble-paved avenues invited me to amble, but the Museo Picasso, a short walk away, was my true destination. Pablo Picasso, born here in 1881, left his artistic mark on the city. Inside, small, hushed groups, art students and couples hand-in-hand paused reverently before his intimate works and those of other renowned artists like Paula Rego. I was the lone biker in this sea of happy visitors, and I shared a glance with the security guard, who asked where I'd come from.

He whistled softly, tilted his head slightly and raised an eyebrow.

'*¡Olé! Sabes más de España que yo,*' he told me flatteringly. (You know Spain better than me.) '*Viajé como tú lo has hecho, quise hacerlo, por conocer rincones, pero ahora hay que ganar la pasta.*' (I want to travel like you do, to see different places, but for now I have to earn some dough.)

He rubbed his thumb and forefingers together rapidly and smiled ruefully. Not for the first time on the trip was I reminded of my good fortune in living this life.

He continued in Spanish. 'I spend my days inside here. Evenings I go off to ride, to escape. Those fantastic coast roads, the mountains. You know Ronda?'

I told him of my visit there. His eyes almost misted over at the thought.

The cool interior and spacious galleries offered a blissful contrast to the heat outside. Several works echoed Picasso's masterpiece, Guernica, that heart-wrenching anti-war witness to the bombing of the Basque town. After a couple of hours in the gallery's calm, I felt refreshed and ready for the city's elegant streets and its Roman Theatre, unearthed as recently as 1951. But first, a treat: pistachio and coconut gelato in a bustling pavement café. Two young girls, a whirlwind of energy and enthusiasm, squeezed onto my table. They were art students from Sheffield, their faces full of the optimism and excitement that comes with exploring a new city. Sipping their *horchata*, they peppered me with questions about my motorcycle journey, about Picasso, about life on the road. Their carefree chatter was fun, a contrast to the relative solitude I'd embraced for the past few days. For a moment I was transported back to my own university days, remembering the thrill of new experiences and the boundless possibilities that lay ahead. They directed me towards the nearby Roman ruins before vanishing down a side street, leaving me to my own reflections. Ah, to be young and unburdened.

I stood in awe before the Roman theatre, located tight against the foot of the Alcazaba fortress. The red sandstone stands were built over the *vomitorium*, its odd name not the result of too much wine, but the passageway through which crowds once poured after witnessing spectacles. Soon, it was my turn to exit. The way out was complicated by a German BMW GS parked so close to my Honda that it was inaccessible from the left, the 'normal' side. With careful manoeuvring, I managed to extricate my bike backward and avoid an international incident, knowing that if I stumbled there'd be a domino-effect of toppling bikes. German swearwords have a particular resonance, especially in my accent. The *Dummkopf-Motorradfahrer* (stupid biker) wasn't around to hear them, unfortunately.

I stuck to the N340, the old coast road, from Cádiz to Barcelona, often called Spain's Route 66. It was now long supplanted by the motorway. It was a gentle road that threaded through the resorts and villages that bordered the sea. Some of the places I passed through were clean, with well kept streets and shops. On the edge of kempt towns roundabouts with large ornamental boats were artfully installed, the name of the boat being the name of the place.

Other, grottier locales had clearly seen their best days a long while ago, and the paint peeled off buildings like sunburnt skin while awnings rusted under the endless sun.

Long-disused terraces once bustling with card games and laughter were now choked in litter and dirt and dog shit. An abandoned nightclub stood like a broken toy, its windows smashed, staring vacantly, and its once bright façade crumbling and plastered in fading circus posters and angry graffiti. Another tawdry looking building advertised itself as a club. The skimpily clad dark-skinned girls lounging outside left little doubt about its real purpose, a reminder that the Costa del Sol's glittering façade concealed a darker underbelly.

Dusk painted the sky as I rolled into Nerja. For a welcome change my room offered a sea view, a breath of salty air compared to the pine-fresh mountains I'd been riding through. Exhausted from the ride, I unpacked lightly, grabbing only the essentials. Leaving stuff on the bike was always a gamble (a lesson I would later learn the hard way), but tonight, disturbing the returning dull ache in my broken ribs felt like waking one of those vicious dogs.

I showered and strolled into the bustling town centre. Packed with people, bars and restaurants, it throbbed with life. The whitewashed buildings lining the narrow streets glowed invitingly that almost created an illusion of midday, except for the cool evening breeze. Guitarists strummed for customers and women in floaty summer dresses mingled with men in shorts.

The excited chatter of holidaymakers and locals enjoying a night out filled the air and bounced off the walls. It was as busy as anywhere I'd seen so far. And I suddenly felt alone. I was usually very happy with my own company, but the friend groups and happy coupledom around me made me wish my wife were there with me. She wouldn't ride on the bike. She wouldn't fly in light aircraft, even when I was the pilot. Actually, probably *because* I was the pilot. I missed her, though, and that night it hit me. I wasn't hungry and didn't particularly want to sit in a restaurant on my own, so I just window-shopped.

Sometimes, like an unwelcome guest, melancholy descends on a journey, a touch of angst amidst the adventure. Sea urchins, steak tartare, tapas variadas, the tempting aroma of gazpacho, none of it sparked an appetite until a sweet, slightly toasted smell wafted by. I came across a shop, *Sabor a España*, overflowing with the region's famed caramelised almonds. I found myself inside before I knew it. The dark eyebrowed girl, a cheeky glint in her eyes, wearing braces, a stripy Yorkshire flat cap and giant red leather oven gloves lifted a large copper bowl brimming with the little beauties onto the counter. She poured the rich brown crusty nuts onto a cooling tray. They glistened invitingly under the lights and settled like molten lava. The aroma was intoxicating, and my wallet materialised as if by magic.

'*Doscientos gramos de almendras caramelizadas, por favor*,' I declared. She poured them into a bag, still warm and delicious.

'I'm here until late if you want more treats once you've eaten these,' she said, arching one of those seductive eyebrows.

The almonds tasted great. I didn't go back to find out the other treats on offer.

Nerja to Mojacar

The following morning while struggling into my kit I discovered that my bike trousers were falling apart again so out came the tape once more after breakfast. The fact that they hardly fitted me after all the Spanish food should have sent me in search of a decent motorcycling shop. However, I had more pressing matters to deal with as east of Nerja the coast road lay in wait with its sinuous curves, carrying me towards Salobrena. Here, I'd finally bid farewell to the sea and plunge back into the heart of the Sierra Nevada, aiming for Lanjarón, the source of the bottled water brand sold over Spain.

The Michelin map had designated this route a scenic masterpiece, marked in green for good reason. It was pure motorcycling bliss. This great road almost topped the Ronda road for sheer fun. The hills were cloaked in stunted woods, and to my right, sheer drops led down to tiny, rocky coves nestled against the cliffs. The road snaked over countless bridges, each one traversing a gully that emptied dramatically into the sea.

Suddenly an enormous dual carriageway in the sky erupted out of a tunnelled mountain face to my left. It must have been a hundred feet above me, on slender stilts. That's where all the traffic must have been, leaving this incredible coastal route to me and the occasional suicidal rabbit.

The ascent into the mountains marked a return to the familiar monotony of the viaduct-strewn motorway, heading towards Granada. The landscape morphed into an increasingly arid expanse, with stumpy green-brown shrubs dotted amongst tomato-red rocks and piles of ochre rocky rubble, utterly different to the lush coast. The motorway offered swift, uneventful progress. Lanjarón awaited, tucked away in the foothills of the mighty Sierra Nevada, its barren and remote peaks dominated by Mulhacén, the highest point in southern Europe at 3,482 metres, jutting out to the northeast. On a clear day, mountain guides say, you can see Africa from its slopes.

Lanjarón is Spain's Buxton, a spa town steeped in history. Once a bustling stop on the ancient Moorish silk route, it now serves as the portal to the Alpujarras, a region where whitewashed villages cling to the southern slopes of the mountains. Everywhere I turned, I encountered the lifeblood of the town: gushing *fuentes* (drinking fountains) dot the streets, a constant reminder of Lanjarón's most precious resource.

The town's heart, Constitution Square, beat with a playful tribute to its namesake water. A modern sculpture titled *Viva* took centre-stage, a fountain where bronze children splashed playfully amidst cascading water. And beside them, an older, more stoic couple sat hand-in-hand, also cast in bronze. It was a charming tableau, a celebration of Lanjarón's water that transcended mere commerce. No logos, no branding, the quality speaks for itself. Everyone knows it's Lanjarón.

I'd settled on my parked bike by the fountain, fumbling with a selfie, when a man in shirtsleeves, long trousers and toting a man-bag offered his help. With a grateful smile, I handed him my phone, and he clicked away enthusiastically from different angles. My curiosity was piqued by the clusters of red polka-dot buckets and plastic roses adorning the statue.

'What's with the decorations?' I enquired.

His eyes lit up.

'Ah, it's only been two weeks since the fiesta of San Juan, *hombre*. We had a blast; the whole town went loco. At midnight, the streets were packed, people drenching each other, laughing. The fire brigade even joined in, hosing us down, and buckets, water guns, everyone was in on it. You should have been there, *Inglés*.'

The central street offered a calm contrast as I rode through, lined with shops showcasing beautiful baskets and pottery. Normally such a lavish use of water would be unthinkable in drought-prone Spain. But here, where the streets had flowed with it, there was a spirit of celebration.

Outside the town, my path into the Alpujarras was marked by another souvenir of Spain's Civil War, a weathered gun emplacement. Further on, before reaching the small town of Órgiva, an unassuming patch of scrubland by the *El Carrizal* ravine featured a discreet memorial. I stopped to read, struggling to comprehend the unspeakable horror that unfolded there: over 5,000 people (no one knows the true count) executed, their bodies brutally tossed into the ravine. This is believed to be Spain's largest mass grave of mostly Republican prisoners from across Granada. Of the Civil War sites I'd encountered, the stories here felt the most harrowing.

I read a shocking account from a simple goat herder, a woman who bore witness as a group of civil guards prepared to murder ten people.

'Are you going to kill me?' a fourteen-year-old boy shouted to one of the Civil Guards.

A gunshot pierced the silence, the boy fell down dead.

"Everyone knew that the fourteen-year-old was the civil guard's illegitimate son", the report read coldly.

The bones of many thousands still lay in that desolate, god-awful ravine with the darkest of dark histories, awaiting a time when Spain can be properly reconciled with its bloody past. It was more evidence of a side of Spain that few visitors perhaps appreciated or, understandably, even wished to know about.

I walked back to the bike, shaking my head in disbelief.

I've always found that one of the greatest pleasures of a road trip is the accidental discovery of things unknown. Such unearthings can change my mood in an instant. What would the next bend, village or town bring, and how would it affect me? Sometimes, as with El Carrizal, the place would provoke sadness, and it was in that frame of mind that I left that high and tragically historied *pueblo blanco*.

However, the road itself soon had me feeling positive again, demanding full concentration to avoid crashing into the dusty, rocky scrubland which bordered the unfenced Möbius-like strip of mountain majesty, and punctuated by the occasional clatter of loose stones dislodged by my tyres. My spirits lifted as the simple act of riding on this challenging road became my total preoccupation. In the absence of distracting traffic, I could focus on picking my line, balancing speed and braking, shifting my body weight subtly, and applying a light pressure on the bars to make a quarter tonne of metal, rubber and plastic do as I bid, accurately and predictably. This was an almost spiritual experience, a seamless connection between tarmac, tyres, machine, body and brain, an activity almost unique to motorcycling. I smiled with the sheer fun of riding, thoughts of my *incident*, as I now dubbed it, tucked as far to the back of my mind as possible. This intoxicating dance with the road was what I had come for.

There was less in the landscape to distract me as hilly scrubland began to take over from the lushly wooded lower slopes. The villages and towns made up for the landscape, however. I passed through Lobras, the smallest municipality of Granada, a curious place with miniature stone-built houses, like a model village, littered alongside the road. Its peculiarities didn't end there. A nearby field contained a collection of randomly scattered yellow-topped milestones, like a roadbuilder's graveyard. Abandoned mercury mines littered the hillsides, the deadly ores long mined out. Elegant slender-pillared bridges and curving viaducts made for seamless progress, while the old switchbacks remained the domain of the occasional donkey and trap, still a familiar sight for the ageing rural population in these parts.

In Cádiar, I stopped for lunch at Ruta, a bustling town centre restaurant. Everyone was on the terrace, seeking shade under parasols. The family owners ran a tight ship, taking orders and serving delicious food with impressive speed. The smaller of the brothers, sporting a thick grey mop, bushy eyebrows, and bearing a close resemblance to an Iberian Kevin Keegan, brought me my *raciones* – local cheese, jamón, and, of course, a bottle of Lanjarón *agua con gas*. Conversation hummed at a low level as people enjoyed their tapas.

I overheard English voices from the next table, a middle-aged couple. She had strikingly red hair and large, dark sunglasses; he was coot-bald, also in shades, with a magnificently eye-catching floral purple shirt and a substantial blue sling. He moved his food around the plate with his free left arm. After I'd finished lunch and paid the bill, I gathered my map and helmet. Dictating notes into my phone hadn't gone unnoticed. As I passed their table, the woman caught my eye and said 'Hello.' We fell into easy conversation about my journey's origin and destination. Ex-pats, Paul and Judy had lived in the village for six years.

I asked about his arm.

'I'm a keen cyclist. Road biking's my thing. It's one of the reasons we moved here. The roads here are wonderful.'

I agreed, the morning's ride still vivid in my mind.

'Two weeks ago I was descending a fast hill near here, and on the bend, I lost it. Hit the barrier, thank God, would've gone straight over the edge otherwise. It was on a road shiny from the heat and tyre rubber. I've broken my collarbone, so I'm out of action for a while.'

I winced sympathetically.

'I did something similar on the motorbike three days ago. Slipped on a roundabout; dangerous surface; broke my ribs.'

'Ouch, that'll be sore, especially with your journey ahead. When it rains in the autumn, I won't even go out cycling, it's a lethal combo.'

I wished Paul a speedy recovery and headed back to the bike, hoping the skies would stay dry.

A fabulous new section of the A348 guided me east from Cádiar, a gentle descent from the Alpujarras into the moonscape of the *desierto*—the bad lands dotted with sparse desert plants and wind-sculpted mounds of sandy rock. This harsh terrain nonetheless supports one of the region's biggest industries: agriculture. The Costa del Polythene, as some call it, is Europe's market garden. Your salad greens likely grew under those acres of bright plastic, mammoth greenhouses that I flashed past on both sides of the carriageway. Lorries laden with leafy cargo zoomed incessantly towards Madrid, Munich, Milan and Manchester.

This arid and uncompromising region made a good living long before agribusiness came around. Those scrubby, Arizonan landscapes? Ideal for Spaghetti Westerns in the

'60s and '70s. *The Good, The Bad and The Ugly* was filmed here, which is why I'd found myself on a mini-Hollywood film set decades ago, back when I worked in marketing for Shredded Wheat. Our advertising agency dreamed up TV commercials based on Henry D. Perky, the pillow-shaped breakfast cereal's US inventor, which had first brought me to Spain in the early '80s. We filmed a Wild West-themed advertisement (three Shredded Wheats helped the postman outrun the bows and arrows of the Native Americans... I know, different times). I wanted to revisit the place where we'd shot the film so Almería's Tabernas desert, unique in Europe, was my next destination. An afternoon's blast from my past awaited.

With dust swirling with every turn of my tyres, I pulled up at the *taquilla* (ticket-office). A bored-looking woman took my cash and slid my ticket into a rusty tin. The wooden palisades of the fortressed town film-set emerged over a rise. It was late in the day, but I figured a few other gringos might be around. Turns out, I had the whole place to myself. The set looked familiar, but it had been forty years and I couldn't be sure I had the right Wild West town. They probably all blurred together anyway: saloon bar, stables, hotel, the gallows... the faded, semi-decrepit look fit the movie bill. Was that a careful recreation of the Wild West, or the strain of tough times and brutal sun?

Hanging my hot jacket on the noose, its arms dangling limply, I swaggered into the Saloon like a lone gunslinger. The only sign of life? A man and a woman on the other side of the bar. My boots squeaked on the dusty floorboards as I pulled up short. Still as statues at first, but then a flicker of movement. She had a smock, a creased forehead, and slightly greasy, lank, brown hair. Not your typical saloon siren.

Apparently, my ticket entitled me to a 'free' beer. There was an Estrella Damm beer fount on the bar, which slightly ruined the Western illusion. Bike rules, so I ordered instead a *gaseosa*, that burp-inducing, slightly insipid lemonade beloved of the Spanish. She dug into a fridge hidden out of sight and poured it into a slightly grubby, chipped glass and slid it across the bar to me. A red pen mark on my entrance ticket said I'd now had the freebie.

The man had been leaning against the corner of the kitchen and roused himself to slouch the few feet to where she had been serving me. She moved over as he approached, casting him a glum sideways glance. His clothes told a tale, unkempt, ragged and dust-filled, with the odd ambiguous stain. He would have passed for a character in a spaghetti western, but it was not an act or a costume. This was who he was. He thumped the bar with his fist. She poured some beer into a glass and set it down in front of him. I mentioned my visit forty years back. His words cut her off the moment she tried to speak.

As he slurred, I realised my hanging jacket was not the only legless thing in town. The beer tap's steady hiss, the day's draining heat, those maddening western tunes... it was a potent mix. A sour waft of stale beer hit me, making me step back.

'Pshht. Forty yearsh, yeah. Us. No, no... fourteen years. Was good then. Now nobody cares for westernsh. Less people come now. You're only the shecond today.'

His desperation tinged the air, and pity filled me for both of them. Their lives played out in a dusty echo of a bygone era, itself more myth than reality. The market was changing, leaving them stranded. Those bustling sets I hazily recalled were gone, replaced by an emptiness echoing across time. The Wild West's thirty-year reign was shorter even than the gap since my last visit. How long would the memories of gunslingers linger here?

I was struggling to follow his drunken tumble of words. A swift exit was needed, like many a cowboy before.

'*Adios,*' I said.

'*Adiosh.*'

She followed me outside. Out of his sight, her hand touched my arm, a plea.

'*Él no es un mal hombre, solo está un poco perdido.*'

Apparently he was not a bad man, just a little lost. I nodded, feeling her sadness, a flicker of a wistful smile crossing her worn face.

'You got room on that bike?' she asked, her laugh half-hearted, half-desperate to get away from her lost husband.

A few kilometres down the road, the 19th century was abruptly replaced by the swinging '60s. Route 66 Tabernas, a roadside bar, was a riot of winged Cadillacs and Buicks, some parked on the roof, others amidst old gasoline pumps and nostalgic Americana. It looked like some entrepreneur had raided Kentucky scrapyards and shipped the whole lot to Spain. Outside a couple of girls were smoking and chatting animatedly, probably singers for the live music promised on the advertisements. I suspected that if I poked my head inside the joint a bottle of poor-quality but expensive cava and a scantily-clad dancer or two might rapidly have appeared by my side. I decided to snap a photo (my Honda magically transported to Route 66) before making a tyre-squealing exit.

By early evening, the *pueblo blanco* of Mojácar welcomed me with a much-needed shower to rid me of the grime and sweat of the day's especially dusty travel. I was in a basic hostal. I couldn't afford to stay in a parador every night. I downed the dregs of a cold beer by the small pool, my pongy gear spread out on the grass to air. Nobody would want to nick it, so I left it lying there as I went in search of a refill.

The hostal overlooked the beach and main road, a relaxed spot to reflect as this long initial leg neared its end. Claiming Europe's southernmost point, the limit of my travels this year, was more than the excuse for adventure, the framing device for the next challenging upward section to North Cape, Europe's opposite extremity. This trip was opening my eyes to the diversity of Spain, its amazing landscapes, fascinating culture, turbulent history and its delicious food. I was enjoying the experience of solo travel. Mostly. The people I'd met had given me an opportunity to practice my Spanish, still halting and ungrammatical but more fluent than ever.

The journey was changing me, too, I must confess. I set out with the most basic of plans, with only a few key ferries booked. I'd left everything else up to chance, making it up as I went along. As long as I reached Tarifa and Mallorca, that was what I wanted to do.

It's not my usual way. Over the winter I'd planned everything. My spreadsheet itinerary was full of details, distances, times, stops, accommodation, even Honda dealers, should I need one. I'd left no room for spontaneity and exploration. I'd approached my adventure like I used to manage my working life, mapped out, timetabled, planned. Very corporate, a bit OCD, less fun, more facts.

One day I'd printed out yet another version of my itinerary. Judith, long-suffering, brought it to me, a cup of tea in hand.

'How many of these are you doing?' she asked, slightly exasperated.

'I'm experimenting with a couple of different routes; I think this one might be better.'

'No offence, but aren't you being a bit obsessed about planning?'

'*Moi*? Obsessed?'

'Look, I thought the clue was in the name. Adventure travel. Where's your adventure if you've buttoned it down like this?' she added.

She was right. I had an epiphany. I'd chuck what I'd done, embrace the spontaneous and the unplanned. It felt different, uncomfortable, exciting.

Don Quixote nailed it: "The road is always better than the inn."

It was the journey that mattered, not the destination.

5

Cartagena–Costa Blanca– Mallorca

Mojacar to Jávea

The coast road to Cartagena clung tightly to the shore, but this was far from the tourist-packed resorts of Torremolinos or Fuengirola. Parts of the route could have been in Cornwall. The coastline was rocky, with slabs of slate glinting from the hillsides where they'd been carved away for the highway. Abandoned chimneys clung desperately to steep slopes leading to the sea, crumbling reminders of the silver and lead mines that once brought prosperity here in the mid-1800s, as did tin to the Cornish miners. Later, smugglers used those same mines to hide contraband tobacco. There were no smugglers in sight today, but plenty of campervans dotting lay-bys and clearings off the road. Seasonal regulars or smugglers' lookouts? Who could say? This whole southern Spanish coastline was a hotbed of illicit activity, with La Linea near Algeciras as its narcotics epicentre.

A little later, as I reached the city outskirts, a flurry of police activity caught my eye. At a toll booth beyond a short stretch of motorway, heavily armed officers with automatic rifles were pouring out of police cars. I'd pulled over to put my gloves back on after paying the toll by card. One of the officers sprinted towards me, questioning why I'd stopped. His right hand hovered over his pistol. Why hadn't I driven straight on? Where had I come from?

I gestured towards my gloves.

'*Guantes*,' I said.

'*He venido de Mojácar.*'

Brevity seemed wise. He walked to the bike's rear, checking my registration plate.

'British?' he asked in English.

'Yes.'

With an exaggerated sweep of his arm, he gestured for me to get the hell out of there. Whatever was happening, I wasn't sticking around to find out.

Cartagena, a city where Roman ruins stand shoulder-to-shoulder with modern architecture, offered a fascinating blend of old and new. I lost myself in the maritime archaeology museum, marvelling at centuries-old artefacts, until the arrival of a gaggle of schoolchildren sent me in search of a quieter refuge. That refuge turned out to be a relic of a more recent conflict: a Civil War air raid shelter, another reminder of that turbulent chapter in the city's history.

In 1936, this Republican stronghold was a prime target for Franco's Nationalist forces. In 1937 a huge underground shelter designed for 5,500 people was built here. Now there was a massive crater, blasted by a 250-kilo bomb through reinforced rock, which spoke of the awful fear that must have gripped the poor citizens caught inside.

I was a lone visitor to the museum, absorbing the exhibits, the grainy footage and haunting sounds, imagining life here eighty-five years ago. In a large cavern, gazing at bombs hanging from the ceiling like menacing bats, I was approached by one of the young museum attendants, Carlos.

'You are interested in the Civil War?'

'Yes, it both fascinates and horrifies me. There are so few museums about it. I've been to a few places where there's no information,' I said, thinking of the concentration camp at Aranda de Duero.

'It's difficult for us Spaniards but the younger generation, like me, we want to know about it, too. It's our past isn't it?'

I mentioned my trip the previous year to Teruel, the site of a brutal Civil War battle that resulted in a staggering 110,000 casualties. It's surprising how little is done to acknowledge this pivotal moment in the war. There are few memorials or markers to guide visitors, and the echoes of that terrible conflict seem to have faded into the background of the city's modern life.

He nodded. 'I know, I've been too. The challenge for the museum is to tell both sides of the story. Feelings in Spain still run deep. Franco's memorial at the Valley of the Fallen is very controversial.'

It was unusual to discuss such matters even now.

'The International Brigades were crucial in the conflict,' he said. 'Your George Orwell was shot, you know.'

'I do. He wrote of it in *Homage to Catalonia*.'

Carlos walked me through some exhibits, speaking passionately about civilian life under siege. As I signed the guestbook and shook his hand, I left into the blinding sun, heartened that a new generation of Spaniards was beginning to grapple with the past.

It was time to hit the road again. With only a couple of hundred kilometres to go before my next stop in Jávea I could take it easy, so I swung out into the busy traffic of the city and headed north on the Costa Blanca coast road past the crowded resorts of Benidorm and Torrevieja. My route wound through the coastal tunnels, past endless beaches and built-up resorts. The roads were manic, a far cry from the remote solitude of Andalucía. Drivers darted across all the lanes to reach exit slip roads; cars were bumper to bumper despite doing over 100 kph.

In the distance I spotted the recognisable Penyal d'Ifac, near Calpe. You can't miss it. It's a giant limestone block which rises a thousand feet straight up out of the sea. I pulled over to admire it from afar, its rocky magnificence casting long shadows over the partying tourists on the beaches below.

I was back in a parador for the night, next to Jávea's lively Arenal Beach. By now I had precious few clothes that looked even moderately presentable so I did some shopping for tee-shirts, a pair of shorts and some underpants. The old ones wouldn't survive another sink wash. Now I was ready to hit the town.

Jávea's characterful bars and its maze of laid-back restaurant-lined cobbled streets contrasted with the concrete jungle clamour of Benidorm, where mass tourism had taken off in the 1950s. It is altogether a lovelier place to be for an evening out, which is what I decided was on tonight's schedule. You know how these things go: first a couple of pints in a bar just metres away from the golden sands, R&B music (not my usual taste) filling the seaside air with cool beats, then a mosey along past Mediterranean, Dutch, Asian fusion, seafood, tapas, Mexican restaurants. Oh, that Dutch one looked different. I darted in.

'Frikandels, yes, And a gin and tonic too. *Gracias* or is it *Dankjewel*.'

The sausage snack only partly filled the sides so back along the boardwalk I went to the tapas bar for *albondigas, gambas, patatas bravas, arroz*. Nice red wine to wash it down, too. Maybe another *cerveza*. Oh, there's an Irish bar. I never go into Irish bars abroad, except in Ireland. Until Jávca.

'*Una jarra de Guinness, por favor*.'

The evening, fuelled by a steady flow of libations, culminated in a hazy, euphoric blur on the dance floor of a pulsating nightclub. Under the strobe lights, surrounded by a sea of youthful energy, I unleashed my own unique brand of dance, a chaotic symphony of flailing limbs and questionable rhythm. I'm sure I provided ample amusement for the onlookers, attractive girls included, who likely witnessed an aging, slightly disheveled man attempting to recapture his long-lost youth. But with each sip of Rioja, the ache in my ribs faded further into the background, replaced by the intoxicating rhythm of the Costa Blanca nightlife. I was hooked.

Jávea to Mallorca via Dénia

The next morning my chest wasn't the only thing that ached again. My overnight revelling made a strong café solo a morning necessity and I knew where to find one. I had some free time before I was due to board the Baleària ferry at nearby Dénia to Ibiza, then on to Palma de Mallorca.

My coffee stop was some way up a winding road in the Montgó Natural Park hills on the way to Dénia. It felt like a lifetime since my first visit on a family holiday almost thirty years ago. Yet, the bar-restaurant, Amanacer, stood almost unchanged, with its refreshing pool, bright dining room, and ice cream kiosk.

My waitress brought me coffee and a croissant. Her hair was brown, her lipstick red. She smelled like flowers. Her dress had the restaurant's logo. She smiled and seemed to enjoy her work despite the heat. Something about the place—ancient memories—made me want to tell her how happy we'd been here.

'We loved coming here with our kids when we were on holiday nearby,' I told her, nostalgically. 'This was always our go-to spot. They'd get ice cream, then we'd swim in the pool. That was many years ago. The kids are grown up now and have their own families.'

If I closed my eyes I could still see my kids as small girls, splashing in the pool.

She laughed. 'Well, it's nice to have you back at last.'

Then, pointing to the pool steps, 'You're welcome to use it, if you like.'

'Perhaps another time,' I replied.

I lingered, lost in memories. Where had those years gone? They say you should never go back... maybe true in some cases, but here, surrounded by echoes of happy family moments, nostalgia washed over me. I ordered another coffee. She brought it minutes later, along with an ice cream from the kiosk of my memories. On the house.

This leg of the journey was almost complete, and the promise of a hot Mallorcan summer filled my thoughts. The restaurant had reminded me that the kids and grandkids would be arriving there soon, ready for poolside fun and family time. But first I had a crossing to make, long planned, from Dénia.

I settled into my cosy seat and fell into a deep sleep. The night on the town was taking its toll on me, reminding me that I couldn't do late hours like I used to. Or booze.

The ferry to Palma had another trick in store. I'd been nursing my ribs carefully which were still feeling tender despite the steady stream of painkillers. In the evening I stood on the stern of the ship, watching the white propeller wash disappear into the golden sea when the boat lurched. I stumbled, whacking my chest on the metal flagpole. It hurt. A lot.

It's only a short distance, half an hour or so, from the port of Palma to our apartment in the southwest of Mallorca but by the time I disembarked it was almost midnight. It had been a very long day and I was knackered.

Nobody was there. No flags flying or welcoming party. I was on my own. Judith was flying in tomorrow. I left the heavily laden bike in my parking space. Unpacking could wait. I walked away and then turned around, the bike visible in the glow of the streetlight. A wave of gratitude washed over me, an odd kinship with this inanimate machine. Sure, it was merely a collection of metal, plastic, rubber and liquids, yet it had carried me on this long journey. Every twist and bump of the road, every adventure and yes, even the mishaps, had brought me closer to experiencing the real Spain. I felt I knew both the country and myself more than before I set off.

This route through the Iberian Peninsula had shown me an extraordinary diversity of landscapes, the country's rich and varied history and people who were helpful and engaging. I'd realised that travelling alone brought special opportunities for discovery and adventure, but also that I missed companionship, especially when times had been tough. But I had enjoyed the journey immensely, and although I needed a rest now I was already looking forward to the next one later this summer.

'*Gracias, amigo,*' I murmured to the Honda, giving its saddle a goodnight pat.

Part Two

THE PYRENEES

'It's all just about the motorbikes. It always has been, it always will be.'

Ewan McGregor

6

Barcelona–La Seu d'Urgell– Andorra

Palma to Barcelona

After thousands of kilometres of relentless adventures, my trusty Honda was finally getting a well-deserved rest. It would see only occasional use that summer, carving through the mountain roads of the Tramuntana, Mallorca's rugged northern spine. But for the most part it would rest in the garage under the swimming pool, a bit more battered than when it departed Derbyshire 2,877 kilometres ago.

A steady stream of family and friends filled my days with laughter and new memories, temporarily pushing aside the trip, while the occasional work meeting in England tugged me back to reality. As I flew over Spain and France in a mere 2½ hours I looked out of the plane's window and recalled with delight my journey to the Balearics. How quickly I could fly over places that took days to reach on the bike. How different and yet still vast the landscape seemed from 30,000 feet. How great to have explored it close-up on the bike.

Soon, though, the summer days were over and we had our Mallorcan place to ourselves again. The Pyrenees were calling, and I had to ride home to Derbyshire so the bike could be fixed. Besides, I was looking forward to spending some time on my own again.

My plan, loosely worked out, was to sail across the Med from Palma de Mallorca to Barcelona, a mere 200 kilometres across the Balearic Sea, then cut through the Pyrenees before catching the long ferry from Bilbao to Portsmouth.

The dockside was a furnace, devoid of shade. Stripped down to the bare essentials, I draped my clothes over the motorcycle, transforming it into a makeshift clothesline as I awaited the boarding signal.

It was the day of Queen Elizabeth II's funeral, and I watched the sombre ceremony on my phone, shielding my eyes from the sun's searching glare. Finally, the queue began to move, and an official's whistle roused the small group of waiting bikers. We hastily donned our gear and rode aboard.

Sometime later I entered the ship's cafeteria where a screen was streaming the funeral. The soldiers were carrying her coffin, with infinite care and dignity, into Windsor Castle. There was a hushed, respectful crowd behind the barriers and the immense, shiny black hearse pulled gently away. Its work, like the Queen's, done.

Beer in hand, I sat down on a blue plastic chair next to a Spanish family, kids, mum, dad and grandparents. They were glued to the large-screen TV in the centre of the deck, as were several other travellers dotted about the room, mostly Brits if their clothes were a reliable guide. My jacket was draped over the back of the chair and my helmet lay on the table next to the cold Mahou beer. I hadn't booked a cabin for the daytime crossing. Lugging my gear around was a hassle but saved me money I'd rather spend on the road.

The *abuela* (grandmother), a woman in her sixties with a kindly face and a touch of silver in her hair, turned to me. Her cream trousers and light blue blouse shimmered in the sunlight filtering through the portholes.

'*És molt trist però és un cerimònia preciosa,*' she said in Catalan.

'Yes, it is sad, but she had a long life,' I replied in my halting Castilian.

'Your Queen was wonderful. We love the royal family here in Spain—yours too,' she said in BBC-accented English, making me feel rather linguistically inadequate.

'It's historic,' I replied. 'And we Brits do pomp and circumstance well, don't we? The crowds in London are incredible. People from all over.'

'She made a historic visit to Mallorca in 1988, you know,' she offered with a sad smile. 'I was lucky. I met her and Prince Philip at the Marivent Palace. I was one of the interpreters for the day.'

A touch of pride lit her eyes.

Maria Pilar, it turned out, was a retired languages teacher from Sitges near Barcelona. Her family had a villa tucked near Alcudia, that sweep of golden beach in the northeast of Mallorca.

'Tell me,' she leaned forward intently, 'where is your motorcycle taking you?'

I gave her a potted list of places.

'Head up into the mountains of Montseny if you are going to the Pyrenees. It's north of Barcelona and a beautiful area, a natural park. Sometimes we go there for a picnic.'

I thanked her and told her I'd check the map. She was right, it was on the way that I had in mind. I ordered another beer at the bar. When I sat back down, Maria turned to me, a glass of red wine in hand. We clinked glasses in tribute.

'The Queen.'

The TV coverage became increasingly difficult to watch. Those excitable studio commentators—couldn't they take a solemn breath? I waved my new Spanish friends goodbye and headed up on deck for some fresh air, where I came across Juan, an Argentinean who lived in Palma. I'd briefly chatted to him in the ferry queue earlier. He was also riding a Honda, an Africa Twin.

This was going to be a challenge. My Spanish was being sorely tested; he had a strong South American accent and, unlike Maria, spoke no English. I'd had only a couple of beers but my Spanish often turns to mush after a few. I struggled to follow what he was saying but the gist was that he planned to ride off-road the whole way to the aptly named town of Hondarribia in the Basque Country. He'd be doing some seriously gnarly tracks on his own, which struck me as far riskier than my solo trip.

Before long, our little biker huddle outside on the stern deck, sheltered from the stiff breeze, grew with the arrival of Karl and Jutta. They were from Malmö, Sweden, and were riding a Harley back home, where more machines lurked in their garage. Karl had lost count, but he claimed he had fifteen motorbikes.

'We come down to Mallorca on the bike from Sweden most years. We take a long break from the clinic, you know? Karl's an orthopaedic surgeon, I'm an anaesthetist. Keeps us busy,' said Jutta.

'Have you seen some bad motorcycling injuries?' I asked Karl, raising a quizzical eyebrow.

'*Naturligtvis*, I've had to deal with some bad ones, but being a biker, I get it. You patch them up and hope they keep their nerve enough to get on a bike again.'

'Doesn't it put you off, knowing what might happen?'

'It does if you really think about it but I think it was Ewan McGregor who said: "It's all just about the motorbikes. It always has been, it always will be."'

'It's made us more careful riders, especially on the long journey here from Malmö. We don't take any silly risks.'

I thought of the contrast with Juan, who was standing only a few feet away.

Did I feel a twinge shoot through my ribs? A reminder to take care? I didn't mention my fall to the docs.

Lucky was the word everyone used at Marchena wasn't it? Sometimes luck is all that separates us from disaster.

A few years ago on an isolated highway in Aragon in the centre of Spain I'd stopped to look at a monument that marked the Prime Meridian. Momentarily distracted, when I rejoined the highway I missed a VW Golf that was overtaking another car, by only a foot or two. It scared me shitless.

Luck saved the day. Again.

The dusk painted our arrival in shades of orange and purple as the *Ciudad de Palma* ferry docked in the busy port in Barcelona. My stomach rumbled in protest; the ferry ride had been a culinary wasteland. Not far away a large yellow arch heralded a McDonald's and I turned in for a burger.

As I settled into my corner booth, a rumble of a different kind announced the arrival of a large group of Hell's Angels. The aroma of fries mingled with the sudden influx of leather and exhaust fumes. The existing customers cast glances filled with a mix of curiosity and apprehension as one black-clad biker after another pushed their way through the rotating door. They were courteous and well-mannered, yet I felt a quiver of unease. Twenty or thirty young, bearded men in worn leather emblazoned with skulls and crossbones made for an intimidating sight. I finished my meal while they were still being served and slid away quietly without being noticed, feeling more ageing rocker than renegade.

Barcelona to La Seu d'Urgell

My overnight was not far from the *Circuit de Catalunya*, scene of many F1 and MotoGP races. The following morning I planned to have a closer look at the course and visit the museum and shop. I pulled up at the imposing metal barrier guarding the entrance. Far from the welcome I'd imagined, an officious, pimply youth appeared, his face a mask of disapproval before I'd even uttered a word.

'*Non*,' he said, 'the circuit does not open for you.'

I explained I didn't want to race round it (I did, obviously, but hadn't even considered the possibility).

'Museum, shop, all shut. Go away.'

It was unusual in these parts to find someone so rude and unhelpful, especially when it was obvious I'd made a special effort to come there. I felt a twinge of anger flush my cheeks. He wouldn't even open the barrier so I could do a safe U-turn. He made me push-reverse which, because of the slight upwards slope, was difficult and hard work. I cussed him under my breath and deliberately went slowly. I gave him the one finger salute. As I get older I have less tolerance for obnoxious idiots. I was keen to get back onto the open road again, frustrated at such pettiness. With a final, deliberate twist of the throttle, I left the silent circuit behind, the insolent youth fading in my rearview.

The Natural Park of Montseny was delightful, as Maria from the ferry had said it would be. I rode ever higher on an exquisite winding mountain road that followed the Tordera stream as it cut its way through the *arroyo*. Sunlight dappled through the leaves of trees that lined the road, their scent filling the air as the branches rustled in the breeze. A smile stretched across my face as the road twisted and turned, each bend revealing a breathtaking new vista. I was having fun.

Suddenly, after one blind curve, I came upon a battered old parked Peugeot, its rear end sticking out into the road, doors open. I slammed on the brakes, swerving to avoid the old banger, its hazard warning lights winking feebly. Two middle-aged guys and a small grey dog appeared out of the woods next to it and I pulled over to remonstrate with them about their crazy parking. They were carrying a wicker basket apparently full of large brown bread rolls.

One who was wearing a Brooklyn Brewery tee-shirt went to shut the car door, apologising.

'Mushrooms,' he declared, his voice warm and friendly.

'We're gathering them for the local restaurants. They fetch a good price. These chanterelles are really delicious,' he added, rummaging in the basket.

His mate, who sported an Elvis-style haircut and sideburns, camo trousers and a dirt strewn brown shirt, was the real mushroom guru, Brooklyn said.

'At least, he's not poisoned himself yet,' he laughed.

Elvis asked if I'd like to take a few with me for dinner, but fortunately both my panniers were chocka and I had no mushroom room. I thanked them, impressed by their dedication to foraging, if not by their parking skills.

The views over the distant mountains towards Andorra were dazzling in the crystal clear air and I stopped more than once to simply stare and take some photos of the jagged peaks, still snow-capped in the gullies, sharply contrasting against the deepest of blue skies.

There were signs, however, that all was not well, particularly in the dried-up reservoirs that appeared near Guixers, in which deep earthy cracks gaped like open wounds. The previously submerged tracks and buildings were now visible, covered in grey silt and appearing like ghosts out of the past. A kayak station was marooned high above the remaining aquamarine water line, a sign that Spain's severe drought continued.

Thoughts of water made me realise I'd pushed on for too long. I had been hours in the saddle since having a proper rest and refreshment. I came across a small restaurant with the unlikely name of Casanova in the village of Odèn. A lively crowd of pensioners filled the terrace—weathered faces etched with laughter lines, hands gesturing as voices rose cheerfully in conversation. Beer and wine glasses covered the tables.

I couldn't break into their circle. It was enough to enjoy their happiness from close by. Taking out my notebook, sipping my drink, I jotted down impressions of this first full day back on the road, trying to capture village life in this sun-baked corner of Spain. It was a timeless place. Take away the few modern cars and the occasional satellite dish and it could have been a hundred years ago. There was even a donkey and cart in the field opposite.

As I rose to leave, the old guys turned to me and touched the brims of their flat caps, carrying on their conversation without pausing. A friendly act I appreciated.

It was back to enjoying the winding mountain roads. My destination for the evening was La Seu d'Urgell, on the Andorran border, a mountainous former Olympic venue. The canoeing competitions in the 1990 Barcelona Olympics were held here. After dinner I wandered through town alongside the waterway, artfully engineered with massive boulders and over-strung with wires, hung with slalom poles like Christmas decorations. It was an impressive sight and is still used for races today. Less impressively the central streets of La Seu were festooned with red and white barriers, diggers, piles of rubble and roadworks, the whole place seemingly a building site. My route to the hotel car park had taken me in ever more confusing circles until I eventually solved the problem by taking the direct route down a closed off partially dug-up street, one of the few occasions I went *off-road* on the whole trip.

My route back from Barcelona to Bilbao was a meandering one, a deliberate choice to savour the journey rather than rush to the destination. Maybe Ralph Waldo Emerson had it right after all, when he said, "It's not the destination, it's the journey". Besides, with the Pyrenees beckoning, why hurry to the ferry and the Bay of Biscay crossing? I had all the time in the world to explore these winding mountain roads. In the hotel car park, a few other bikes were parked, including one that caught my eye: battered, mud-spattered, and sporting a

UK number plate. It looked like it had seen some serious adventures. No sign of its rider, though. A pang of longing hit me. Solo travel has its freedoms, but sometimes a bit of company, someone to swap stories with, is also nice.

La Seu d'Urgell to Arties

On my way back to the peace and enjoyment of mountain roads I passed through Andorra, stopping to have a look at some of the tax-free shops. There were enough knives, coshes, guns, pepper sprays, tasers and handcuffs on display in some of the windows to equip a small militia. The accompaniment for this startling array of window weaponry were large bottles of whisky, gin and vodka, with hookah pipes and cigarettes on parade too.

Drugged up, drunk and in charge of lethal force, hell, those customers would be tough cookies.

Andorra might be wealthy but it's not a pretty place and was extraordinarily busy with tourists and cars, some of whose drivers may well have taken advantage of the low duty rates on alcohol that morning. I had more close shaves with erratic motorists in the short time I was in the principality than at any point on the entire trip from Tarifa to Nordkapp. They seemed incapable of doing anything predictably. A particular speciality was pulling out of a side junction at the last moment in front of me, even though we'd made long, lingering eye contact. The friendlier the terms they seemed to be on with me, the more likely they were to try to kill me. In my entire biking career only the Italians near Palermo and Naples beat the Andorrans for highway lunacy. I escaped Andorra after a soothing herbal tea to calm my nerves.

I pointed the bike in the direction of the Port d'Envalira, the highest paved mountain pass in the Pyrenees (2,408m). The road wound steeply back and forth, but it was wide so finding the right line round the tight bends was easy and a joy. The only blots were the tar snakes, zigzagged streaks of smooth in-fill tarmac poured into road cracks, which were slippery on the bends and tended to unsettle the bike on the straights. Despite that the day was brilliantly clear, sunlight glinting off the sawtooth peaks and views stretching into infinity. It was one of those bluebird days when being on a bike, in the mountains, away from Andorran lunatics, was pure happiness.

As I crossed the border into France near the lovely spa town of Ax-les-Thermes, my phone pinged with a text message from BT, cheerfully announcing my arrival in a new country. I realised that using GPS had cost me over £30 in data roaming charges for the privilege of taking my short trip to Andorra. The country is excluded in the small print from the long list of places in Europe where roaming is included in my contract. Sneaky.

I tucked into a second helping of lunchtime gâteau to sweeten the blow. It was too easy to settle into a satisfying torpor after lunch, especially when the sun invited a blissful afternoon's siesta. Maybe I was becoming increasingly Spanish. Maybe I was just tired. I should have taken a day off, done nothing, slept in and chilled out. There were times when it would have been good just to stop and linger a while longer. This was one of those days but the lure of the open road was ultimately stronger. Surrounded by workers, lovers, friends enjoying each other's company with simple food and wine in the pretty square I roused myself slowly from my chair and headed back to the Honda, its white paint job blindingly bright in the sun, the stickers on the top box almost fading before my eyes.

My route took me on the French side of the Pyrenees, through Foix, with its magnificent castle, which I'd visited five years before, then on to the Ariège, one of the most unspoiled parts of France, with wooded mountains and fast-flowing clear rivers. It was an hour and half of glorious riding. The weather was lovely and there was little traffic, so

I could relax and enjoy watching the scenery unfold. The border between France and Spain is sinuous in this part of the Pyrenees. The road crossed back and forth over the border several times, often without me knowing it. Eventually I had to turn southwards to find my hotel for the night back in Spain, so I took the N125 to the Pont de Rei, where the old border crosses the River Garonne.

This historic spot was where many Spanish refugees fled north to safety in France during the Civil War. Sadly, only a few years later it was persecuted French and German Jews who made the border crossing in the other direction into neutral Spain, escaping the Nazis. Today, a simple stone marker post indicates where they eventually found safe haven.

I parked the bike exactly on the border, its front wheel in Spain, its rear in France, and took a photo as the last slivers of the sun disappeared below the nearby peaks. The valley plunged into rapid darkness and the suddenly cool evening air, scented with pine and damp earth, had me zipped up for the rest of the day's ride to the parador of Artíes.

It had been a long but rewarding sector, a day etched in the memory, and I treated myself to *pa amb oli*. The paper thin slices of *jamón* melted on my tongue with their rich, salty flavours. Simple and delicious. I slept well that night, lulled by the faint tinkling of goat bells, a chorus against the star-dusted night as they wandered the meadows nearby.

7

Artíes–Jaca–Saint-Jean-de-Luz

Artíes to Jaca

The crisp mountain air flooded my senses as I flung open the balcony doors. Coffee and croissant consumed, I packed the bike, eager to lose myself in the best riding roads Europe has to offer. But before that, work, unfortunately, couldn't be completely ignored. With a sigh, I settled into a quiet lounge and logged into a virtual meeting, board papers replacing the thrill of the open road.

Still, it was a contrast to the stuffy boardroom my colleagues were in back home. In that post-COVID period, the brewery I worked for part-time was still holding some online meetings, which suited me down to the ground, especially as I'd flown back for one only a few weeks earlier. I sat in front of my laptop in my riding leathers and boots, a contrast to my suited-and-tied colleagues. I tried not to let my attention wander.

A couple of hours later, the meeting over, I made a Le Mans start, scooting out of the car park as fast as I dared. A few kilometres down the road lay the ski area of Baqueira-Beret, Spain's most popular winter resort. The snow had melted long ago and the place had a slightly desolate air that out-of-season ski areas have, the grey tows and chairlifts casting long shadows across the lush green slopes. Back on the proper track, the border crossing into France at the Col du Portillon marked the true beginning of my day's Tour de France challenge.

The mountainous miles flew by in a blur of exhilarating switchbacks and spectacular scenery. The distant high peaks of the Pyrenees wore a mantle of white cumulus clouds above the hazy blue of the arêtes, *cwms* and valleys but immediately above me was an intense deep purple sky pierced by scorching midday sun. In Arreau, between cols and temporarily back at ground level in the Vallée d'Aure, I parked the bike under a shady oak tree for a coffee in the pretty main square. It was thronged with cyclists out doing some of the climbs the hard way, dreaming perhaps of Tour de France glory on their own *étapes*. I was full of admiration for their efforts.

I approached one of the riders clad in logo-covered blue Lycra, arms tanned and whippet-thin, his muscles defined like a Grecian statue. 'Which way are you heading now?' I asked.

He gave a friendly nod. 'We've come from Bagnères and now go up the Col d'Aspin and then to Tarbes. It's an easy day today. Yesterday from Pau, conquering those other passes, that was *sacrément difficile.*'

I wished him and his mates *bon courage*. They'd need it.

The roads became ever steeper as I dropped down the gears. Sitting on top of 1,100cc of internal combustion engine I was powered up the winding, narrow roads to the sound of the exhaust reverberating off the rocks.

As I carefully overtook group after group of sweating cyclists, it seemed no self-propelled day on two wheels in this glorious countryside could be classed as easy. It was hard enough on the motorcycle, managing some hairy bends, with little or nothing by way of a barrier against the long plumbline drops. Sharp switchbacks disappeared round sheer cliffs and tight corners where only one vehicle could possibly pass. I prayed nothing was coming the other way.

Tribes of goats and, on the Col d'Aspin, a herd of cows, stood stationary in several places on the road, four-legged bovine boulders leaving slippery brown deposits to catch the unwary. I was forced to crawl past, my feet dangling just centimetres above the surface, ready for an abrupt stop.

I was aware of my buttocks clenching, gripping the sides of the fuel tank harder, as the bends tightened, and the exposure became almost overwhelming. I fought hard to try to relax my grip on the handlebars, reminding myself that the secret to smooth and safe cornering was a delicate touch on the controls, not the grip of death. At the summit of most of the cols I pulled over, taking in the stupendous wide-angled vistas which helped to shake away the nerves.

My arms simply weren't long enough for a panoramic selfie so I swapped phones with an Austrian rider so we could both capture the grandeur of the scenery on camera.

I sat down on a rock to drink some water and to contemplate just being there. I'd started the morning back in the world of work but here I was doing something I loved, being in a place that was simply beautiful and in glorious weather to boot. I had no worries, other than staying safe. I had hours still to ride, enjoying the physicality of being on my machine. It was joyful, memorable... and I still get goosebumps when I think of it now.

There are some occasions when the ride is about the destination, when the weather or traffic or the lack of diverting scenery make the day a bit of a chore. Then there are days like this one, a day I didn't want to end.

Large brown metal signboards that displayed the name of the pass and route profile were plastered with stickers by countless cyclists and motorbikers, souvenirs of the enduring popularity of these roads.

Nearing the summit of d'Aubisque, a giant heart painted on the tarmac stopped me in my tracks. Above it, boldly inscribed, was the name "Judith". My wife's name.

Astounded, I walked back down the col, phone clutched in my hand, to capture this strange coincidence and to send it to her.

She replied, via WhatsApp, in a masterpiece of bluffing: "I painted it earlier for you. Glad you spotted it. Keep going. Love you. XX".

As I continued to ride majestic peaks, their summits shrouded in wispy clouds rose on all sides. Deep valleys, carved by ancient glaciers, plunged into the earth, their slopes blanketed in a patchwork of green meadows and dense forests. The air was thin and crisp at this altitude, carrying the scent of pine needles and wildflowers. A refreshing breeze whispered through the trees, offering a brief respite from the scorching sun. I was riding with my visor up, the better to see the road ahead but also to dry the sweat that trickled down my cheeks. On my left, as I rounded another sharp bend a waterfall cascaded down the mountainside, fed by snowmelt from high above, its roar echoing through the valley. Nature was raw and visceral in its power here.

A vast expanse of mountains stretched out before me, their peaks forming a jagged horizon that seemed to go on forever. Tiny villages nestled in the valleys below, their red-tiled roofs glinting in the sunlight. Vehicles, far beneath me, seemed like tiny ants crawling up the tarmac zigzags.

Each conquered pass—Peyresourde, d'Aspin, Tourmalet, d'Aubisque—felt like a personal victory. It was a grand cru of motorbike touring. A vintage day.

It was nearly seven o'clock in the evening by the time I made it to the Spanish border at the Col du Portalet, the shadows growing long in the valleys. At nearly 1,800 metres it was decidedly chilly; I pulled on more layers and thicker gloves for the rest of the day's 280-kilometre journey to

Jaca, in the fading light that soon dimmed to an inky blackness.

As I drew to a halt by the Hotel Oreol and parked the bike down a narrow alleyway, I sighed with deep satisfaction. I was completely knackered from the physical effort (yes, even on a motorbike) and the sheer concentration I'd expended.

That had been one of my most unforgettable rides ever.

Jaca to Saint-Jean-de-Luz

Night had brought with it a fantasy of weird dreams, scenes where a cow was on my pillion and goats were riding cycles. At one point I'd skidded on ice but didn't fall over until I came to a halt, when I promptly dropped the bike. My brain must have been whirring all night.

Jaca is a lovely city and one that's on the regular tourist path if you're travelling on the Camino de Santiago pilgrim route. The scallop shell symbol was on the pavements, street signs and walls, all over the place. Thousands walk the route annually, but as I headed out to visit the small cathedral and walk some of the narrow and historic streets it was quiet and still slumbering.

The alleyways were lined with small shops packed with Camino souvenirs and the smell of freshly brewing coffee and baking bread wafted through the narrow passages. A small café looked promising for breakfast. It's difficult to get something as simple as a croissant and coffee wrong. But this place managed it. Pre-buttered, marmaladed and toasted to a blackened crisp, the croissant was inedible. The coffee failed to make amends, insipid, like lukewarm milky bathwater. The unshaven waiter almost threw them onto my table and then disappeared before I could complain. His disinterest was almost a work of performance art. I halved the bill, left a couple of euros and made an exit myself.

I headed out to see the Ciudadella, the impressive pentagon citadel that is Jaca's jewel. I especially wanted to see its Museum of Military Miniatures, a collection of dioramas and figurines in scenes of battle from different conflicts, frozen in time at 1/32 scale. I reflected on Ukraine where battles were happening for real in that very moment. Few other people were in the museum and citadel, even midmorning, so I had the place to myself. The quality of the exhibits was outstanding, and you didn't have to be a model soldier buff (I'm not) or a history fan (I am) to appreciate the miniature storytelling.

I was also putting off the moment of departure from Jaca for a while as the weather was changing. The clear skies of the Pyrenees had disappeared overnight. Heavy clouds gathered as I headed back to the bike. So with a sigh I wrestled into my bright yellow rain gear, which immediately made me both feel and look bloated and ungainly. But little is more energy-sapping and uncomfortable on a bike than being wet—and inevitably cold.

I headed up the N-330 to the destination etched in my memory from studying the map—the curious and enormous former international railway station at Canfranc. It's a town and place that is full of historical significance, a hotbed of spies and refugees in WW2. Because of its cross-border location, Franco's regime used Canfranc to exchange tungsten, vital for tank production, for Nazi gold. The station, which was being renovated to its former glory with EU money, was 250 metres long and has 365 windows. A luxury hotel was opened within its walls shortly after I visited.

Unfortunately all I could do was peer through the fencing from a distance, as the rain began again, a drenching drizzle at first. I couldn't begin to imagine who might be willing to stay in one of the 104 luxurious rooms at up to £400 a night, in the middle of nowhere, with no international train service yet planned. The old behemoth hotel used to be known as the Titanic of the Mountains. Would this project sink without trace, I wondered, as I clambered back on the bike. Or was there a deeper intrigue behind today's story of

Canfranc, as there was in the old days when mysterious figures passed through its halls?

The rain began to ease a little as I headed north to France through the 8.6-kilometre Somport tunnel, Spain's longest. Emerging on the French side, a quick glance at the fuel gauge sent a jolt of panic through me. The needle was nudging precariously close to empty. Belatedly I realised the warning light had flickered on moments ago while I was lost in the symphony of engine noise and tunnel echoes.

Thinking fast, I shifted the bike into neutral on a slight downslope to coast, saving as much juice as possible. With the motor only ticking over I could hear the slipstream whistling over my helmet and the whoosh of the tyres over the tarmac. The situation was starting to get tense. I'd no spare fuel can, and the road was still winding and mountainously remote. I felt a rising panic and expected to hear the phut-phut of a fuel-starved engine at any moment when, to my huge relief, I came across an unmanned service station. The Honda's capacity is 20.4 litres. Over 19 litres of E5 went in. I wasn't quite running on fumes, but it was a close thing. Nearly a hard lesson learned; since then I have carried two litres of spare fuel on long trips, which would be vital later in the Norwegian far north.

With the threat of a fuel crisis temporarily averted, I decided to press on towards the French Atlantic coast and the town of Saint-Jean-de-Luz, my intended stop for the night. The allure of exploring Bayonne, Biarritz and Pau remained, but the continual rain had sapped my enthusiasm for further detours. It wasn't a desperate urge for home, but rather a subtle shift in mood, a transition from carefree exploration to a more purposeful journey. Yesterday's leisurely meanderings through the mountains were a memory, replaced by a determined focus on making progress.

Reaching the busy city of Pau, I secured a rare parking spot and gratefully took refuge in a café, the warmth of a steaming *chocolat chaud* chasing away the lingering chill. A brief exploration of the city centre revealed a network of streets under construction, adding to the damp and slightly dishevelled air. Pau joined a growing list of places I vowed to revisit *sans moto* for a more leisurely exploration, preferably with sun not rain beating down on my bald head.

The rain had become torrential by the time I arrived at Saint-Jean-de-Luz, near Hondarribia where Juan, the Africa Twin rider, was headed. I could barely see the road signs through the spray and downpour. My visor was constantly steaming up and my only chance of seeing where I was going was to lift it. This meant the inside of my helmet was being drenched, and I was getting facefuls of cold rain. I kept wiping my glasses with my gloved hand, as water seeped round my ears and down my neck. I was fed up and my Campanile budget accommodation was looking increasingly attractive. Meanwhile the satnav decided it had had enough, too. Water must have entered its works and I stared at a blank screen. I didn't dare use my phone for navigation in case that got soaked too.

I'd been up and down the edge of town road where I thought the hotel was several times. Suddenly I spied it, behind a Courtepaille steak restaurant, and swung off the road abruptly, prompting an irate French driver way too close behind me to blast his horn.

'*Connard,* fucking give me a bit of space,' I swore. Stress was getting to me.

The car park was basically a paddling pool but as the tyres sploshed their way through the deluge I felt overwhelming relief at arriving in one piece. I parked outside the hotel reception door, on the pavement and under cover, where at least I could unpack and lock it up without needing wellies. As I was clicking on the disc lock and chain, a couple of flics (cops) stood nearby under the canopy, smoking.

'You'll be okay here tonight. Look around,' one of them said to me in French and pointed round the corner.

I looked up. There were a dozen police cars and more were joining them down the entrance road.

'There's thirty of us here tonight, so nobody's going to nick your bike.'

Twenty-eight of them queued at the check-in, as I stood for ages dripping on the carpet. Finally, inside my basic room, I flopped onto the bed, wet gear strewn over the floor, my eyelids heavy with exhaustion. I needed a warm shower, fresh clothes and something strong to drink before dinner. I idly switched on the telly and channel-hopped to BBC World.

"*Chancellor Kwarteng announces huge tax cuts. Pound plunges.*"

The realities of home, suspended while I was on the road, began to reclaim me. A sigh escaped my lips, a mingled echo of relief and a faint pang of regret as the simple pleasures of my journey began to fade into the inevitable gravitational pull of the quotidian once more.

8

Saint-Jean-de-Luz–Zierbena

Saint-Jean-de-Luz to Zierbena

There's always a moment of trepidation in the morning, emerging from an overnight stop to check on the bike. Will it still be there? Sadly, bike theft is a common phenomenon these days. However, I was confident today that my bike would still be where I'd left it. The Honda was surrounded by a large group of cops in a blue haze of cigarette smoke, a growing ring of fag-ends encircling it. These guys were the CRS, the tough riot control specialists, not to be messed with. It was like having my own personal security force looking after the bike. I never did find out why they were there. Saint-Jean-de-Luz seemed an unlikely place for a demo. Maybe it was a police awayday.

Today would be my last day's riding before catching the Brittany ferry back to England. I was hoping for glorious weather to finish my southern leg of my journey on a high note. Unfortunately, the non-stop rain had other ideas. The car park was a miniature lake by now. I lingered over breakfast, hoping it might ease.

By half past ten it was clear that the bad weather system was going nowhere. With a resigned sigh, I prepped myself for the final soggy leg. Gritting my teeth, I pulled onto the motorway, the roar of the engine barely audible over the drumming rain. Visibility was down to mere feet. The only guides were the flashing white lane markers, a blurry streak in my peripheral vision. The visor steamed up constantly, forcing me to squint through a watery haze, perpetually scanning for the dreaded red glow of brake lights. This wasn't riding, it was an exercise in blind faith and cold courage. Every mile felt like a minor victory, a hard-won step closer to the sanctuary of the ferry and, hopefully, drier times ahead.

At San Sebastián I simply had to come off the motorway and rest, such was the concentration and tension of the riding. I grabbed a coffee and *pastel de nata* in a small bakery, a pool of water gathering by my feet. The warmth of the room and the enticing scent of the cakes lulled me back to life.

A middle-aged man, kind eyes crinkled at the corners and sitting at a nearby table, smiled at me pitifully, and said in English with a hint of the north, 'Welcome to the Basque Country.'

James was a British architect who had lived in this part of Spain for nearly twenty years.

'I wouldn't go back to England now. I love the Basque people, the food and wine but not the weather. That's just like where I came from.'

'Manchester?'

He laughed. 'Right first time. It's green here for a reason. We get more rain in San Sebastián than any other city in Spain.'

The Basque Country, home of the Guggenheim Museum and the Kursaal Congress Centre, has an outstanding reputation for modern architecture, which had drawn him there, despite the local language barrier.

'Do you speak Euskara?' I asked.

'A little, but it's totally different from Spanish. The Basques are so proud of their heritage,' he said, pointing to the red, blue and white Basque flag on the wall, curiously like the Union Jack

'Bit like how different Welsh is from English,' I replied, thinking of my 100% Welsh wife who spends time every day reading in her native language. I could have gobbled down one of her Bara Brith cakes with my coffee right now.

'*Etxerako bidaia segurua.* Safe journey back home,' said James, as I picked up the bill to pay at the counter.

The black ribbon of road merged almost seamlessly into the dark and threatening sky for the last 140 kms to Zierbena on the west side of Bilbao, where the ship *Salamanca* was waiting to depart for Portsmouth. I hunkered down on the saddle, sheltering as best I could behind the windshield, peering through a slit at the bottom of my visor, like a mediaeval knight. Great gobbets of water clattered on the screen, splashing violently and seeping round the edges over me. Dampness eked its insidious way down my neck into the seams of my trousers and began to pool between my buttocks. I simply had to keep going and out of trouble for long enough. At a steady 70 kph or even slower it took a long while before signs for the docks started to appear. I rode through a large industrial estate, past oil tanks and over numerous speed humps. Mercifully, by the ferry there was no queue, and the orange-vested staff pointed me towards Border Control; I was passport-stamped out of the Schengen zone and rode rapidly up to where the vehicles were embarking.

It was with mixed emotions that I rode gingerly up its slippery checker plated ramp. This summer's riding had been challenging and rewarding, and I felt a hint of loss at the conclusion of my journey to the southernmost tip of Europe.

But mixed with that feeling was a stronger emotion— anticipation for the next chapter of my adventure, the road trip with my riding mate Ralph to Nordkapp, the northernmost point of the continent. He'd not been able to join me for Iberia but was up for Scandinavia. While I'd been busy in Spain, he had been using his spare moments to modify and equip his BMW for northern climes. What stories would unfold on that journey? Who would we meet? What adventures and surprises would we have? Where would our journey lead us?

And, most personally, how would that next experience shape me, as this one had?

There were dozens of different ways I might have gone to Tarifa and then to Mallorca this summer. I will never know what might have happened on the roads I didn't take. But I let serendipity shape most of my route rather than planning everything down to the last spreadsheet cell. I had enjoyed this new approach to travel, and felt a freedom I'd not experienced before—and even loved its sometimes chaotic spontaneity.

I'd always thought of myself as a lone rider and still clung to being self-reliant. I liked being totally at liberty to do as I pleased, beholden to nobody. I wondered how different that would be with Ralph. I would have to adapt.

Yet I also had felt the loneliness of crowds and appreciated more than ever the joys of sharing great moments, whether in nature or in culture or just with a simple laugh.

My Spanish had improved (a little) as I'd pushed myself to speak the language. There are still plenty of places where little English is spoken and the effort of making a connection with someone in their native tongue adds to the fun.

I learned much about the history of Spain, especially its bloody Civil War and began to appreciate why it's so difficult a topic to confront for the Spanish.

The people I'd met had mostly been delightful and helpful, especially the police I'd come across. Even the French cops, not usually noted for being pussycats, were amicable.

A fortnight and more of good eating, drinking and less exercise than usual (especially with broken ribs) had added a few inches to my waistline, but I'd enjoyed an exceptional variety of local dishes, not all of which I've shared in the book for fear of being too foodie. The Hairy Bikers have that market sewn up.

The landscapes through which I'd travelled had been utterly varied and intriguing, shifting from region to region. Even the desert-like areas around Tabernas had a raw beauty.

There was a clear sense of poverty and rural deprivation in many places, especially in the north, which contrasted sharply with the wealth of the big cities and parts of the south. But throughout the country there was also a sense of unity and pride in place, even with the Catalonian independence issue. I wondered how Britain might feel by comparison, as the fleeting news from home seemed to emphasise deepening strife and division.

And then there were the roads and the bike.

Ewan McGregor said, 'It was all about the motorbikes.'

I think we know that's never the full story. For me, it wasn't about the motorbike, my trusty Honda. The riding was never just a means to an end. It was the essence of the journey, a liberation from the ordinary. Each day, I looked forward to the open road, the freedom to choose my own path, to explore hidden corners and conquer challenging routes. The bike became my passport to adventure, a key to unlocking the secrets of Spain and the Pyrenees. Whether carving through mountain passes or weaving through city traffic, I was in my element, connected to the world in a way that only a rider can understand.

Yes, there was always the motorbike. And the motorbiking had been good.

Coca Castle

Segovia

Spanish pork scratchings

Noel and the author in Avila

My Honda after the incident in Marchena

Puente Nuevo in Ronda

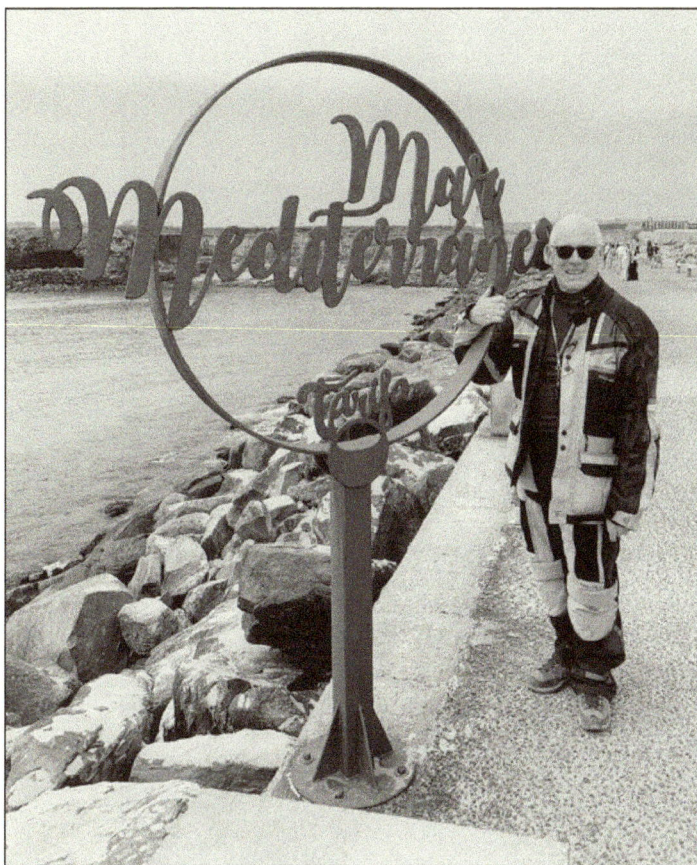

Tarifa – journey's end in the south

Mezquita in Cordoba

Pyrenees, near Col du Tourmalet

Ralph and his BMW at Arnhem Bridge

Storseisundbrua on The Atlantic Road

Survived the Trollstigen

Bronze Age porn at Tanum, Sweden

Breidalsvatnet near Geiranger—in June

Having devilishly good fun

The beautiful River Namsen

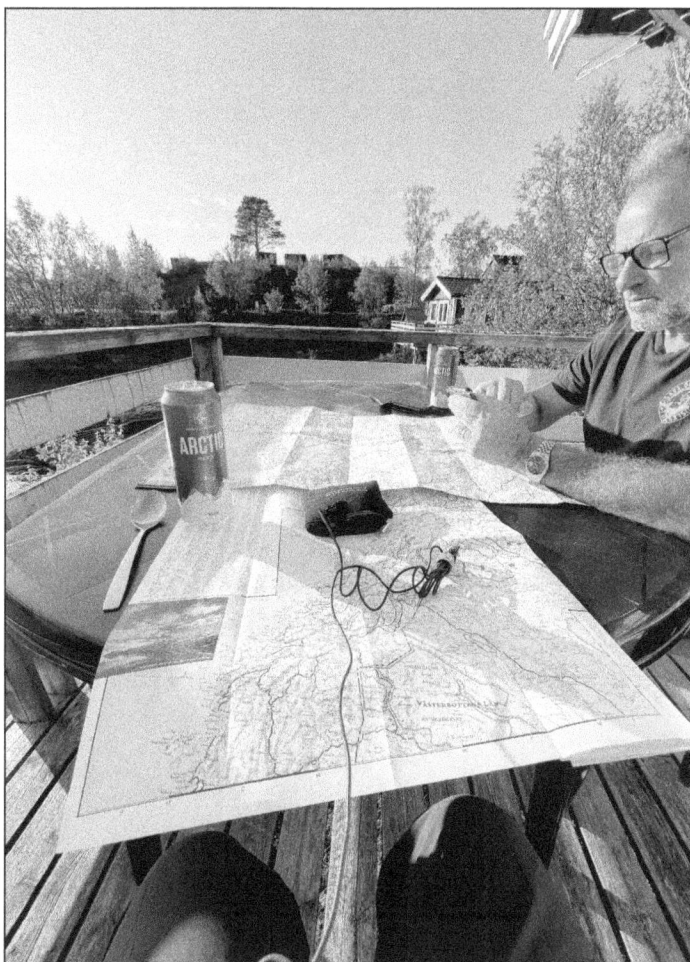

Planning the next day at Yttervik

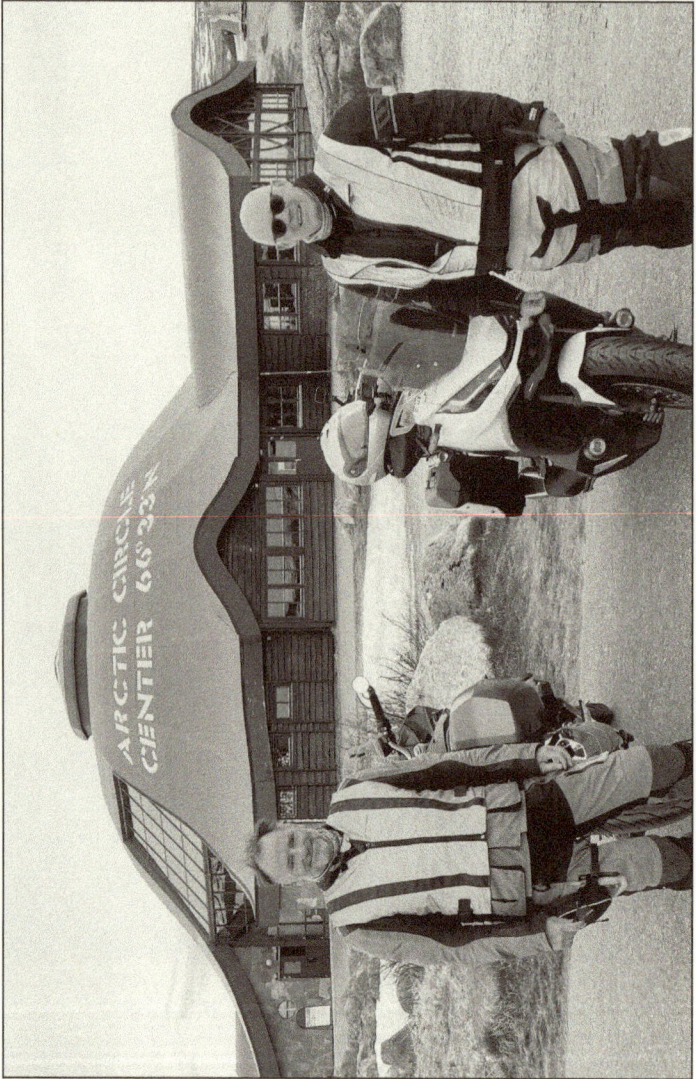

Crossing the Arctic Circle

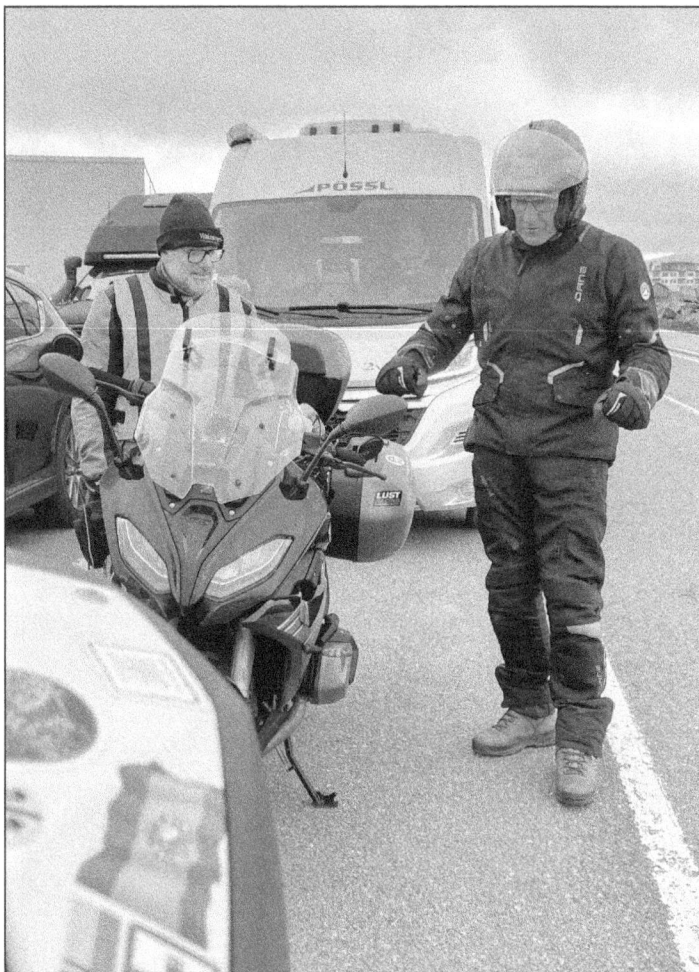

Ralph and Klaus, the crazy Dutchman

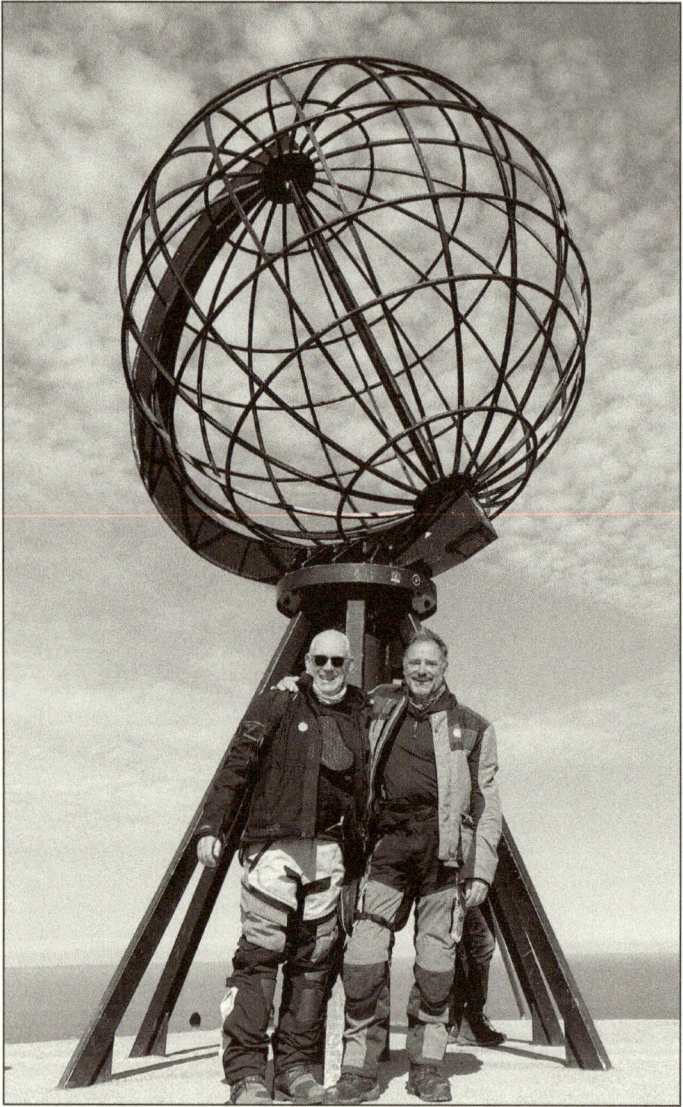

Journey's End northwards – at Nordkapp

Schengen Border.
Restricted area
Adgang kun for
reisende
Border crossing only
Въезд только для
лиц, следующих
SCHUBERTH
SHOEI

Russian border crossing point at Storskog

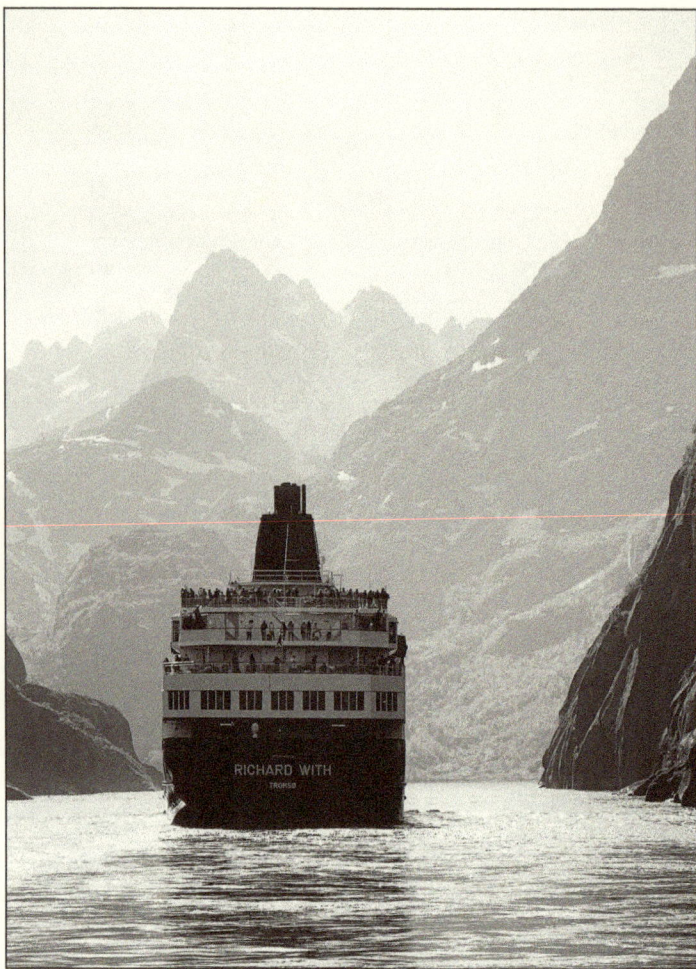

The Hurtigruten ship *Richard With* on the Trollfjord

A well-travelled bike on the quayside at Bergen

Part Three

TO NORDKAPP

To go north, you must go south. To reach the west, you must go east. To go forward you must go back. To touch the light, you must pass beneath the shadow.'

George R.R. Martin

9

'Got a crazy idea for you'

Derbyshire, Rotterdam, Bremen

I pulled the bike out of its winter resting place in the garage. Spiders scuttled away. I blew dust off the faded Ronda and Córdoba stickers on my top box, souvenirs from the previous year's sun-baked Andalucían travels. Seeing them now stirred a nostalgic longing. It seemed a long time ago but now it was time to swap the warmth of Spain for the icy and unbounded wilderness of Norway's Nordkapp, the northernmost point of mainland Europe.

I'm not a fan of winter riding. I know plenty who ride all year round but cold, wet and foggy days on the bike do nothing for me. Instead, I rode in my mind, using the winter months to dream and plan.

My dining table turned into a map-strewn command centre, a place for charting routes and researching new and unfamiliar places to visit. The spontaneity of Iberia was to be sacrificed to a rigid schedule of itineraries as I, or rather we, headed north to Norway.

Why so different an approach? Partly because the distances would be far greater and the logistics more complex, but mainly because I would be doing this trip with a riding buddy for the first time. For joining me was my good friend Ralph, a seasoned rider but a continental virgin embarking on his first tour on the wrong side of the road aboard his powerful BMW RS1250.

The fact that Ralph used to be my boss added to the pressure. I felt the weight of responsibility of planning and preparation. I didn't want to wing it and make an arse of myself—he'd seen me do that many times before at work. I was supposed to be the competent one at this motorbike touring lark, so I was leaving nothing to chance.

I had meticulously planned our route, a lengthy meandering that traced the rugged beauty of Norway's entire coastline, as well as a good chunk of Sweden's. A spreadsheet listed dates, legs, distances, times, stops, places of interest, possible accommodation, even motorbike main dealers. Highlights were marked up in yellow. There was a lot of yellow.

The itinerary in outline went like this:

Hull – Rotterdam – Bremen – [Puttgarden–Rodby ferry] – Copenhagen – [Oresund Bridge] – Gothenburg – Oslo – Otta – Molde – Trondheim – Namsos – Mosjoen – Bodo – Lofoten Islands – Tromsö – Alta – Honningsvag – Nordkapp.

I'd had time over the winter months to buy the North Sea ferry tickets and book some key city accommodation with secure bike parking. Our machines were expensive and highly nickable. I was aware that it might be hard to find hotels or lodging in some remote places so I'd planned that we would stay on campsites for a stretch along the coast of Norway. I didn't think Ralph would be too keen on the idea of slumming it in a tent, but he was surprisingly enthusiastic and promptly popped out to buy one.

Weeks blurred into a whirlwind of kit lists, shopping and the inevitable nagging fear of forgetting something crucial. Ralph and I couldn't possibly pack enough clothes for a month on the road, so laundry gel and a sink plug became essential travel items.

As the day of our departure drew near the art of minimalist packing reached its zenith. I figured that I couldn't stuff in everything I wanted, so every item was meticulously reconsidered and designated essential. Nice to haves were simply discarded. Every nook and cranny on the bike, even mouse-sized spaces under the saddle, were put to good use. Finally all the panniers were snapped shut and straps tightened with a thrill of anticipation.

Our plan to camp en route had added another layer of complexity to our gear needs. Fortunately my mountaineering days had left me with a cache of expensive lightweight gear, chair included, for those midge-infested Scandinavian evenings with a lakeside beer. Ralph, starting from scratch, made new friends with his local outdoor store and had a stash of shiny new kit ready for Nordic action.

Motorcycling through unpredictable summer weather, especially in the far north, demanded a wardrobe of warmth and waterproofing. This meant splurging on gear like my Rukka Nivala jacket. New Alpinestars Revenant Pro trousers replaced the ones I shredded in last year's Spanish mishap. None of this came cheap but I'd learned the hard way that safety and comfort attracted a vital premium.

Every spare inch of my Honda concealed essential tools, tape and cable ties (learned my lesson), which turned the bike into a mini mobile workshop. But that nagging doubt lingered: have I forgotten that one crucial item? One item I couldn't forget were my meds. My ticker needs regular drugs to keep it turning over smoothly and they wouldn't be easy to find in the middle of nowhere. I counted them all out carefully, added a spare few as a margin for error and stashed them in different places for security.

Our departure for Nordkapp was suddenly upon us. It seemed like only yesterday we were dreaming of fjords and midnight sun, and now... here we were, practically ready to go. It was time to take to the road again on my longest ever motorbike tour.

And what of the Honda NT1100 itself, the machine that had carried me over 3,100 miles through the heart of Spain the previous summer, emerging battered but not totally broken? When the insurance assessor surveyed the damage on my return, his grim demeanour and sharp intake of breath had spoken volumes. The dealership's repair estimate topped £5,000. A few more dents and they might as well have written the whole thing off.

I argued that the estimate was absurdly expensive. The claims assessor had a ready explanation: 'Your policy demands the bike be restored to its brand new condition. That's why we're replacing most of the left side.'

It seemed a rare occasion where the client argued for a cheaper repair. Still, the company covered the costs, and the dealership transformed my battle-scarred Honda back into a pristine white warrior, ready for its next road trip.

I wandered back into the house where Judith offered a cup of tea.

'So, are you nearly ready for this jaunt of yours and Ralph's?'

'Almost. Only a few last-minute things to chuck into the bags and then we're good to go.'

'Enjoy your romantic cruise on the Hurtigruten ship together,' she replied, keeping a straight face.

I grinned sheepishly.

It wasn't meant to be this way. In fact, instead of Ralph, it should have been her on the ship with me. Her little dig reminded me of how this whole cruise had been planned a couple of years earlier, before I headed off to Tarifa.

I vividly recalled the conversation after I'd booked a surprise birthday present. She'd opened the envelope that I'd lovingly decorated and filled with a card showing a ship, fjords and the Northern Lights.

Her lowered glasses and icy glare should have alerted me to an emerging problem.

'Hang on. You booked us on a twelve-day cruise?'

'Yes.'

'And this cruise is in Norway?'

'Correct. A Northern Lights tour.'

I was starting to feel I may have blundered.

'You know I hate ships and sailing. I get seasick in the bath.'

'Er, well—'

'And when are we going?'

'December.'

'Is it warm and sunny in Norway in December?'

'Not... exactly.'

'Of course it's not, you idiot. It's dark, freezing, miserable.'

'Well, the ship's cosy, I'm sure.'

My voice trailed off into a feeble attempt at optimism. It was clear that my surprise birthday adventure was off to a disastrous start, and this bargain Hurtigruten trip to see the Aurora Borealis, sailing up the Norwegian coast and back, was headed straight for the rocks.

'Stephen, after forty years of marriage you should know better. I don't do cold, I don't do seas, and this brochure says we barely even dock. Why on earth would I like this?'

'You love seafood. There's a lot of it on the menus.'

The look I got suggested that I was far from convincing her, so I quietly let it drop and found a different birthday present instead. I slunk away; the thrill of adventure replaced by a pang of regret. I'd been carried away, forgetting that while our differences are what kept our marriage exciting, they also demanded consideration.

Time to make amends. Forget winter wonderlands. Go in the spring instead, I decided.

Fortunately, the travel company were very helpful. After the woman on the line stopped chuckling (I must make a mental note not to tell the truth when ringing up customer services) they said they'd happily swap the twelve-day winter expedition for a rather more abbreviated seven-day, one-way trip from Bergen to Kirkenes in the far north of Norway. In

May. This would at least solve the darkness problem, though as the friendly tele-sales lady pointed out (rather superfluously I felt), 'It will still be on the sea.'

She made it clear that the hefty deposit would soon be forfeited without a decision. Covertly, I rebooked for Spring 2020.

Round two, the spring version, required my best sales pitch.

'Love, I know wine's pricey onboard, but with pre-booking, we might stretch to a whole bottle... for the week... each.'

She didn't say no, well not exactly anyway.

Then, of course, a lethal bug threw a spanner into everyone's travel plans across the world. At least now I had time to craft more convincing arguments. But selling the idea of a small ship, a floating petri-dish of post-COVID anxiety, to a nervous sailor—warm weather or not—was going to demand all my skills of persuasion.

Then the nails arrived for the coffin of my travel proposal. The BBC broke the news: the cruise ship *MV Viking Sky* lost power off the perilous Hustadvika coast, forcing the dramatic evacuation of 1,300 people. The fact that it wasn't a Hurtigruten vessel was irrelevant to Judith—a sinking ship was a sinking ship. Her told-you-so look needed no translation. My cunning plan was holed below the waterline.

There are two ways of looking at a situation. Either as a problem or an opportunity. I had been planning to ride from Tarifa to Nordkapp on my motorbike anyway. What if I could ride north, far north, and then sail back? Hurtigruten were happy to let me join the ship at any point I wanted and to take the bike onboard. Sorted.

Fortunately after over forty years of marriage Judith is very tolerant and knows my restlessness borders on clinical. A begrudging but nonetheless signed month-long pass was the ultimate seal of approval.

As a seasoned solo traveller, the thought of tackling this far-flung trek North to Nordkapp alone gave me pause. A journey as grand as this one craved shared moment, the comradeship of the road. With a mischievous grin, I fired off a text to Ralph, one of the few friends I knew who might share my passion for two-wheeled fun.

"Ralph, got a crazy idea for you. I know how busy you are, so plenty of notice. This summer we head to Tarifa, in southern Spain. Then next year even bigger trip. Destination: Nordkapp, the northernmost point of Europe you can reach on wheels. We'll weave through Belgium, Holland, Germany, Denmark, Sweden, Finland, and Norway. Booked my bike on the Hurtigruten ferry from Kirkenes – that's practically Russia – in mid June. Six days at sea, then ride back via Denmark and Rotterdam. It's a 5,000-kilometre marathon, about a month in the saddle. Currently riding solo, but would you be up for the insanity?"

Two days stretched like an eternity, then the reply pinged through.

"Wow. Thanks for asking. Can't do Spain but Norway sounds amazing. Which bike you taking? I'm torn between the stylish Speedmaster or swapping for a tourer. Louise is already rolling her eyes at the bike videos."

"Might invest in the new Honda NT1100 for this one," I texted back. "Made for long hauls, and its cruise control sounds a good idea, especially with those Norwegian speeding fines."

And that's how, a year and a half later, Ralph and I found ourselves standing in Kirkenes, Norway on the edge of Russia, him on his road-worn BMW RS1250, me straddling my filthy Honda, a shared sense of achievement buzzing between us.

Derbyshire to Hull

D-Day (Departure Day) dawned brightly, and the sun was shining, which I took as a good omen. Ralph had ridden over to North to Norway Road Trip HQ in Derbyshire and we'd done the last minute checks.

Flags and bunting fluttered bravely, as if ready to wave the intrepid travellers off on our grand adventure. In truth, they were remnants of the recent local carnival, and the cheering crowds were conspicuously absent. Our send-off consisted solely of Judith, who gave a perfunctory wave before disappearing back inside to resume her ironing.

Ralph's BMW RS1250 was not lightweight at 243kg—not counting luggage and rider. Hefting a quarter of a tonne of machinery around required some strength, especially at slow speeds. On my driveway Ralph was manoeuvring his bike on tip toes when he slipped on a bit of loose gravel that was lying in wait on the tarmac. Over on its side it started to go and it was probably only adrenaline that gave Ralph the strength to drag it back to vertical. A close call, and we hadn't even started. A timely reminder that even the tiniest slip-up can derail a grand adventure.

Together we set off northward, our sights set on Hull for the evening P&O ferry to Rotterdam. By nightfall, we were sound asleep in our cabins aboard the *Pride of Rotterdam*, while a large posse of bikers who were clearly up for all night revelry chugged Morettis below deck. Grimsby faded in our wake; its gritty cityscape replaced on the coastal horizon by low, grassy shores as we slipped out of the Humber estuary towards the North Sea.

Rotterdam to Bremen

By dawn's first light we approached the dock in Rotterdam's sprawling Europoort, which triggered a frenzy of metallic clanking and muttered curses. Bikers descended upon their machines, a symphony of ratchets tightening and straps snapping into place. Nerves jangled like loose chains. Nobody wanted their pride and joy to topple in the rough sea. The air crackled with a mix of anticipation and clumsy chaos—gloves on, gloves off, a misplaced helmet, the forgotten earplugs. Finally the cavernous car deck doors creaked open, spilling a sliver of dawn into the smoky dimness. A chorus of engines roared to life, their deafening rumbles a prelude to motion. Bikes lurched forward, riders wobbling precariously, braced against an ill-timed slip. The ignominy of dropping your bike here would linger as surely as the stink of diesel. But with each rider finding their balance, the swarm thinned, feet snapped firmly onto pegs, and we surged up the ramp into the open air. A deep breath, laced with the tang of salt and exhaust fumes, signalled a release. The journey proper had begun.

We pulled up to border control, got the obligatory stamp in our passports and then the barriers rose, a silent signal of freedom. Ralph mirrored my wide grin, and with a synchronised revving of engines, we catapulted into motion, the dockside blurring past. Our Nordkapp adventure, a wild dream transformed into roaring reality, was finally, undeniably, underway. In our minds we were buccaneers, sallying forth. To anyone watching, though, we would have seemed like two older geezers on bikes laden with lots of bags tentatively trying to escape Rotterdam.

We faced a hefty stretch of 450 kilometres across the Netherlands and Germany, but the weight of history first compelled a detour to Arnhem. Here, a desperate attempt to secure a key bridge during Operation Market Garden became a bloody turning point in WW2. Over 1,600 British soldiers fell in the fierce battle, and the rebuilt bridge (now named after Major-General John Frost) stands as a silent memorial. Even amidst the bustling normality of modern Arnhem, the echo of that sacrifice lingers in the many museums, monuments, memorials and carefully preserved military hardware that dot the town. A pink rose, a single stem, was lodged in the handle of an anti-tank gun, dedicated to the people of Arnhem by the 3rd Parachute Battalion. Information boards by the bridge briefly told the bloody story of 17th September 1944, but we wanted to find out more.

'You know, Ralph, sometimes I stop and think about how lucky we've been.'

'Our generation you mean? Yes, you're right. We were the Make-Love-Not-War generation, born into the swinging sixties, and here we are, still vaguely capable of swinging a leg over a motorbike in our sixties.'

'We've literally dodged a bullet, haven't we? Imagine growing up with rationing and air raids. Blimey, no thanks.'

'Quite right, and nowadays the only tanks we have to think about are the ones on the bike, filling them up and heading off across the whole of Europe,' said Ralph.

'We grew up with the Beatles, not bombs. That's worth celebrating.'

'I suggest we commemorate Arnhem later with a Beck's in Bremen. Tally ho.'

We left the John Frost Bridge. Then, a crackled cry came over the intercom:

'I've left my glasses on the saddle. They might have fallen off.'

'I'll go back,' I offered, U-turning with a mix of resignation and amusement.

Moments later, I returned: 'Do you want the good news or the bad news?'

Ralph's specs were on the ground where we'd parked, but in more pieces than normal. This was when our just-in-case list proved its worth. A spare pair meant he could avoid squinting his way to Bremen. Trying to fit the original bits together with sticky tape and glue, like an optical jigsaw, would keep him occupied late into many nights. And afterwards he still looked like Coronation Street's Jack Duckworth.

We arrived at the Oorlogsmuseum on the outskirts of Arnhem, the first of many such poignant stops we would make on our journey. These museums, often meticulously curated by dedicated individuals, ensured the stories of the past wouldn't be lost to time. Walking through their halls, we felt a deep respect for those whose lives were forged in the fires of war.

From the multitudes of hidden victims of the Spanish Civil War to the bombed-out towns of northern Norway, and the unsettling echoes of the current war in Ukraine, the shadow of war seemed to stretch across the European continent.

Some ancient BMWs with rusty skeletal frames, seized engines and ancient cracked tyres attracted our attention. These Wehrmacht messenger bikes had spent thirty-five years buried in the soggy Dutch soil, gradually disappearing. They looked staggeringly uncomfortable to ride, even for those times, and I contemplated the naked terror the young riders would have felt in the face of the Allied attack, as "our boys" attempted to take the bridge.

The thump-thump of Kraftwerk's *Autobahn* blasted from my helmet speakers, my off-key rendition echoing across the far-reaching expanse of German motorway. Little did those 70s electro-pop pioneers know their anthem would soundtrack two Brits on bikes, hurtling along the fabled autobahn nearly half a century later.

'Speed. It's a relative thing, not an absolute fact,' interrupted Ralph over the intercom.

It is empirically true. Question: when does 140 kph (87 mph) feel slow? Answer: when you're on a derestricted German autobahn being overtaken by cars doing more than 200 kph.

Not that I'd try to use that relative line if pulled over by a stern-faced *Polizei* with a radar gun. Still, there's a strange thrill in watching the needle hover at 140 kph while being overtaken by Porsches doing double that.

Truthfully, though, the Rotterdam-to-Bremen via Arnhem dash was always going to be a schlep. With so much ground to cover before reaching those glorious Norwegian curves, those tempting B-roads had to be sacrificed to the gods of efficient mileage.

And so, after our Arnhem detour, we submitted to the monotony of the autobahn, punctuated by bursts of white-knuckle overtaking. Even on their unrestricted stretches, I felt like a tortoise amongst hares, those BMWs and McLarens a blur in my mirrors. Every glance over my shoulder for a potential guided missile up my rear was a tense reminder of the risks that came with the thrill. We were not so much living life in the fast lane, as trying to survive in the slow one.

The adrenaline rush of dodging warp speed racing driver wannabes faded into the tedium of a massive traffic jam, stretching from Osnabruck to Wildeshausen. My eyes glazed over the endless taillights ahead. The Germans were investing in their fast roads, no doubt delivered on time and under budget. While we crawled along, they probably also had a sleek high-speed rail network connecting these same cities. I thought of the contrast with the UK's clogged motorways and haphazard rail network.

German drivers, though quick, were disciplined and as soon as there' was a *Stau* (traffic jam) they created a *Rettungsgasse*, an impromptu emergency vehicle carriageway, by pulling over to the left or right of their lane. We feigned ignorance and shot down the middle. I've no idea as to the legality or otherwise of this move for non-emergency vehicles, such as two bikes from the UK, but our high viz vests and yellow stripes on the front of my white motorcycle with lots of bright lights seemed to impress the German *Autofahrer* and we made surprisingly good progress. Ralph followed in my wake; I couldn't see if they were all shaking their fists at him.

Once free of roadworks German drivers adopted an F1 approach, as though they were accelerating off the grid. We were being passed at crazy speeds even though Ralph and I, riding in tandem, were both already exceeding the UK speed limit by a criminal amount.

Ralph burst into song over the intercom:

'*Don't let's be beastly to the Germans when we've definitely got them on the run.*'

He warbled his version of Noel Coward's WW2 satire, firstly in an upper-class accent and then in cod German when it came to '*Don't let's be beastly to the Hun*'. At this point they were being beastly to us as one Porsche owner hung a few feet off my rear, suddenly shot out and then squeezed back in between us, forcing me to brake hard.

I was finding it hard to agree with Coward's lyrics at this point. Juvenile, I know, but when you've a 911 up your chuff it's strangely comforting. Ralph started a new rendition.

Hiss... '*only got one ball*' (crackle), '*Göring has two, but they are small*' (more crackling).

Silence. Our intercom banter was rudely cut short. Ralph and I had exceeded the limits of our radios' range; neither of us had any idea where the other was. Mr Porsche had broken up our mini convoy.

'Are you receiving me? Over,' I squawked into the mic.

No answer. I tried again.

Minutes passed and by now I was cursing the fact we'd not fixed any form of Plan B rendezvous.

After a few hints of static noise I spotted a familiar looking pair of headlights in my mirrors.

'Coming up your rear, Stephen.'

My mate's Scots lilting laugh rang loud and clear again. The team was back together.

'I saw flashing blue lights and slowed down. Thought it was the cops.'

'Was that the ambulance that went past about five minutes ago?' I asked.

'That's the one. I still couldn't catch him afterwards.'

It was a long haul to Bremen, and by the time we finally rolled into the city, exhaustion had settled into our bones. Ralph, to his credit, had never ridden on the wrong side of the road before, so tackling 450 kilometres on his continental debut was impressive.

I've always had a soft spot for Bremen, one of those grand old Hanseatic cities. As a teenager on an exchange visit, I'd stayed in a stately mansion near the Bürgerpark, owned by the surgeon parents of a girl named Inge. She was smart, kind, and completely out of my league. Any ideas I might have had of forging closer Anglo–German relations than was the aim of the exchange came to nought; not least since my first real girlfriend, Wendy, was on the same trip.

Years later I returned often to Bremen as I worked for the UK importer of the city's most well-known brewery, Beck's. I was keen to show Ralph a few of my old haunts. After landing at our hotel, the promise of a few steins in the charming Schnoorviertel spurred on a quick shower and change. Several beers and a hearty *Wienerschnitzel und Frites* later, we wandered into the main square, swaying to the beat of some live jazz and marvelling at the meticulous reconstruction of the Rathaus, a symbol of the city's post-war resilience. We popped into the cavernous *Ratskeller* (town hall pub), admired the massive statue of the burgher Roland (symbol of the city since 1404) and then for luck rubbed the donkey's leg of the Stadtmusikanten, the landmark bronze of a donkey, dog, cat and rooster. A proper tourist's evening after a long day in the saddle.

As we strolled, fuelled by beer and post-ride contentment, our conversation meandered through politics and music as well as remembering the times we'd spent working together. I had known Ralph for years and we'd always got on well, both in the office and outside. We'd not spent a long time together socially, though, more a pint or so after work, and the odd short skiing trip, a shared passion. This trip was going to be much more intense and both of us were unsure how it would work out. Practical preparations didn't include chemistry lessons.

I recalled that nearly twenty years before I had handed him my resignation letter. I was responsible for a big part of the company that ran tenanted pubs. UK licensing law was changing and all our 3,000 pubs had to be relicensed, a huge task. I had fallen behind the plan and felt I'd let Ralph, my boss, down. He tore up the letter, looked me in the eye and didn't say a word. I got the message. *Just do it.* In the end it all worked out and Ralph remained my mentor and guvnor for many more years. He was someone I could trust, he had faith in me and that was why this time I had planned the trip so diligently. I wanted it to be spot on.

10

'You will not see them again'
Bremen–Copenhagen–
Gothenburg

Bremen to Copenhagen

Early morning. Hotel car park. A blue strap dangled by the pannier, my yellow rain gear bag limp at its end. The pillion seat glared empty, the usually taut net flopping uselessly. In my stomach I felt a gut-twisting realisation. My carefully packed bag, with tent, sleeping bag, stove, those essential bits for Norwegian wild camping, all gone.

A quick glance at Ralph's bike confirmed it. His, too. Shit.

I'd gone down to the car park before breakfast to cast a casual eye over the bikes. I was still standing there, waving my arms around and cursing, when I heard footsteps behind me. Ralph's.

I'm a glass half-empty type; panic is not my style, but I will vent my frustration. Ralph, though, displayed an almost preternatural calm.

'At least the bikes are still here and rideable,' he offered.

'And they didn't bust open the panniers, so we've got the rest of our kit.'

He was right, I thought, admiring his calmness under pressure. That's why he was a CEO and I wasn't. Losing the camping gear was a blow but not the end of the trip. Still, I'd chosen the hotel and it was me who suggested that with CCTV in the parking lot we were safe to leave our bags on the bikes. This was not the start I'd imagined. I'd cocked up. Again.

Back at the Rotterdam ferry, I had chatted with a pair of German bikers, crowded together on a GS with luggage and gear. Turned out they'd started their journey with two BMWs, but one had been nicked in Ireland—an unfortunate emerging trend in the Emerald Isle, apparently. Losing our bikes would have ended our trip before it truly began. As it was, we'd only lost the camping gear. Replaceable, if a major pain in the backside.

Off we shuffled to *Polizei* headquarters, two grumpy bikers with a tale of severed straps and vanished gear. The young cop was sympathetic, but clearly unimpressed by the puny scale of the crime. We patiently filed our reports, the hotel promising to scour their CCTV footage. Frankly, we both knew it was a lost cause.

'Your hotel is near the train station,' the officer explained, a hint of weary resignation in his voice.

'Sadly, addicts will nick anything to feed their habit. Forget about those bags. You will not see them again.'

Well, that was that. A quick rummage through nearby bins had confirmed our suspicions, and dashed our hopes. On the other hand, the thought of some street person using my sleeping bag... let's say it wasn't an image I wanted to dwell on but I knew it would keep them warm. Our list of losses was easy (if lengthy) to compile; we simply consulted our kit list. Translating it all into German was a vocab test that I hadn't anticipated. With our *Bescheinigung* certificate (for the insurers) in hand, we trudged off to the nearest McDonald's, desperate for caffeine and a mental reset.

Truthfully, the loss stung. That tent, my faithful companion through countless Scottish Munro-bagging weekends in the Highlands, was gone. Should I replace it ? Was it worth it at my age? I shoved those questions aside. For now, we'd focus on the open road, not the gear that had bought a cheap fix or two for some Bremen druggie.

I thought back to Spain and having to make decisions on the hoof. I'd done it then and we could do it again now.

'Well, that's a game-changer,' Ralph muttered, breaking the silence.

'Looks like we're stuck with hotels from now on unless we want to spend a morning traipsing about looking for tents.'

'I wouldn't want to risk it again. Looks like you're right,' I sighed. 'Though my wallet's already shrivelling up at the thought of Norwegian hotel prices.'

'We could try to find one of those cheap hostels,' he suggested.

'Work for our beds, share a mixed dorm with the backpacker crowd? Might liven things up a bit.'

I thought he was joking but the flicker of mischief in his eyes suggested otherwise. I let out a snort of laughter.

'Sharing a room with a bunch of twenty-somethings? Our snoring would have them chucking things at us.'

'Fair point, though some of the other inmates might be better looking than you,' Ralph conceded with a wink.

'Maybe we can go self-catering,' I said, trying to find a sliver of cost-saving optimism.

'We could try to cram a few extra essentials into the panniers.'

'Hmm. Think we can live off sauerkraut, tinned herring and crispbread?' Ralph asked.

'Sounds about as appealing as that dorm room. Just think of the farts.'

We both went quiet for a bit, pissed off about losing the camping part of the trip. But then we just started cracking up. Another obstacle? No biggie. This adventure had started to surprise us, and we were ready for whatever came next.

And as to Bremen's less fortunate resident who now possessed my camping kit? Well, I hoped for their sake it brought them a flicker of the joy it once gave me.

Our Bremen disorientation was painfully clear as we left *Polizei* HQ and promptly made a left turn straight onto the tram tracks. A brief bout of impromptu off-roading over the pavements got us back onto the R27 and by good fortune no pedestrians or trams were heading our way. Once safely back on *Bundesautobahn* 1, we settled into our routine: Ralph leading, me playing rear gunner, warning him of those pedal-to-the-metal German drivers approaching from behind.

If you're of a certain vintage you may remember BBC radio's Terry Wogan and his double-entendre Janet and John stories? Ralph had an uncanny ability for mimickry, swapping into a gentle Irish lilt.

'*John goes to the village shop,*' said Ralph over the radio.

I start to titter as I anticipate his impromptu episode in a spot-on Wogan impression.

'*Janet is out of flour,*' he continued.

'*Janet is making muffins. Janet gives John the money and tells him not to talk to any strange women.*

See John skip down the street.

Ding-dong goes the shop bell.

'*Hello John,*' *says Mrs Roberts. Mrs Roberts is Welsh. See the consonants. Mrs Roberts is looking for something.*

'*Have you lost something, Mrs Roberts?*' *says John.*

'*Two jugs with wooden clothes pegs,*' *says Mrs Roberts.*

'*I can't put my clothes on the line without them,*' *she adds, helpfully.*

'*Oh, here they are. Hold them for me, John. Anyhoo, what would you like today, John?*'

'I'd like some flour please. Janet is making muffins.'

See John give Mrs Roberts the money and pocket the change.

Mrs Roberts asks John: 'Could you make me some more wooden pegs, please, John?'

Mrs Bickerdyke says: 'You are good with your hands.'

John knows what a chisel is. Clever John.

John skips home to see Janet. Janet is waiting in the doorway with a big cherry pie in her hands.

'Sorry I was so long,' says John. 'Mrs Roberts asked me to hold her jugs because she had no clothes on and she knew I like a bit of muffin. Mrs Bickerdyke said I was good with wood and can handle my chisel.'

See a rolling pin land on John's head.

Do you know how heavy they are?

Janet does. Poor John.

Ralph's deadpan comic delivery had me laughing so hard I could barely keep the bike steady.

Our music hall routine of daftness had resumed and was getting quite polished when we slammed into another massive *Stau* near Lübeck. We'd planned to see the historic city but with our enforced late start and Copenhagen nowhere near, we binned the plan and cracked on to the ferry at Puttgarden, 242 kms without stopping. The lengthy traffic jam reduced our pace to a crawl and somewhere in the queue I lost Ralph again. As I filtered gingerly through the endless line of cars and lorries I had a dilemma. We were out of radio range and I didn't know for sure if he was in front or behind me. We had a ferry to catch so there was no alternative but to go for it and see what happens.

Nearing Puttgarden, the endless flat steppes of fields punctuated by high voltage lines gave way to a view of the Baltic Sea, with little harbours and sailing boats bobbing on blue waters. At Grossenbrode I pulled into a garage with a good view down the road. No sign of Ralph. By now I'd guessed I was ahead of him. After refuelling, I pulled into an access road nearby. Brake lights suggested drivers took me for a police motorbike. Ten minutes passed and still nothing. Then suddenly I saw a pair of familiar headlights and a white Shoei helmet I recognised. I pulled out behind him. A surprised thumbs up and we were back in touch.

As we rolled to a halt at Puttgarden to catch the Scandlines ferry to Rødby in Denmark, Ralph revealed that he'd been riding on fumes for ages. Desperately short of fuel he called into one petrol station which turned out to be shut. By the time he found some go-juice he'd resorted to coasting downhill, going as slowly as he dared on these fast roads. It was a close call once again.

'Next time, maybe fill up before the orange warning light comes on?'

Even as I said the words, I recalled that I'd so nearly run out of petrol myself back in France by the Somport Tunnel. Who was I to talk?

He shot me a sheepish grin.

'Awa' an boil yer heid.'

Which I think means get lost.

With our bikes brimmed with fresh E5, we boarded the ferry for Rødby en route to Copenhagen. We sat on deck in the warmth, supping a cold drink. Time for a quiz.

'Think of Denmark: what springs to mind?'

'Pastries. Bacon. That wee mermaid. Søren Kierkegaard. Peter Schmeichel. Carlsberg, of course'.

A cold Carlsberg sounded particularly tempting as we pulled up several hours later to our hotel in the heart of the city. A rowdy stag party was spilling out of the reception area, beardy blokes togged up as women in lurid pink skirts, lipstick, inflatable breasts. I cringed at the prospect of a noisy night. There was probably a reason it was named the Wakeup Hotel.

Next to the hotel was a multistorey car park. We had learned our lesson, so scoured it for the safest place to leave the bikes before emptying them of everything, even though it was a laborious and unwelcome task. Padlocked together and with disc locks on the brakes, the motorbikes were made as difficult as possible for opportunist thieves to steal. We hoped.

Those beers had our names on them. We slung our gear into the room and headed into town.

We found ourselves in a surreal scene: Aloha, a Hawaiian-themed gay bar, Mexican beers served by a Spanish waitress. It was a summer's Saturday night in the heart of Copenhagen, and the whole place was out for a good time. I squeezed my way through a dense throng of brightly dressed young chaps to the bar, which was stacked high with glasses and cocktail liquors. I was struggling to see a beer tap amidst the gaily coloured bottles. Cocktails and mocktails flashed past me over the countertop to waiting customers who danced and downed them almost without pause.

A beautiful dark-haired girl, wearing a low-cut, exotically floral dress and a fabulous lei flower garland asked me for my order. I was admiring her pineapples at the time (they were printed all over her costume).

'Two beers please,' I stammered, feeling shamefaced. I'd not even learned the Danish for this classic request so had to ask in English. Terrible.

Her name badge said Esmeralda. She didn't look typically Danish.

'Madrid,' she replied, when I asked where she was from.

'I'm at the uni here. I am doing a doctorate in philosophy,' she added, in passing.

She handed me a couple of Coronas. I retreated through the sweaty crowd, slightly humbled.

'*Nunc est bibendum*, Ralph', I shouted, over the music, as I handed him the bottle.

He looked quizzically at me.

'Now's the time for drinking,' I translated.

'Braw philosophy that,' he replied, quaffing down his beer.

Esmeralda wasn't unique; across Scandinavia, we encountered Portuguese, Spanish, Argentinian and Croatian hospitality workers. Next time you're in a UK pub or restaurant short on staff, they're likely to be in Oslo, Copenhagen or Stockholm. And the missing Polish plumbers and builders? They're probably in Norway too. The bar's crowd grew a bit too jam-packed for comfort, so we retreated to an outdoor bench near a group of women in their 20s enjoying an office party. Their excellent English made it easy to overhear their teasing comments about 'Grandad' and 'past bedtime'.

I was feeling quite wobbly after Aloha. I wasn't not sure if it was tiredness, the beers, hunger or the array of Hawaiian shirts. We needed food and walked to the characterful waterfront of Nyhavns Kroen. It was a short distance off but it took an age to walk there. We waited ten minutes for a break in the bike traffic before crossing the road. Copenhagen is a cyclist's haven but pedestrians need to be vigilant. A wrong move here and you'd be wheeled into hospital.

We savoured baked salmon, asparagus and potatoes on a warm evening bathed in golden sunlight. The waterfront was thronged with people strolling past the multicoloured merchant houses. Under a canopy of branded parasols, a group of bagpipers from Stouby, Denmark gathered before a piping competition, a big deal here, apparently. Dressed in corporate pipe band attire, they had left their instruments behind, raising only glasses of Tuborg instead. We could enjoy our dinner in peace, though I think Ralph would have been partial to a blast of *Scotland the Brave* on the infernal windbags.

'Well, Stephen,' Ralph muttered, shaking his head as he sipped his lager. 'Right stramash this morning, wasn't it?'

'You can say that again,' I replied, still feeling annoyed about the stolen camping gear.

'Two years of my planning up the Swanee.'

Ralph shrugged; his expression taciturn as ever.

'I was scunnered too but we can't do much about it now, can we? Best not dwell on it. Bawbags aw the same.'

He slipped effortlessly into Scots. It seemed to fit the mood, or maybe the pipers had inspired him.

'Onwards and upwards, eh? Literally,' I replied.

'That's the spirit,' Ralph encouraged.

'I guess your hero Rabbie Burns summed it up well: the best-laid schemes o'mice an' men gang aft agley.'

Ralph calmly ordered another Tuborg.

'It's part of the adventure. Didnae things go aw wrong for you in Spain, too? Now we get to stay in some decent howffs instead.'

'Posh bothies. That's about all our budget'll run to,' I reckoned.

'Nae bother,' Ralph exclaimed, a mischievous grin spreading across his face.

'Mony a mickle maks a muckle, you know. We'll have to be a bit clever with our bookings, save cash wherever we can. Think of it as a challenge.'

I smiled at his infectious optimism.

'All right, Captain Rambunctious,' I said.

Ralph winked. 'We'll just need tae play it by ear.'

Copenhagen to Gothenburg

Playing by ear, busking it, winging it. That's precisely what we did the next morning. My original plan, meticulously crafted over two years (thanks to COVID-related travel delays) involved a mix of cheap hotels, lodges, small pensions and a bit of camping in the far north, where accommodation was scarce. Six nights under canvas in total. Rapid rethinking was needed.

My improvisational approach, honed during my time in Spain, came in handy now. After breakfast, we transformed some window seats in the hotel lobby into our Operations

Centre, maps sprawled out and phones ready to grapple with TripAdvisor, Hotel.com, Booking.com, and the like. It was a stroke of luck that we were on the cusp of the high season in Norway, where our camping had been scheduled. Any later and finding last-minute accommodation would have been challenging. As it turned out, the couple of hours spent replanning unearthed some wonderful *hytter* and *rorbuer* (traditional Norwegian cabins and fishing huts), highlights that would become a refreshing antidote to chain hotels.

For the second day running we were late departing. We left Copenhagen behind and headed for the famous Øresund Bridge, that connected Denmark to Sweden. It's a superb feat of engineering: the longest combined bridge and tunnel crossing in Europe. Five miles of bridge stretch from the artificial island of Peberholm to the Swedish coast, followed by a four-mile tunnel linking it to Denmark. This would be the first of many impressive tunnels we'd traverse on our journey to Nordkapp and back.

The bridge also served as a test for our new Flyt tags, windscreen-mounted transponders acquired for Norwegian toll roads and ferries. We approached the barriers and, after a hesitant pause, they lifted, allowing us to proceed. Faffing with toll money wearing gloves is always awkward. I've literally thrown money away in the past. The tags were a breeze.

The weather was fantastic for riding. A light wind, sunny and warm, but not too hot—a Goldilocks day, just right. For motorcyclists, ideal conditions are a narrow window. We hate wet roads; our two small tyre contact points are all that keep us upright. Gusty winds play havoc with balance, cold temperatures numb fingers and distract, and excessive heat causes sweat to sting our eyes and dehydration to fog our concentration. Present conditions, however, were perfect for the long bridge traverse ahead.

Reaching Malmö in southern Sweden, we headed northwards on the E6. A car was pulled over on the hard shoulder, hazards flashing. Behind it, a cycle rack had detached from a tow bar, scattering parts across the road. A silent wave of gratitude washed over us as we realised we hadn't been following too closely when the car and its bike rack became unhitched.

Ralph came on the intercom: 'That's going to be a hell of a repair job. There's bits everywhere.'

'Like your glasses,' I replied.

Today we needed even more luck on our side, as we still had 340 kilometres to reach Gothenburg. The E6, running up Sweden's west coast, is one of Europe's longest roads. We could theoretically stay on it for over 3,000 kms from Malmö to Olderfjord, south of Nordkapp, and continue into Finland as far as Kirkenes. However, despite it being the 'short route', we wanted to explore the fjords and Lofoten Islands in western Norway, so we planned only to follow it as far as Otta in Norway, 850 kms away.

An hour and a half north of Malmö we stopped in the seaside resort of Båstad. On such a warm day, it was a good spot for an ice cream break and the chance to stretch our legs. It's famous as a tennis hub, where Swedish greats like Björn Borg have played, and it hosts the Swedish ATP and WTA tournaments. My Mallorcan neighbours, Giuseppe and Maria, also call Båstad home, and I was keen to drop in for a cuppa. Alas, they were in Spain when we arrived. Instead, Ralph and I strolled along the charming seafront, indulged in liquorice ice cream, basked on the golden sands and generally ogled happy Swedes at play. It was so impossibly idyllic that we felt compelled to lower the tone by snapping selfies in front of various Båstad signs. My goofy image attracted an embarrassing number of likes on social media.

By mid afternoon the sugar rush from the coal-black *lakritsglass* had worn off. We stopped for fuel, and the siren song of a *korv* sizzling on the counter lured me into buying one. Allegedly made from meat, this sausage-shaped comestible resembles a saveloy—remember those fish and chip shop bangers of dubious ingredients? I returned to Ralph with an enormous sausage in a bun and a restorative Red Bull.

'That's a richt stoater o' a sausage, but it'd be even better wi' a dollop o' curry sauce oan tap!' Ralph said, struggling to gobble down the meaty morsel.

After polishing them off, we swore to stay off such culinary indiscretions... until the next time.

By now, any pretence of reaching Gothenburg at a reasonable hour had vanished. We ambled up the E6 and soon stumbled upon the coastal town of Varberg. We stopped solely because our local tourist guidebook mentioned a castle that was worth a visit. I'd been suffering castle withdrawal symptoms since leaving Spain and we'd forgotten to visit the magnificent *slott* (castle) in Malmö.

As we threaded our way along pristine suburban streets, we were stopped by a friendly traffic cop.

'Can't go into the centre, lads. There's a college leaving party going on and the roads are closed. Turn round and go next right.'

What style. The Swedes shut down their town centre in the middle of the day so that sixth formers can celebrate leaving school. We followed his instructions and soon found ourselves at the *fästning* (fortress) close to the sandy beaches that attract tourists from all over Sweden. The place was teeming with lithe young people, immaculately turned out, alongside cyclists with small children squatting on those curiously practical continental cargo bikes. It was a scene of pure summer Scandi-bliss.

The fortress was built straddling the beach, the tide lapping up to the base of its imposing walls. It looked the kind of castle from which long-haired blond Vikings would hurl by hand great boulders at the Danish invaders before wringing the neck of a chicken for lunch. Not to be trifled with. And speaking of tough Swedes, a slightly battered Volvo estate pulled up, from which emerged a big-boned, slightly haggard-looking bloke, strolling across the promenade to greet us.

To non-bikers motorcyclists can either seem dauntingly severe and unapproachable, especially if they're sporting studded leather jackets with "Satan's Children" death-heads plastered everywhere (as in the MaccyD's in Barcelona), or, as Ralph and I like to think of ourselves in our more subtle gear, really nice chaps worth having a word with.

Volvo-driving Lars introduced himself and enquired about our bikes, where we were from and going to. This is often a prelude to the interlocutor's own tales of derring-do. And sure enough, it was.

Lars, an ex-biker in his early 70s, told us his back and neck were injured and he had to sell his Honda Goldwing (those things weigh nearly 400kg). He couldn't pick it up when he dropped it, which he used to do with alarming regularity, apparently. In his prime—presumably when he wasn't dropping the beast—he'd toured the UK and Ireland and told us how much he loved the Wild Atlantic Way and North Coast 500. He was also a monster-miler, once riding from Varberg to Calais (1,300 kms) in a single day. It put our puny day's effort into perspective.

As he turned to leave, he casually glanced at Ralph's Beemer and remarked, 'By the way, your pillion foot peg's loose.'

Sure enough, it was. The cotter pin had vanished somewhere along the way. We wondered what else was about to drop off en route.

Lars wished us well. I could tell from the slightly rheumy look in his eyes that he'd given up his beloved road trips with the greatest reluctance. It was another reminder to make the most of every opportunity to go on adventures of my own.

The remaining journey to Göteborg (Gothenburg), Sweden's second-largest city, was uneventful until the last kilometre or so, a routine which soon became the norm. Ralph and I developed an uncanny knack for messing things up on final approach. The city's extensive roadworks made following the satnav's instructions a nightmare, especially when roads seemed to vanish into thin air.

At a set of lights Ralph disappeared down a tunnel, while I took a side lane that led directly to the Comfort Hotel at Stenpiren on the waterfront. I had parked up, checked in, hauled my luggage to the room and was about to crack open a beer in the bar when Ralph finally arrived after driving round the city in ever decreasing circles.

'Unbelievable,' he exclaimed, when eventually he turned up.

'I ended up in a labyrinth of one-way streets and those bloody roadworks again. How'd you get here so fast?'

'Oh, I just saw the hotel sign and rode straight up to it,' I said, nonchalantly flipping the crown off the bottle.

We had rolled into Göteborg during its 400th anniversary festival. Talk about timing. The free electric ferries at Stenpiren were proving to be immensely popular, shuttling hordes of people across the water to Frihamnen, the former banana import hub-turned-music-venue that was now going, well, bananas. We were sorely tempted to catch the legendary '80s band Suede in concert, but the prospect of some quiet beers and a proper meal won out.

Standing on the pier, we watched a massive, joyful crowd dancing to Caribbean music blaring from giant speakers mounted on a sack truck. The infectious pleasure was palpable and this wasn't even party central. The mass of parked bikes hinted at the revelry on the other side of the river.

Gothenburg was a city in flux, transitioning from its industrial roots. Amidst the ubiquitous roadworks, an ultra-modern tram system and avant-garde high-rises were sprouting up like mushrooms. The heart of the city remained solidly red-brick, with arched windows and verdigris-tinged roofs in classic Scandinavian style. It exuded wealth, history and confidence. Yet the centre was eerily quiet, even for a

Sunday evening. The festival had seemingly swallowed the entire city.

We were about to resign ourselves to another street sausage dinner when we stumbled upon the Steampunk Bar. They'd taken the theme seriously. The black-clad, Gothy bar staff, sporting welder's goggles in the dimly lit interior, were harder to spot than a black cat in a coal cellar.

Thanks to some help from our table neighbours, we deciphered the gothic Swedish menu. We were tempted by some of the weirder offerings, like fermented herring and fish balls but opted for more familiar *burgare* with chips. A few Pilsner Urquells slipped down, too. It had been a long day and, feeling the need for further refreshment, we ambled to the local BrewDog pub, only to find it deserted, apart from one man and his dog. Everyone else was at the party, of course.

We downed a couple of the Dog's finest beers, agreeing that even they didn't have a pedigree like Pedigree, and wobbled our way back through the strangely empty streets toward Stenpiren. The golden sun was setting gently behind a distant dock crane and warehouse. It would be a while before we would see another sunset, as we neared the Land of the Midnight Sun.

Silhouetted against the industrial backdrop, a middle-aged woman danced alone at the pier's edge. Her silver hair shimmered, her light top and dark cargo pants flowing with her movements. As the battery-powered ferries glided silently past, she danced with effortless grace, her mobile phone and headphones her only tether to reality. Ralph and I watched from afar, captivated. It was a mesmerising moment: she, ethereal, lost in the music; us, mesmerised by her ecstatic reverie. Unexpected and extraordinary, like the best moments of any road trip.

'D'you think she missed the boat?' I said, breaking the spell.

Ralph shot me a look that said *You numpty.*

11

Ancient Swedish Porn
Oslo–Rondane Mountains–
Trollstigen

Gothenburg to Oslo

The consequences of having been an idiot earlier in the trip needed some attention the next morning, courtesy of an urgent appointment at the Ahlqvist Honda Motorcycle Centre. We retraced our steps to the south side of the city, navigating the maze of roadworks with hard won expertise. This time, we didn't get lost.

My Honda NT1100 is a DCT model with an automatic gearbox, though it can be ridden in manual mode too. Normally, bikes are parked in gear, which acts like a handbrake. But mine flips into neutral when switched off, so park on a slope and there's every chance the bike will run away. Instead, there's a parking brake with a small lever on the handlebar. It's effective when used properly but easy to forget. Leaving Rotterdam, I'd managed to ride off with the brake engaged. No wonder the engine was screaming. By the time I noticed the flashing red light and neglected lever, I'd already gone a couple of kilometres. It doesn't take long to wear down brake pads that way.

I was worried about not having a parking brake, especially on the many ferries we'd be taking. A jolt could easily send the bike tumbling, an expensive and potentially dangerous scenario. So, in Bremen, I had called the Gothenburg dealership, hoping they could squeeze me in.

'We're fully booked,' they said, 'but come anyway, and we'll see what we can do.'

While Ralph happily browsed the showroom, eyeing up an MV Agusta Brutale 800, a Honda Goldwing and other massive beasts (he'd ace Mastermind with big bikes as his specialist subject) I wheeled my Honda around back into the bustling service bay. Axel, a mechanic (honestly, not a pun), took the bike from me as if it weighed nothing and effortlessly flipped it onto its centre stand, a feat I struggled with since lowering the suspension. Axel made it look easy, like he was levitating the bike with his mind.

A few deft turns with a couple of spanners (12 mm ring and 4 mm Allen; I made a mental note of these for next time) and the job was done. I filmed the whole process, lest I repeat my muppetry. This prompted one of Axel's colleagues to quip, 'He's a spy.' They wouldn't accept payment. It was another reminder that the motorcycling world is a brotherhood, where help is freely given and gratefully received.

Ralph was about to inspect an Africa Twin when I reappeared, much sooner than expected.

'Let's go. Oslo awaits. Another day, another country,' I announced.

'Fast work,' Ralph remarked. 'Didn't wreck the brakes too badly then?'

'Ouch,' I winced. 'Touché.'

Back we went onto the E6 northbound, but only for a short hop. I had a detour in mind: Lysekil, a coastal town 132 kms from Gothenburg, snugly located on the southern tip of the Stångenas peninsula. Originally a fishing village, it's now a spa and bathing resort with two important nature reserves. It seemed like an ideal *fika* stop, a Swedish term that means coffee and cake, but it's more a state of mind—a pause, a moment of relaxation. If cake is involved, so much the better.

To reach Lysekil, we left the E6 near Uddevalla and took the scenic 161, a winding road flanked by forests and high earth banks. Despite being arrow-straight, the road was dotted with speed cameras, so we maintained a leisurely pace. We arrived at our first road ferry, signposted "Finnsbro Scores", a surprise to Ralph, who hadn't studied my route closely and was wondering which team Finnsbro played for. This is one of Sweden's busiest maritime routes, a 1.8-kilometre crossing of the Gullmarsleden waterway. The bright yellow Tellus ferry is electric-hybrid, and we boarded with barely a vibration or jolt. Moments later, we were gliding away from the quayside for our first of many passages. And it's free. In Scandinavia, especially in Norway, many ferries are simply part of the road system and come at no charge. We barely had time to remove our helmets and cool down in the heat before we were back on the bikes and rolling off the ferry.

Lysekil was charming, once we navigated the extensive roadworks on the sole access road, nipping in and out of traffic. We stopped at the Hamn, the harbour bustling with small pleasure craft and fishing boats. Nearby, a wooden cabin—an ice cream parlour/café adorned with Swedish flags —looked enticing. I went with the liquorice ice cream, cake for Ralph.

Fully *fika*'d, we hopped back on the bikes with over 200 clicks to go to Oslo, but first we were heading back in time to the Bronze Age.

The Vitlycke Museum at Tanum, Bohuslän, south of the Norwegian border, is an absolute marvel. A World Heritage Site spread over an extensive area, it boasts 600 rock carving sites with tens of thousands of images. Alongside the 8,000-year-old carvings, there's a reconstructed Bronze Age farm.

Anna was a very pretty girl who worked in the reception area and spoke great English. She'd studied in Portsmouth and was keen to practice her language skills. We were her willing audience.

'They fucked a lot then,' she said, to our astonishment. 'Well, there wasn't a lot else to do in the cold Swedish winter,' she added. She took a couple of guidebooks off the shelf and handed them to us. 'The best of the Bronze Age sex drawings are on pages forty-five and forty-six.'

Ralph and I flicked rapidly through *Kinky Rockcarvings* (sic) to find these eye-openers. They were inventive, that's for certain. The book cover had the English subtitle "Hooray! I finally solved my erectile dysfunction" and judging by the main illustration it pre-dated Viagra by several millennia.

'When you get to the rock, go to the far end and look right up. There you'll see some acrobatic positions they used to favour.'

'I suppose this is, like, top shelf rock porn,' I said, trying to be helpful.

She looked confused. 'Porn, maybe, but top shelf? I don't understand.'

Ralph and I headed out, guidebook in hand, to find the ancient Swedish porn.

Clomping around in the sweltering heat wasn't exactly what we'd envisioned for this trip, and we felt like we were wearing winter coats in a sauna. Normally I'd strap my jacket onto the bike, a trick I've used countless times in Spain's scorching temperatures. But our Bremen experience had made us wary of leaving our gear unattended.

I slung my heavy jacket over my shoulder and we took a well-marked path to a huge, slanted rock which was covered in petroglyphs, highly detailed rusty-brown drawings of humans, animals and Bronze Age scenes, over a series of rocks. There were thousands of them spread across the site. I found the risqué stuff. Tucked amidst curious drawings of sledges and Viking longboats were some seriously impressive phalluses. One character had a spear in one hand and his knob in the other; it was a toss-up as to which was the biggest.

Once we'd had our fill of filthy petroglyphs, we ducked into the café for *ostfralla* & *skinka,* my Swedish menu vocabulary being limited to 'cheese and ham rolls'.

I was finding it an unusual experience being in a country where I had but the merest smattering of the language. I'd learned a few simple Swedish phrases but for the most part people spoke excellent English, like Anna. It felt like cheating, somehow, not having more than the odd phrase of Swedish.

As we'd entered Sweden, once again we played our country's famous things and people quiz. Among the obvious Swedish contenders, we'd come up with ABBA, Björn Borg, Zlatan Ibrahimovic and Greta Thunberg. Right on cue, as we left the Bronze Age, we passed an icon of 21st century consumerism by the E6.

'IKEA! Ralph, how could we have left that out?'

Surprisingly, it was the only one we saw in Sweden.

Crossing into Norway, the roads transformed. The previously pristine surface became a bit less smooth, the lupins lining the road gave way to carpets of delicate yellow wildflowers, and the flatlands of northern Sweden yielded to rolling hills that grew increasingly rugged. Almost infinite vistas opened up as we ascended, and numerous bridges spanned implausibly pretty inlets, with small boats at anchor and dainty red-roofed houses lining the shore.

By contrast with Germany and the madcap pace of their drivers the placid pace of Norwegian roads was a revelation. Their 80 kph limit (a sluggish 50 mph) initially sounded like torture. But amidst landscapes that demand our full attention, why rush? Plus, there's the small matter of fuel prices that would make a banker weep. Slower means cheaper in this neck of the woods. And then there are the fines... go over the limit by a mere 10 kph? That'll be £170, thank you very much. Push your luck, and you might be selling the house to pay for the privilege. No wonder those ominous and ubiquitous speed camera posters feature ghost-like figures. The Norwegians aren't messing around when they ask you if you're *"Over fartsgrensen?"* (Over the speed limit?)

Who wants to roar past when, at any moment, a reindeer, elk or mighty moose might amble out of the woods? This was reason enough to embrace the slower pace. We witnessed these majestic creatures at various points and, trust me, you don't want to tangle with one at speed.

Because we were sticking rigidly to the speed limits our journey to Oslo seemed to take ages. Eventually, though, as we approached our hotel, the Cochs Pensjonat in the heart of Oslo, we executed our signature move—Ralph veering off in one direction, me in another. I was blindly following TomTom's GPS instructions, which had me circling like a lost pigeon before I finally zeroed in on the hotel. They'd mentioned a courtyard for parking, but a van was stubbornly blocking the entrance. Tired, hot and frustrated, I decided to mount the kerb and sneak around the van.

But in the very moment I was airborne up the high kerb, with no hope of planting my feet down, a woman with a massive dog materialised on my right, mere feet away. Panicking, I twisted the throttle to clear the hump. The bike lurched forward, the front wheel took to the air and twisted mid-flight. I lost control then came to a bone-jarring crashing halt, wedged in the wrought iron gate leading to the courtyard. I was pinned against the wall by a quarter ton of Honda, at a precarious angle. Only the windshield and the brake lever prevented a complete topple and the probability of it crushing me against the brickwork. My helmet took a beating from the wall and my right glove scraped along the bricks, gouging a rip in the knuckles.

Brilliant, I thought to myself, *Just bloody brilliant.*

To add insult to injury, passers-by simply gawked at the idiot wrestling with his bike and the unforgiving ironwork.

'Oh, bugger.' I finally exclaimed, hoping the expletive wouldn't echo too loudly through the courtyard. With a defeated sigh, I killed the engine and took several deep breaths to calm myself.

As I knew from my crash in Spain, when things go wrong on a bike, they go wrong fast. I took a few moments to assess the damage: a) was I hurt? b) was the bike damaged? c) what the hell do I do now?

The answers, as far as I could tell:

a)   no, luckily, though my right wrist throbbed;

b)   the screen was obviously shattered, as it was a hell of a thump against the gate and wall;

c)   get this damn bike upright and stop looking like a fool.

By the time I'd wrestled the bike onto its sidestand, Ralph appeared, oblivious to the drama. With two of us coordinating efforts and clearing the pavement, his bike surmounted the kerb like a trials rider.

I tried to open the metal gate, but it was jammed tight against the brick wall. We pulled and heaved, but it wouldn't budge. After a while, the manager, who must have witnessed our struggle on CCTV, emerged. He couldn't open it from the inside either, not until he fetched a sledgehammer and gave it a mighty whack while Ralph and I pulled in unison.

'Odd,' he remarked, 'I don't recall the gate being stuck like that before.'

I kept my mouth shut, a guilty silence hanging in the air.

As soon as I parked, the broken screen fell off. We'd started the day at a Honda dealership. It looked like we'd be paying another visit in the morning.

This was getting to be a habit.

Oslo to Rondane Mountains

It's a been while since I've had to pad down a hotel corridor in my underpants to go to the loo in the middle of the night.

'I can't believe I had room with the non-suite bathroom,' I grumbled to Ralph in the reception. 'And me, with my prostate.'

Ralph laughed. 'Well, you did say the Cochs Pensjonat was a snip at £60 for downtown Oslo.'

'A bargain that came with free added all-night traffic din and no air conditioning,' I sighed, rubbing my wrist, still throbbing from yesterday's crash.

'How's your wrist?'

'Painkillers not kicked in yet,' I moaned.

'Och well, at least we have this charming little café for breakfast,' Ralph said, gesturing towards the bakery and its shady flower garden next door.

I decided to focus on the bright side. It was a beautiful morning, both the bike and I were (mostly) unscathed and we were excited for a fantastic day of riding ahead.

'Elon Musk must be raking it in here,' I said, sipping my coffee under an apple tree as a parade of electric vehicles whizzed past.

'You bet,' Ralph replied between bites of pastry. 'Norway's the electric vehicle poster child. It's pretty impressive.'

'I wonder how much their oil money is fuelling this,' I mused.

Ralph shrugged. 'Probably helps, but you gotta give them credit for leading the way. Diversification. Guess we'll catch on eventually.'

'Oslo's definitely got its own vibe, hasn't it?' I remarked, wincing slightly as I recalled the £9 pints at the Egon restaurant the previous evening.

Ralph chuckled, 'Yeah, it's unlike Sweden, that's for sure. A bit more... brutalist chic?'

'More Cold War architecture, I'd say,' I countered, 'Rather austere. More Sami influence too, the people look slightly different.'

'They certainly know how to party though,' Ralph said, nodding towards the harbour. 'Did you see those boats last night? Packed to the gunwales with office types, absolutely trolleyed.'

'I know, right?' I exclaimed. 'Monday night and they were knocking back the grog like it was going out of fashion. Must have mortgages the size of Norway's national debt.'

'Or maybe they're all secretly oil barons hiding their riches behind sensible knitwear and a penchant for pickled herring.'

We togged up, checked out, then packed up the bikes for another day on the road.

'I wish we had more time to explore Oslo. So much to see here,' I said, half-hoping for a day off to let my wrist recover.

'Same here, but Lofoten is calling, and first we've a repair job to do on your bike,' Ralph said, glancing at my battered NT1100.

'So, how's the windshield situation looking?'

I sighed, running a hand over the cracked Perspex.

'Not great. Half of it's already gone, and the rest is barely hanging on. Need to find a replacement ASAP, but it's not looking promising.'

'Well, you've got a few thousand kilometres to go before Nordkapp,' Ralph reminded me, like I needed it.

'And the weather forecast up there isn't exactly for sunny skies and beachwear.'

'Tell me about it,' I muttered, tightening the last bolt on the stripped-down windshield.

Oslo is on the same latitude as the Shetlands yet is still 2,000 kms south of Nordkapp. So with that monster distance still to go and the likelihood of poor weather, finding a replacement was an urgent priority. I wasn't hopeful.

'Fingers crossed for a miracle, then,' Ralph said, giving me a reassuring pat on the back.

'Let's hit the road and see what Norway has in store for us.'

By happy chance, MC Oslo, another Honda dealer, was on our route out of the city. We gingerly extracted our bikes from the hotel courtyard, me still fretting about any potential damage to mine. But a cautious test ride revealed everything was in working order: brakes, steering, suspension, the lot. Phew. Lady Luck was on my side once more.

We found the dealers. It was Groundhog Day. While Ralph sat on various bikes in the showroom and generally played like a kid in a toyshop, my hopes of a replacement windscreen were rapidly dwindling. They had nothing in stock, no imminent deliveries and wouldn't even entertain my idea of taking one off a new bike. Even if they had, the £800 price tag was highway robbery.

I was about to give up when the parts chap had a brainwave. He rang a local supplier who happened to have a German-made screen—an exact fit for my bike. The cherry on top? It was a quarter of the price of the Honda original. I happily coughed up the cash, got the address and we were off again.

By now, we'd seen more industrial estates than actual scenery. The parts warehouse was no-frills. No posh reception or even a grubby collection of girly calendars, only a buzzer by a roller door. I pressed it, and as it rolled upwards a pair of hefty boots appeared, followed in order by hairy legs, shorts, a beer belly and finally a huge beard beneath which was buried a bulky bloke clutching a parcel.

'Are you the dude who crashed the bike?' the beard asked, his voice gruff and direct.

I nodded, a bit taken aback by his bluntness. 'That's me,' I admitted to the Viking lookalike.

'Right then,' he said, handing me the package. 'Here's your screen. Don't crash the fucker again, eh?'

I thanked him and shuffled the bike into a shady spot in the car park. The screen fit as promised, and by eleven o'clock we were back on the road, grateful for the swift and efficient service.

However, by this point, our delays were piling up. First Bremen with the theft, then Copenhagen with the accommodation fiasco, Gothenburg with the brake issue and now Oslo with the windscreen saga. It was four days of false starts and frustrations. We needed to get cracking.

The E6 swept its magnificent way northwards, through hills covered in forests, past lakes and rivers; it skirted inlets with charming little harbours all a-bob with dinghies and small yachts. We enjoyed some superb riding on roads that were just made for motorcycles. Great tarmac, no nasty surprises like potholes, and steady and sensible drivers who also obeyed the speed limits and weren't hanging inches away from my rear tyre. There were long sweeping bends and enough gentle undulations to provide variety and interest as we passed through pretty, small settlements, strung out along the road like dainty necklaces.

All the houses lay at the end of long drives set back from the road, their manicured lawns keeping the passing traffic at arm's length. But it was the postboxes that truly captured our attention. These were not your standard, utilitarian metal boxes, but rather miniature wooden houses, each balanced atop a meticulously varnished tree stump. The roofs of these whimsical structures were adorned with thick carpets of grass, varied wildflowers, and the occasional wind-sown sapling, creating the illusion of tiny airborne meadows. It became clear to me that in this part of Norway, status isn't conveyed through the size of one's lawnmower or the make of one's car, but rather through the creative and eco-conscious design of one's letterbox. It was a delightful and unexpected quirk, one that seemed quintessentially Norwegian.

Ralph and I were in high spirits, our intercoms filled with impromptu renditions from *The Sound of Music*, which seemed a fitting soundtrack to the pastoral scenery. He has a surprisingly high voice and does a rather convincing Maria.

As we rounded the shores of Lake Mjøsa, Norway's largest and one of Europe's deepest lakes, the midday sun began to take its toll. With 135 kilometres under our belts since our earlier stop near Oslo, the need for a pee break was pressing.

On cue, a rest area materialised near Biri, south of Lillehammer. Tucked away from the main road in a wooded glade, it offered a welcome haven from the heat. Sleek metal and wood benches were strategically placed along a grassy slope leading down to the lake, inviting weary wanderers to rest and rejuvenate. Several campervans were parked nearby, their occupants enjoying picnics in the idyllic setting. The lay-by bogs, generally places to avoid at all costs in the UK, were top-notch, clean and fragrant, plus well-stocked with requisite commodities of paper, soap and water.

We quenched our thirst with chilled water from our flasks, devoured a gooey chocolate bar and stretched out on the benches for a well-deserved nap. Within moments, the soothing sounds of nature and the gentle rocking of the bench lulled me into a state of peaceful drowsiness. I was vaguely aware of the activity around me, the laughter of children playing by the lake, the gentle lapping of waves against the shore, but I was content to remain still, as if under a pleasant anaesthetic.

The sun's heat eventually roused me from slumber, but Ralph remained comatose, a soft snore escaping his lips. I giggled to myself, stretched, and took in the scene, feeling refreshed and ready to continue our passage through this enchanting land.

A short hop from the rest stop brought us to Lillehammer, the charming town that hosted the 1994 Winter Olympics. While still a popular winter sports destination, it's also home to the largest literature festival in the Nordic countries. But instead of delving into the world of books, we opted for the Lillehammer Art Museum. Having dubbed ourselves the Culture Vulture Bikers we were determined to live up to it.

The museum was a modern, airy space showcasing a wide array of Norwegian art, including the works of Edvard Munch. We were particularly drawn to the whimsical yet eerie pen and ink drawings of trolls. The colossal Norwegian forests seemed like the breeding ground for such creatures, even though we had not actually encountered one ourselves... yet.

As we mounted our bikes to visit the ski centre, we struck up a conversation with Agnes, a Scot who had made Lillehammer her home for the past thirty years. She hailed from a part of Edinburgh which Ralph knew well and they swapped stories about Auld Reekie. It was easy to see why she had fallen in love with this place. Lillehammer offered a lively city centre tucked in amongst breathtaking mountain scenery, with the Olympic ski jump as its crown jewel. *Top Gear* fans may remember the rocket-powered Mini stunt filmed here. We decided to skip doing this on our bikes and opted for a more ground-level view of the enormous structure, but the sheer height of the jump still made our knees wobble.

The traffic in the city was chaotic as we tried to escape, eventually resorting to a back road to re-join the E6. The route followed the scenic Gudbrandsdalen valley, a fabulous stretch of road intermittently marred by roadworks. We soon encountered one such project, where massive excavators gnawed at the blown-up hillside, evidence of the engineers' fondness for explosives. A large barrier blocked the road, with no detour sign in sight. Spotting a yellow-hatted worker on a digger in a nearby yard, I rode over to enquire.

'Excuse me,' I called out. 'We're trying to get to Otta. How do we get around this road closure?'

The worker, clearly unfazed by the disruption, gestured casually.

'Head back about five hundred metres, take the first left, go uphill for a bit, then another left and you'll be back on the E6 by the church. Piece of cake.'

His flawless English served as a timely reminder of how other countries value language learning, a contrast to the often dismissive attitude in Britain. The 2004 decision to make foreign languages optional in English schools had resulted in a significant decrease in language proficiency. I accept I'm biased, but as a Chinese proverb wisely states, *To learn a language is to have more than one window from which to look at the world.*

I was still mulling over these thoughts when, 120 kilometres after leaving Lillehammer, we reached the small town of Otta, its name derived from the river that flowed through it. Our pre-booking efforts in Copenhagen had revealed no available accommodation in town, so we'd opted for a ski hotel stationed within the Rondane National Park. Despite it being June, a nagging worry lingered in the back of our minds—would the roads be blocked by the remnants of the winter's snow?

As we ascended the steep and increasingly rough road towards the hotel, we encountered our first taste of Norway's infamous hairpin bends. Eight in total, several of which were the heart-pounding, uphill, steep-camber, ultra-tight variety. Our brief hairpin practice in the Peak District before leaving the UK felt like child's play compared to this real-world challenge, complete with the added thrill of mortal danger from a lethally long drop on the other side of the barriers.

The road bucked and bumped beneath us, demanding our full attention as we each wrestled with throttle, speed, brake, gears and weight shifting. The heavy luggage piled into panniers and top boxes made its presence felt, as the high centre of gravity threatened to tip us over at every turn. Each hairpin was a test of skill and nerve, but we emerged from the ordeal victorious, rewarded with breathtaking views of snow-capped peaks almost iridescent in the sunlight and satisfyingly dry tarmac, though patches of white dotted the higher slopes nearby.

Shortly after after six o'clock, we arrived at the Rondane Hoeyfjellshotell, carefully navigating the stony parking area in front of the main entrance. The air was noticeably cooler up here and the panoramic views were simply awe inspiring. It had been a long, challenging day, but a good one nonetheless. The mountains of our dreams lay on our doorstep, and our Norwegian quest was truly under way.

As we climbed off our bikes, Ralph let out a long breath.

'Blimey, that was scary,' he exclaimed, wiping his forehead. 'First crack at proper mountain roads; that was brilliant.'

I grinned, clapping him on the shoulder. 'Nice one, mate. Hairpins are always a bit tricky, but you handled them like a pro.'

Ralph grinned wryly, the adrenaline still pumping through him.

'Ha-ha, yeah, a few of those turns were a bit white knuckle, for sure! But hey, we're here now, and the view is absolutely breathtaking, isn't it? Totally worth it.'

I didn't realise at the time just how white knuckle that experience had been for him. I was about to find out tomorrow.

Rondane Mountains to Bud

Mid June in Norway felt like the start not the middle of the holiday season. Even our ski hotel in Rondane was only now shaking off the winter slumber. The upside of this early season lull was having breakfast—the legendary smorgasbord—to ourselves.

A cholesterol-packed Norwegian fry-up tempted us but with the memory of last night's reindeer stew still lingering (and our wallets emptying at the mere mention of Norwegian prices), we opted for a modest calorie intake of yogurt and berries. A wise choice, considering the £36 we'd shelled out for two prawn sandwiches and coffees in Lillehammer. The cheap roadside meals I'd enjoyed in Spain seemed a long time ago now.

Emerging from the hotel lobby to a brilliant blue sky was a delightful surprise. We'd braced ourselves for cold, wet weather, so the sunshine felt like a bonus prize. The hotel's gravel car park, however, presented a different kind of challenge. Its slight slope made it prime bike-dropping territory, so we gingerly manoeuvred our machines back onto the road.

The descent back to Otta was nothing short of spectacular, with heart-soaring views of snow-capped mountains and the deep valley carving through the Rondane range. But the day's route planning took an unexpected turn.

The previous evening over beers and our usual podcast recording, Ralph had confided to me that the exposed hairpins on the steep road up to the hotel had triggered a bout of vertigo. Ralph is blind in one eye, the result of a childhood accident. He had no problems with normal riding but the exposure of the mountains had caught him unawares. He'd done admirably on the way up, but the prospect of facing more twists and turns, including the notorious Trollstigen, filled him with apprehension. He'd watched countless videos of riders tackling this challenging route, so he knew what lay ahead. We needed a Plan B.

We decided to split up for the first part of the day. I would take the low road to Geiranger and conquer the Trollstigen, while Ralph would take the high road to Andalsnes, where we'd reunite. It wasn't the plan we'd envisioned, but sometimes the best escapades are the ones you don't expect.

Back in Otta we parted ways for the first time on our trip— not counting the numerous occasions we'd got lost on our way to hotels, of course.

'You sure you'll be all right on your own?' I asked Ralph, a touch of concern in my voice.

'Don't you worry about me, Stephen,' he replied with a wink. 'I'll simply pootle along keeping my eye open for any trolls. I'll see you later. Have fun over the Trollstigen. By the way, did I tell you the one about—?'

I lost radio contact before he could finish the joke. With a wave we each headed off on our chosen routes. I took the R15 south of Ottadalen, heading west towards one of Norway's most popular regions. The road followed the river, winding its way through the landscape and gradually ascending into the heart of the mountains. It was a glorious day for a ride.

It felt odd riding alone, even though that's my usual state. I missed Ralph's banter and funny stories already. He'd had me in stitches the day before recounting a teenage escapade: sneaking with his pals into a showing of some erotic film— *Emmanuelle*, if I recall correctly—armed with syringes filled with yogurt. At strategic, ahem, climactic moments, they'd unleashed creamy chaos into the unsuspecting audience. He'd had a mischievous glint in his eye as he'd shared the tale. I shook with fits of giggles. It was so unlike the Ralph I'd known in the office.

Riding as a duo was still a new experience, but I was enjoying the companionship and the chance to get to know my old boss better. I'm usually pretty confident and feel I can handle most situations, like that scrape in Marchena, but it was comforting to know my mate had my back, just as I had his. We were heading into some very inhospitable and remote country. A bad accident or a breakdown up in the Far North would be a serious proposition, as the guy I'd met on the ferry to Spain had shown. Two was more than just company, it was safety.

For the moment, however, I was back to being on my own. I rode for over an hour and saw only two cars, a tractor and a naked woman on a pushbike. I let the silence settle for a moment, then filled the gap with music. The Eagles' *Peaceful Easy Feeling* seemed fitting, but a few bars in, I switched off my headset. I wanted to simply be present in the mountains, alone with my thoughts.

I realised then how much I was enjoying this journey, not only for the scenery, but for the esprit de corps I shared with Ralph. Our banter, our shared passion for riding fun and exploration, and the simple joy of being together on the open road all added up to an experience that was greater than the sum of its parts. We'd laugh over beers at the end of the day, thinking back to people we've known, their quirks and the funny things that tended to happen in our world of pubs. He had such a positive attitude; his beer glass was always half full, where mine was sometimes emptier.

Plus, he'd have enjoyed seeing Brunhilde on a bike.

In Våga, I paused to admire one of the famous *stavkirken*, or stave churches. These enchanting wooden buildings are scattered throughout Norway and resemble enormous, fantastical matchstick creations, with steeply pitched roofs and a magical, fairytale quality. Their intricate carvings often depict fantastical creatures, including trolls. They possess a mythical quality and are movingly beautiful. The Våga church, one of Norway's oldest, dating back to 1150, was no exception. Its rich wood contrasted beautifully with the crisp white windows, and even the tiles on its sharply pointed spire were made of timber. I'd heard that trolls were keen gardeners, and the church's impeccably tended graveyard suggested they must live nearby.

The road stretched out before me, empty and inviting. Minutes passed without a single vehicle in sight. I engaged the cruise control, letting my mind wander as I soaked in the tranquillity of the surroundings. As I approached Grotli, the lake shimmered like a sapphire, reflecting the deep blue sky and the jagged peaks that pierced the horizon. The air was still, not even a whisper of a breeze to disturb the serene landscape.

The road itself was a motorcyclist's dream: flawless tarmac, devoid of potholes, tar snakes or debris. The guardrails that lined the route, while reassuring, felt almost unnecessary in such an idyllic setting. The only signs of civilisation were the old, russet-coloured barns scattered on the hillsides, their distinctive grassy ramps leading to the haylofts above.

The once towering pines gradually shrank, their windswept forms hinting at the approaching snowline. The mountains loomed closer, their peaks generously flecked with icy patches. The R15 road flowed effortlessly through the landscape, its graceful curves dancing to the beat of the rugged terrain. I crossed over delicate bridges, their steel frames reminiscent of a child's Meccano set. Few tunnels marred this stretch of road, allowing the journey to unfold in harmony with the natural contours of the land.

Below, rivers raged with snowmelt, the white water crashing over rocks and settling into deep green-blue pools. Quaint clusters of wooden *hytter*, attractive weekend retreats, dotted the riverbanks, their roofs verdant with grasses, flowers and heather. Despite the sun's best efforts, the temperature had plummeted to a chilly five degrees, prompting me to plug in my heated jacket.

In the distance, the imposing peaks of the Jostedalsbreen glacier signalled my turn onto the narrow track road at Langvatnet. The lake, still frozen solid, mirrored the sky's steely grey. The road ahead snaked upwards towards Geiranger, its tight hairpins a taste of the Trollstigen pass that awaited me.

Tall snow poles lining the verges served as indications of the winter's icy grip on this route. A small crew of road workers, their yellow lorry and red cones the only bursts of colour in the monochrome landscape, laboured to repair the damage inflicted by the harsh winter months. Deep banks of snow, their layers of grey, brown and black resembling a dirty collar, flanked the road, rising high above me. To my left, the snow-clad slopes of the mountain soared upwards, their sheer faces plunging dramatically into the lake below.

The temptation to gawk at the scenery was strong, but I forced myself to focus on the road. With only a single track and oncoming traffic to contend with, losing concentration was not an option. A wispy fog rolled in, obscuring the rocks below. As I neared the col, the sun vanished, replaced by thick cloud. The world around me transformed, taking on an ethereal, otherworldly quality.

As I neared Geiranger the number of coach parks and tour buses increased, their passengers herded together like sheep. I was grateful for my ever reliable Honda, which allowed me the freedom to explore this gorgeous landscape at my own pace, on my own terms. That said, this trip wasn't just about conquering miles on a motorcycle, it was also a voyage of self-discovery, a chance to reconnect with myself and to forge new bonds with an old pal.

I eased off the throttle and descended towards the honeypot village, a familiar sight from the decks of countless cruise ships. The bends here were wide enough to accommodate the larger vehicles that frequented the area. In a lay-by, a cluster of seven identical Renault Twizys, tiny electric cars decked out in corporate green and silver, showed a more eco-conscious approach to tourism in these mountains.

I pulled over to gaze down over the fjord that made Geiranger famous, a place that graced countless bucket lists. It's undeniably impressive, a UNESCO World Heritage Site with a natural beauty that takes the breath away. The balance between the tiny village, home to a mere 250 souls, and the throng of people that visits during the four-month tourist season is unsustainably delicate. Over 300,000 tourists disembark annually from cruise ships alone, their sheer numbers threatening to overwhelm this fragile ecosystem.

The *AIDAperla*, another colossal cruise ship, was disgorging its hordes as I watched. I felt a pang of guilt. I too was, after all, part of the problem. While I relished the freedom of exploring on my motorcycle, I was still a tourist, contributing to the issue that threatened to erode the beauty I had come to admire. This paradox, the inherent contradiction of being both a passionate traveller and an advocate for responsible tourism, gnawed at me. It's a dilemma faced by many who yearn to experience the world's wonders while minimising their impact on the environment and local communities. The rise of the anti-tourist movement, particularly since travel opened again post-COVID should make us consider the issues more carefully, but the answers will not come easily. One man's 'bloody tourist' is another's customer and livelihood.

Despite these conflicting emotions, I couldn't deny the allure of Geiranger. The small village is situated at the head of the Geirangerfjord, a setting of natural beauty that is simply awesome. Charming though it is, with colourful red-roofed houses clustered around the harbour, a couple of anodyne large modern hotels and a functional caravan park mar the scene.

Looking closer, I found a row of ancient wooden boathouses, two storeys tall with grass-covered roofs, bordering the crystal-clear waters. I peered down into the fjord and saw the algae-covered stony slipways descending into the impenetrable black depths. Though I was only a few hundred metres away from the village centre, few tourists had ventured even this far, to the authentic fishing heart of the place. Peace reigned there amongst the mossy stones and weathered dark timbers.

The fjord itself was a breathtaking sight, with steep cliffs soaring out of the waters either side and numerous waterfalls cascading down the dramatic mountainsides. The most famous of these are the Seven Sisters and the Bridal

Veil falls, whose milky white waters tumble ferociously hundreds of feet down the cliffs into the deep fjord.

In the near distance, past the cruise ship, I could see the zigzags of the road which led up and out of the fjord. I'd seen Geiranger, that box was ticked. Now the road demanded my full attention again, promising a welcome return to solitude and the single-minded pursuit of the next item on my bucket list: the (in)famous Trollstigen.

Climbing the steep road out of Geiranger, I couldn't shake off the nagging questions about ethical tourism. It's a tangled knot, this relationship between experiencing a place and preserving it. There are no easy answers, no simple solutions. But the responsibility to find a balance, to tread lightly and ensure our presence benefits rather than harms, remains. It's a challenge, a privilege and a moral imperative all at once, and a conundrum I can't quite reconcile.

A mountain and a fjord crossing lay between me and the Trollstigen, but around one of the tight uphill bends on the way to Eidsdal I encountered a massive roadwork project, an example of Norway's seemingly endless appetite for tunnelling. My first delay of the afternoon. I switched off the engine and limbered up as I waited endlessly for the lights to change. At last, they went green. My bike twitched and bucked over the rough tunnel surface, as I tried to make up time. Machinery and pipes intimidatingly littered the dark tunnel, as water seeped down the walls, glistening in my headlights.

Freed from the tunnel's confines, I approached the ferry terminal at Eidsdal where there was a long line of vehicles snaking back from the dock. Typically, bikers are waved to the front of the queue in most places in Europe, but as I confidently filtered past cars, campervans and the occasional coach, a gruff-looking man in a dirty high-vis vest stepped in front of me.

'Back of the queue. Go.'

I stopped abruptly, jamming on the brakes.

'English,' he barked, 'you go back of queue.'

'Hey, why don't you let bikers through to the front?' I asked, slightly taken aback.

'Go fucking back,' he repeated, his tone leaving no room for argument.

I don't think he was singling me out for being English. He did it to some German riders too. Obviously I was dealing with a ferryman with an attitude problem as well as a limited vocabulary. I reluctantly retreated to the back of the line. It turned out that only one of the three ferries that usually ply this route was operating that day, a rare instance of Norwegian inefficiency.

By this point the queue stretched around a roundabout and back up the hill again. I texted Ralph to update him on the situation: "Trying to find my inner Zen. Ferry left. I'm still in a monster queue. Chaos reigns. Been chatting to a Norwegian family who've been waiting 3 ½ hours."

"The obstacle is the path," came his Zen-like reply.

The situation was so dire that the locals, clearly accustomed to such delays, started fishing off the quay. When Grumpy wasn't looking, I stealthily inched my bike forward, squeezing into tiny gaps in front of camper vans and cars. It wasn't as if a motorbike would deny boarding to a bigger vehicle, after all. Two hours had already passed, and I was determined to make a break for it when the next ferry arrived. I was feeling increasingly uncomfortable about the long wait that Ralph was having to endure. It was pressure I didn't need.

Another pissed-off biker, one of the Germans, had the same idea, and we both made a mad dash for the ramp as soon as the last car disembarked. Finally, in the nick of time, I was back on the road, albeit for now one that floated on water. Grumpy hadn't spotted our stratagem and we got away with it.

By this time, later in the afternoon than I'd expected, my plan of stopping at the lofty Trollstigen viewpoint to survey the sinuous beast from above had to be binned. I had watched videos of riders tackling this sought-after road, but riding it was no video game. Eleven incredibly tight hairpin bends and an 800-metre drop to the valley below was a recipe for both exhilaration and terror. I pulled into a lay-by before the road narrowed its way through two large boulders. I needed some favourite music to match my nervous mood.

On went Grieg's Peer Gynt and *The Hall of the Mountain King*. It's full of trolls and goblins. Its insistent, repetitive rhythm and gradually increasing tempo and volume suggest a sense of claustrophobia and impending danger. It seemed the appropriate soundtrack to what some call one of the most dangerous roads in the world, which of course only made it even more enticing. I switched on my cameras. This was one I wanted to see on action replay later. Oh, and to show Ralph over a beer. Maybe several times.

The narrow road clung to the mountainside, with only jagged rocks serving as a precarious barrier. The looming peaks above cast an imposing shadow. Passing through the snow gates and the ominous "10% incline" sign, the road narrowed even further. Navigating Trollstigen's incredibly tight, descending bends demanded a delicate balance of brake, gears and throttle. It was a constant dance to ensure speed and lean angle were synchronised with each curve's trajectory. Going too slow risked stalling mid bend and dropping the bike, inviting a chorus of irritated horns, potential damage, injury and a hefty dose of embarrassment. On the other hand, going too fast was an invitation to almost certain death or serious injury. The Trollstigen is a true test of a biker's skill and courage. Was I ready to face that test?

I rose from the saddle, stood on the pegs and peered through the first turn. No traffic. I took it wide, accelerating out and onto the next short straight. A massive waterfall roared beneath the road, a sight I would encounter several times along this route. The bends tightened, the exits narrowed and the air pressure popped in my ears as I descended. I was at one with the road, speed and balance in harmony. The concrete barrier, because it was so low, formed a potential tripwire into the abyss. The road was mainly clear of snow and ice, despite having only reopened after the winter a few weeks prior. Approaching cars passed me in a blur; all my attention was focused on setting up the bike for the next bend, right line, right speed. The front tyre twitched as I crossed some wet pebbly run-off from the constantly eroding cliffs. My buttocks clenched and I tightened my thighs' grip on the fuel tank. Another very narrow bridge, a car waited on the other side and then began to move towards me while I was mid bridge. Shit. He's not seen me. I opened the throttle wide, slipping by inches through the narrow gap left by the car and barrier. 'Fuck, that was close,' I screamed.

And then, there it was: Trollstigen, the road of a thousand videos (plus another one just filmed), a legendary route in the biking world. Suddenly, it was over. A few more twists and turns remained, but the road widened and flattened, a bit of an anti-climax after the heart-pounding descent. I pulled over to snap a selfie by the enormous troll biker-girl monument at the café, joining a group of BMW GS riders who were doing the same. I'd passed the test of the Trollstigen. A gentle smile of satisfaction brightened my lips. Another box ticked.

A short ride later, I arrived in Andalsnes, where Ralph had been waiting for 4½ hours parked by the Norse Visitor Centre. I rolled in, exhilarated yet slightly guilty that he hadn't experienced the same thrill. Over strong coffee and a late lunch of chewy chocolate bars and the tang of salty liquorice sweets, we swapped tales.

'Ralph, you should have seen me on that second hairpin,' I bragged, unable to contain my excitement. 'Almost got my knee down.'

Ralph raised an eyebrow, a wry grin spreading across his face.

'Oh yeah? The only time you ever get your knee down is checking the tyre pressures,' he deadpanned. 'And falling off your bike in Spain.'

'Ha-ha, funny,' I retorted, rolling my eyes.

'But seriously, I'm glad you didn't do it with me. To be fair, it's a tough one and you made the right decision. It's no place for vertigo.'

He'd waited ages for me to arrive and I could understand his keenness to get going. More tales of my bucket list day would have to wait.

With a long ride to our overnight stop in Bud and at least one more ferry crossing ahead, it was time to saddle up, switch on the comms, and continue our travels. Bud—the Norwegian village, not the American beer—wasn't on our original itinerary, but it became a necessity after our camping gear was nicked, forcing us to book a last-minute cabin. Happily, the ferries from Andalsnes to this charming coastal village ran smoothly. We arrived late, tired, thirsty and hungry from a long day in the saddles.

Ralph grabbed a few beers from the camp shop while I hunted for dinner. He settled on the front terrace of our cosy *hytte*, two Isbjørns in hand, content to watch the calm waters and ignore the pungent aroma of our biker boots wafting from within.

Dinner that night proved challenging. Bud is not big. The supermarket was shut, as was the local fish restaurant. The Spiseri og Catering, a take-away joint, came to our rescue. I ordered a massive pizza that wouldn't fit in my top box. I rode back from the shop with it hanging out of the sides. We devoured it, washing it down with more excellent Norwegian beers.

'Did you see any trolls on the Trollstigen?' asked Ralph.

'No. Apart from the big one by the caff at the end. Did you?'

'Och aye. I met a group of them while I was hanging about in Andalsnes or wherever it was. They were teaching me some troll phrases.'

'Interesting,' I said, intrigued. 'Give me an example of some.'

Ralph swigged down a mouthful of lager, drew himself up and declared in a liltingly trollish way, *'Tha am fear a tha a' creidsinn ann an trolaichean air chall.'*

'Wow, that's pretty impressive. You learned all that today? What's it mean?' I asked.

'Anyone who believes in trolls is mad... It's a Gaelic saying.'

'Ah.'

12

Geology Lessons
Trondheim–Namsos–Yttervik

Bud to Trondheim

Our campsite was a geological wonderland: Lewisian gneiss, quartz, feldspar, granite. Ralph, a geologist by training, transformed into an enthusiastic tour guide. He was literally in his element.

'... and that, my friend,' he gestured towards the ground, 'is what we're standing on. The oldest rocks in the world, like those in Scotland. Lewisian gneiss. Four billion years old. It's a granite that at some point has been metamorphosed.'

I concentrated on his explanation as he pointed to different bits of rock, most of which looked similarly stony.

'You can see the big quartz and feldspar crystals and how it's been stretched out, and there's a lenticular shape in the middle.'

Keen to add to the scientific discourse I chipped in. 'I see, it's been stretched like a... stick of rock,' thinking of something with "Skegness" written through the middle.

There was a pause.

'Hmm, not *like a stick of rock*, it *is* rock.'

Geology was all around us and his passion was contagious. I gently began to walk back to the bikes, otherwise I could see we were set for a whole field trip. Today we had the Atlantic Road (*Atlantershavsveien*) to conquer, a third bucket list item in less than twenty-four hours. As we walked back over the mossy outcrops, I couldn't help but grin at the quirky scene. We were surrounded by grass-roofed huts made of corrugated iron, weathered caravans plastered with ropes, buoys and random shipwrecked nautical items. One even had an old tuba and a trumpet stuck on its sides.

Some call the Atlantic Road the world's most beautiful drive. No doubt other roads lay claim to that title too, but it's undoubtedly a contender for the premier league. Spanning over eight kilometres, a mere sliver of Norway's lengthy coastline, this route packs a punch. Eight bridges, causeways, and a scattering of tiny islands and skerries weave together a tapestry of coastal beauty, a highlight reel of Norway's most stunning scenery.

Connecting the island of Averøy to the mainland, the road is a whirlwind of visual delights. It's almost overwhelming trying to decide where to focus as the sea sneaks through rocky crevices beside you or vanishes beneath a graceful bridge arcing skyward. The Storseisundbrua Bridge is the star of the show, a sinuous structure that twists mid-air before descending back to earth. You might even recognise it from Bond's battle with the baddies in his Aston Martin DB5 in *No Time to Die*. We had paused in a lay-by before the bridge to set up the GoPro. The Armco was covered by a slightly faded patchwork of stickers left by fellow travellers. I added my own Honda Wanderlust sticker. I had already stuck mine onto various bits of street furniture along the route, adding to their growing international collection.

Motorhomes trundled past on the opposite side of the bridge, no one in a rush. The sky, a canvas of heavy clouds broken by shafts of sunlight, painted a dramatic scene as the beams danced across the mirrored sea.

We didn't talk during the ride, both of us lost in the simple thrill of piloting our bikes through gorgeous scenery we'd never experienced before. It was so stirring I could see how musicians and artists flock here for inspiration. Not for the first time did I feel a visceral joy at this adventure. I tried to lock the sights and smells and sensations into my neocortex, where long-term memories are stored. Something to retrieve later when my adventuring days are over, should the key still work. God willing.

Ten minutes later, we reached Kårvåg. It was over. We toyed with the idea of turning back, reliving the magic, but some experiences are best enjoyed once. With the rest of the magnificent coastline calling, we pressed on.

Our next stop, Bremsnes, lay thirty kilometres to the northeast. We were on the hunt for the ferry to Kristiansund. Normally crossings were well signposted, but the boat sign we followed led us to a ferry-less dead end. A garden centre was nearby. Surely someone there would know. Besides, we were craving a coffee. Norwegian garden centres, however, stick to the basics. Plants, tools, compost; no café in sight. They haven't yet discovered retail diversification.

We spotted an elderly couple in the car park and asked for directions. Their school-lesson English seemed to have faded over the years, so I had to consult my Norwegian–English phrasebook.

'*Unnskyld*,' I began, '*Vet dere hvor fergen til Kristiansund går?*' (Excuse me, do you know where the ferry to Kristiansund goes?)

The old man furrowed his brow. '*Ferge? Nei, nei... den går ikke lenger.*' (Ferry? No, no... it doesn't run anymore.)

His wife chimed in, '*Tunnel nå. Under fjord.*' (Tunnel now. Under the fjord.)

With some back and forth, a mix of broken English and Norwegian, we pieced together the story: the ferry had been replaced by a 5.7-kilometre tunnel beneath the Bremnesfjorden back in 2009.

Coffee-less and slightly bemused, we retraced our route, re-joining County Road 64. Suddenly we plunged 250 metres down into the undersea tunnel, one of the deepest in the world. It was a spookily steep hill, a descent into Hades. The tunnel is a spectacular feat of engineering and we were blissfully unaware of the many leaky struggles during its construction.

Tunnels became a recurring theme on our Norwegian road trip, each one a unique experience. Some were ancient, their gloom punctuated only by flickering lights that left a sooty patina over our bikes, a badge of honour we wore proudly. Others were modern marvels, well-lit and airy, with smooth asphalt that seemed to stretch on forever. Most were free, and many were surprisingly long, five or six kilometres being commonplace. We even tackled one behemoth stretching over ten clicks. Norway, of course, boasts the world's longest road tunnel, the Laerdal, at a staggering twenty-five kilometres.

One constant, however, was the noise. No matter how normally effective my earplugs, a resonant frequency always found its way through, booming off the tunnel walls. I experimented with different speeds and gears, but the cacophony—my own bike's roar mingled with the reverberations of other vehicles—proved incurable. It was a wearying physical assault on the senses. Then there was the cold. Heat struggles to penetrate these subterranean passages and the temperature could plummet from a pleasant 21°C outside to a shivery 3° within moments.

'It's Baltic in here,' shouted Ralph over the din, as we reached the chilly depths a quarter of a kilometre below the waves, the point where the road started to climb again.

But even with the noise and the cold, there was a certain thrill to these journeys through the heart of the mountains or underwater. Each tunnel felt like a portal to a hidden world, a passage through time itself.

Emerging from the depths we were greeted by fresh air and the relative quiet of Kristiansund's outskirts. We were desperate for that overdue coffee by now. Finding a parking spot proved another challenge. Not wanting to risk a run-in with the traffic wardens by stopping on the pavement, we rolled to a halt in the town's official car park. I somehow managed to pay twice using an infernal app-based system, chucking away the advantage of squeezing our bikes into a single pay-and-display space.

Kristiansund (not to be confused with Kristiansand, our eventual departure point in the far south) is a major fishing port. We took a walk along the quay to admire the *Klippfiskkjerringa* sculpture on the harbourside. This gritty, realistic artwork pays homage to the women who laboured in the klippfisk (salted cod) factories; it was one of many remarkable sculptures we'd discover throughout our travels, each celebrating the resilience and hard work of Norsk women.

We darted into a dockside café and sipped a warming brew as ferries, fishing boats and specialist vessels for the salmon industry played maritime dodgems on the cold waters of the *havn* (harbour).

Soon after departing Kristiansund, we were back in the rabbit hole, diving into another undersea tunnel to the island of Bergsøya. The E39 hugged the coastline, the sea a constant companion for the next hour until we reached Kanestraum and the ferry to Halsa, our entrance route into the region of Trøndelag. The distant mountains still wore their early summer dusting of snow.

We arrived at the ferry quay in good time for the afternoon departure. Our pre-registered Flytpass dongle proved essential, as cash and card were useless here for paying the seven quid it cost to cross. Norway is no place to be a tech-Luddite.

The half-hour crossing offered time for a loo break and give our heads and necks a break from the heavy helmets. My right wrist was aching, so I slathered on more Voltarol gel for relief. It was an ever-present reminder to take care, a little souvenir from Oslo.

We landed on the slipway and with practiced aplomb swung our legs over the saddles to get away before the motorhomes. I was all for pushing on hard today. It's my style.

'We've still 150 or so to go. Let's crack on. I'm not hungry, are you?' Ralph, however, possesses a more pragmatic approach.

'I could use a wee piece of something. Next decent-looking place, that's not a garden centre, let's pull over.'

The afternoon remained café-less, however, until we stumbled upon Valsøya, a camping and restaurant site. Its exterior was underwhelming, with a carpenter busily wielding a chop saw amid scattered tools. But stepping inside was like entering a luxurious ski lodge—rustic wooden beams, polished crystal glasses, and elegant linen tablecloths. The food was delicious: *skagenrøre*, a delectable shrimp salad and tangy *rabarbersaft* (rhubarb juice).

I wiped my lips with one of the fancy napkins.

'Well, that was quite the morning, wasn't it?' I remarked, stretching out my legs and spreading out the map to trace the day's route.

Ralph ran his finger over the Atlantic Road and beyond.

'Yeah, yeah, yeah,' he uttered under his breath. I could tell he was reliving it, the bridges, the tunnels, the ferries, every last drop of it.

'Just fantastic.'

'Indeed,' I replied. 'Did you count how many tunnels we went through? Felt like we were moles for a while there.'

'Lost count after ten,' he replied with a grin. 'But that Atlantic Road, eh? Water everywhere, beautiful inlets, gentle pace.'

'Where are we now?' He looked up, confused. His finger hovered uncertainly over the map and then jabbed it conclusively. He beamed brightly when he worked out that Valsøya was both a restaurant and an island. It was sometimes impossible to tell if we were on mainland Norway or not.

'Sooo, as long as we keep the sea or is it a fjord on our left for the next half hour we're heading in the right direction, right?' he queried.

'Right. Then keep right on at Vinjeøra, then turn next right, sticking on the E39. That'll take us right to Trondheim. Right, got that?'

'Righty-o. Don't forget your heated vest.'

He gestured towards the chair where my electric underjacket lay draped, its wires dangling suspiciously on the wooden floor.

'Thanks,' I retorted with a smile. 'I'm going to need it on those mountain passes. You'll be begging to borrow it.'

'Too big for me'.

He grinned as we donned our gear once more, ready to tackle the road to Trondheim. The long morning's gentle pace and wonderful scenery had recharged us, and despite the occasional tunnel-headache, we were eager to get back on the road again.

Motorcyclists have a number of pet hates. In city centres these include tramlines, cobblestones and deep ruts. I wondered what lay in wait in Trondheim. Imagine our delight, therefore, as we rolled up to Hospitalgata, a charming 18th-century wharf area, only to be confronted by a large patchwork of treacherous cobbles and a deep drainage channel right outside our Airbnb. Still haunted by my windscreen shattering faux pas at the Cochs Pensjonat—a move we had since dubbed GateGate—we gingerly walked our bikes through the obstacle course. Ralph and I were taking no risks. We tucked them safely into an extremely narrow passageway and locked the door for the night.

Marcus, the owner, was in the process of restoring the old merchant's house, having transformed a former stable and warehouse into a surprisingly decent gaff. However, I'd not spotted in the write-up that there was only one bed, so we tossed a euro to decide our sleeping arrangements. I lost, and the narrow sofa became my bed for the night.

The evening air was balmy, the sun casting a rosy glow on the city. While I busied myself with the usual post ride rituals of unpacking and laundry, Ralph, clad only in his underpants, sprawled out on the wooden veranda, leaning against the grey clapperboard wall, soaking up the warmth. I saw steam gently wafting off him as he closed his eyes and nodded off. It was a chance for both our gear and us to finally catch our breath after another long day on the road.

I woke him from his slumbers by noisily hanging out my washing on various rusty nails that stuck out of the wooden boards. A shadow now partially covered his resting place.

'Just shut my eyes for a minute then,' he declared breezily.

'Thirty, actually.'

'Must be time for a beer in that case. I was dreaming of Brunhilde.'

Our borrowed city map, dog-eared from use, directed us towards the historic treasures of Trondheim, once the capital of Norway. We made a beeline for Bakklandet. In the warm, golden light of the cloudless evening, it was a sight to behold, a charming neighbourhood full of brightly painted wooden houses delicately balanced on stilts along the Nidelva River, crossed by the Gammle Bybro, the old town bridge. The area retained its authenticity, resisting the urge to become overly touristy. A handful of pubs, including a crowded floating beer barge, were doing brisk business.

'Well, that settles it then,' I said, nodding towards the barge. 'Beer first, sightseeing later.'

Ralph gave me a dry look. 'Beers first, second, maybe third. Sightseeing can wait.'

'That sleep did make you thirsty,' I quipped.

We compromised, agreeing to a quick cultural pit stop before slaking our thirsts.

A short walk away, the imposing silhouette of the Nidaros Cathedral dominated the skyline. The magnificent structure, the largest medieval building in Norway, encapsulated both faith and history. Its intricate Gothic façade, adorned with menacing troll gargoyles, whispered tales of a time when Nordic paganism clashed with the burgeoning tide of Christianity. Saint Olav, the Viking king who brought Christianity to Norway, met his end in the Battle of Stiklestad in 1030. The cathedral, built over his burial site, became a pilgrimage destination for centuries, drawing the faithful from across Europe.

The dog-eared map was proving rather informative.

It's a pity Nidaros was closed and we couldn't go in to pay homage to the man who shaped the spiritual destiny of a nation.

Suitably enlightened, however, we sought refreshment at the nearby Øx Taproom.

'Right, then,' Ralph said, scanning the menu. 'What'll it be? "Satanic Rites" or "Two Grumpy Old Bastards"?'

'Hmm,' I pondered, stroking my imaginary beard.

'Given I'm sharing a room with you, let's go for the Two Grumpy Old Bastards.'

'Excellent choice,' Ralph replied with a grin. 'Here's to Saint Olav and his beer-loving descendants.'

We clinked glasses, the rich, dark ale slipping down effortlessly.

Trondheim to Namsos

I woke with a stiff neck and sore back from sleeping on the narrow sofa. I was putting away all the bed linen when Ralph breezed in, stretched and yawned. He'd slept well.

He took one look at the makeshift bed, reached down and pulled at some lever beneath it, yanked at a handle and the thing suddenly expanded into a proper bed.

'You should have asked,' he said, as he I stood there gobsmacked.

Trondheim effortlessly earned a spot on our lighthearted Top 5 Places I'd Like To Move To list that we were constantly debating throughout the trip. It was a charming city, walkable, safe and unassuming, with a burgeoning foodie and microbrewery scene. Given the region's propensity to throw up all four seasons in a single day, we were blessed to have only the summer experience. The glorious weather we enjoyed added to our delight at the city, which evidently had a large population of very attractive women.

Fortified by a café breakfast of *gudbrandsdalsost* (a peculiar-looking brown goat's cheese) and tart huckleberry juice, we wheedled our bikes back out over the pavement hazards, then mounted our luggage before setting off for Namsos 210 kms away. However, a short early detour was in order. We had to visit Hell.

Yes, Hell. Another odd place-name to add to my growing collection, joining the likes of Condom, Cockbridge, Penistone and Lady Hole Lane, visited on previous trips. Not to mention Bastād, our earlier encounter on this trip. One day, I'm determined to devise a truly Profanisaurus road trip itinerary, it would be Firkin great to ride. (Firkin is on the bonny banks of Loch Lomond, incidentally.)

But back to Hell. If anyone's wondering about its whereabouts, I can pinpoint it precisely: thirty-two kms east of Trondheim.

'To Hell with you, Stephen,' Ralph quipped as we set off, a mischievous glint in his eye.

'With pleasure,' I replied with a grin.

'Marcus's back passage was so tight; I had the devil of a job extracting my bike out of it. Didn't you?' he added, rising to the infernal theme.

The jokes flowed as freely as the sweat as we headed east, making a pitstop at another Honda dealership to snag some lightweight summer gloves. The weather was living up to Hell's reputation, with the mercury climbing towards a blistering 28° C. In Norway, of all places.

'Well, if this is Hell,' Ralph said as we cruised along, 'they've got a wicked sense of humour. Who knew the devil was such a fan of sunshine and sweltering heat?'

'Perhaps he's trying to lure us into a false sense of security,' I replied, wiping sweat from my brow. 'We'll probably hit a snowstorm the moment we reach Namsos.'

Our route was a series of brief disappearances into the cool darkness of tunnels that offered momentary respite from the heat. Roadwork crews were out in force, leaving us to navigate endless stretches of what we'd come to call squirrel, that annoying delaminated tarmac. The squiggly lines left by the milling machines made for a frustrating ride, the bikes following the grooves like they were on railway tracks. The only solution was to relax (easier said than done) and let arms and wrists hang loose and let the bike find its own way.

I discovered that flashing my hazard lights kept other drivers at bay and my blood pressure in check.

'Where's your L plate?' Ralph teased as we emerged from yet another spell of squirrelling, me leading a line of traffic at a snail's pace.

'Hey, if it keeps me upright,' I retorted. 'Besides, wouldn't you rather have an intact mate with a low blood pressure than a stressed out one with a buggered bike?'

'Ah cannae argue wi' yer logic,' came his droll reply.

Hell isn't quite what you might expect. It's lacking in the molten lava, fire and brimstone department. It was a modern town that boasted a new airport (Trondheim's) and a sprawling retail park. Not a bad consolation prize if you miss out on a ticket to the more appealing sounding Heaven, in Texas.

We made our way to the wooden clapperboard station, where a railway sign bore the town's fiery name rather humbly. No horny devils or infernal imagery, a platform for selfie-snapping tourists like us. The additional sign, "Gods-Expedition", was a delightful bonus (it meant "goods", not anything ecclesiastical). We carefully navigated yet another treacherous gravel forecourt, not wanting to mar our Instagram-worthy photos with a toppled bike or two before seeking refuge in the air-conditioned haven of a nearby coffee shop for a well-deserved *fika*.

Earlier, we'd considered a detour to the charmingly named Stiklestad, Norway's equivalent of Bannockburn, where King Olav II met his sticky end at the hands of his own subjects in an ambush. However, I was quickly learning that distances in Norway were deceptive. Every day's journey, no matter how short on paper, seemed to stretch into eternity thanks to the strict speed limits and the constant visual feast of the landscape. We reluctantly abandoned the Stiklestad idea and continued north.

The road snaked through undulating hills that caressed the edges of fjords and the tips of lakes. Traffic was sparse, allowing us to fully immerse ourselves in the gentle rhythm of the ride. The scenery transformed before our eyes, shifting from rolling green hills akin to the Scottish Lowlands to majestic peaks like those of the Alps. Seemingly endless expanses of forestland gave way to rugged mountains, their slopes dotted with wildflowers. Crystal clear streams cascaded down rocky ravines, while the occasional glimpse of a secluded wooden cabin erected amongst the trees added a touch of human warmth to the wild beauty. It was very picture postcardy.

We pulled into a lay-by near Sparbu, parched from the unscripted heat. It wasn't supposed to be this hot.

Dehydration is a thief, stealing away focus and leaving a mental fog in its wake. As we gulped down ice-cold water from our Thermos flasks, a rather battered BMW GS motorbike rolled to a halt. Laden with tattered bags, dented panniers and a spare tyre dumped precariously atop everything, the bike looked like it had circled the globe. As indeed it had.

Gunnar, an Icelander, had been traveling for eighteen months and was on his way home, taking a scenic detour through Norway. He'd picked up the spare tyre in Romania, a wonder it was still attached as it was lashed on with a few flimsy straps. He was disarmingly modest about his adventure; an inspiring motorbike nomad. We felt like amateurs in comparison. Before setting off to conquer the planet, he'd done a tour of Europe, caught the travel bug and simply kept going. He'd spent the pandemic holed up in India.

As he lugged his epic juggernaut bike off into the distance, a scruffy English campervan pulled up. The familiar registration plate was a welcome surprise; it was the first UK vehicle we'd seen in days. Even though Norway is practically next door to the UK, it's not an easy destination for Brits to reach. Germans and Dutch, always intrepid explorers, seemed to be everywhere, of course.

Malcolm and Diana, the van's middle-aged occupants, were keen bikers too. Both ex-police, now retired early, they were on an extended Scandinavian journey, though not as far as we were headed.

'So, you two are riding up to Nordkapp. Impressive.' Malcolm's voice held a hint of envious admiration.

'That's the theory,' Ralph replied, with a touch of self-deprecating humour. 'We're doing okay so far, loving the country and these great roads. It's just a long way still to go.'

'And back,' I interjected, 'though we've a cunning plan for that. We're taking the boat back to Bergen. It's a bit of a cheat but we're looking forward to a rest.'

Diana nodded, a flicker of jealousy in her eyes. 'We're both bikers at heart but we came in this thing this time around. Gives us a bit more comfort, I suppose.' As she said this she looked back at the battered campervan with a scowl.

'Plus, it's a good way to make the most of our budget. We're determined to keep going until the cash runs out. Or, of course, until we kill each other,' Malcolm chortled, blithely. Diana's expression hinted at the latent possibility.

'I'm glad we're not doing this trip in that grotty campervan,' I said to Ralph as we swung out of the lay-by onto the highway.

'So am I,' he responded. 'I'd never escape your snoring or those ponging boots.' There was a pause. 'We're not in a tent tonight, are we?'

'Nooo.'

With the mid afternoon sun blazing, we enjoyed the cooling breeze of the open road. The eighty-eight kilometres to Namsos wound their way through a blur of IKEA-esque place names: Bangsund, Klinga, Sjøåsen, Sprova, and my personal favourite, Spillum.

We entertained ourselves with telling crap jokes.

'Did you hear the one about the fight between two campers? It was in tents.'

'Fred gets pulled over by the cops for having defective rear lights. He goes round to the back of his car and breaks into a panic. "Come now, sir, it's not so bad, just a brake light offence." "I know that, but where's my caravan?"'

'What's a polar bear think when he sees a camper in a sleeping bag? Sausage roll.'

An hour and a half later we reached our campsite – an early arrival for once, and just in time as we had run out of witticisms and Ralph was on the verge of another Janet and John story.

Rolling into Namsos Camping, complete with its own crystal clear lake, we quickly dumped our gear in our *hytte* (we'd upgraded from the tents on offer) and eagerly embraced the on-site amenities. Swimming trunks on and straight into the snowmelt waters we plunged. Even Ralph, a seasoned wild swimmer used to the frigid waters of North Wales, found it a tad bracing. But after a day's hot riding, this icy shock was the tonic we needed, or so we tried to convince ourselves. Besides, several Norwegian teenagers nearby seemed completely unfazed, so we persevered, for king and country. Well, we couldn't let the side down, could we?

Namsos was not especially scenic but was strategically positioned on our journey. Apparently the number one sightseeing attraction is the *Bjørumsklompen*, a series of observation points overlooking the town, a place with a turbulent past, having been twice ravaged by fire and then destroyed in World War II. A series of information panels helpfully showed the old wooden town as it was before the Germans flattened it by bombing in April 1940.

Namsos to Yttervik

We awoke to news that felt oddly distant. Boris Johnson had been found to have lied to Parliament by the Privileges Committee and had resigned as an MP. 'It does feel a world away,' said Ralph.

'I have no clue what else has been happening back home,' I replied. Sometimes ignorance is bliss, though normally I'm an avid news watcher. So far it had been good to have a detox from grubby political matters.

'Are you going to get a sticker for your bike that says "Tory Scum"?' asked Ralph, knowing that I was not, to say the least, a fan.

'No. But it is one of my passwords,' I replied.

This was the second surprise of the day, and it wasn't even 8 a.m. In the pre-dawn hours, I'd stumbled to the bathroom, half asleep, and thanks to the sunlight streaming through the window, narrowly avoided stepping onto a mirror shattered into a thousand tiny shards. Ralph, roused by the sound of my nocturnal clean-up, emerged bleary-eyed. We jokingly concluded that a bear must have visited during the night, though we couldn't fathom why it hadn't at least had a nibble on us. Perhaps it was disgruntled that we'd finished all the beers. We never did find out why the mirror would randomly drop off the wall but we certainly hoped it wasn't a bad omen.

Amidst the shenanigans and the scenery, we realised that our bikes were finally due for some attention. Aside from cursory morning checks, we hadn't properly serviced them since the journey began. Today, for the first time in almost a week, we wouldn't have to hunt down a dealership. With our pre-flight checks of tyre pressures, oil and coolant levels complete, we bid farewell to our first campsite.

At this stage in our journey, we'd adopted a strict no-fuel-opportunity-wasted policy. We meticulously monitored our bikes' fuel consumption, remarkably similar at around 65 mpg, and kept a constant eye on our remaining range. As a precaution, I'd strapped a 2-litre reserve tank to my pannier. We were determined to avoid a repeat of Ralph's near-empty tank incident on day two and mine in the Pyrenees.

We rolled into a service station at Grong. Despite miles of empty roads, we were surprised to find a large group of Norwegian and Danish bikers. They were tucking into massive *pølse i lope* (sausages in bread), a staple of Norwegian filling stations. Suddenly two fellow Brits—the only ones on bikes we'd encounter on our entire Norwegian adventure—materialised as if by magic. Sausage in a bun clearly has a strange allure.

The sun shone warmly at 24° as we drove alongside the Namsen River that rushed over rocks through a broad valley, and the only sounds were the low rumble of our Honda and BMW engines and the soft rustling of leaves. We spotted a clearing under a canopy of trees where a lone campervan was parked and decided to stop. Its shiny paintwork told us it wasn't the one driven by Malcolm and Diana. A well-trodden path lined by pines and silver birch trees beckoned us down to the riverbank. The peaceful setting and lack of sleep were too much for us and we gave in to a nap. Ralph stretched out under a tree, while I found a lichen-covered rock beside a small pool of water. It was a moment of pure, blissful relaxation.

The day's ride continued with a series of tunnels, many extraordinarily long and dusty. One, the Korgfjell tunnel, stretched over eight kilometres. At Trofors, we crossed into Nord-Norge, or Nordland, one of the three counties of Northern Norway, alongside Troms and Finnmark. These counties comprise a third of Norway's landmass, yet only 10% of the population lives here, around half a million people. We were entering a true wilderness of harsh beauty, a tundra landscape with long, long distances between small settlements. It was simultaneously invigorating and intimidating. The E6 highway was marked by a theatrical arch adorned with colourful stakes resembling organ pipes, a symbolic entry into the land of ice. I'm sure it's even more dramatic when there's six feet of snow on the ground.

I sensed a shift, not just in the scenery, but within us. We were gaining confidence in our abilities, recognising our progress and the rhythm we'd established. Our daily routines were smooth, packing and unpacking were efficient and we were becoming a team—and it was enjoyable. Any doubts about traveling with Ralph had disappeared. We genuinely enjoyed each other's company. I felt like Ernie to his Eric. Each morning, I looked forward not only to the ride but also to our conversations and the unexpected moments that might arise.

Traveling by motorcycle in convoy is a unique experience. It's not like sitting side-by-side in a car. We both had to be actively participating, sharing the same yet distinctly individual experience of the day. There were long stretches of silence when we were out of radio range or had nothing to say, but it didn't matter. The stunning Norwegian landscape was always there to fill the void.

Late that afternoon we arrived at our second campsite, Yttervik, south of Mo i Rana, having covered 320 kilometres of exhilarating riding. Our tyres slithered over the hard-packed dirt track as we weaved through parked cars to our classically brown-painted *hytte*, nestling on the edge of Ranafjorden. Though forty-two miles from the open sea, the skies above our wooden terrace were teeming with gulls and seabirds in a cacophony of calls and cries. This was paradise for Ralph, a closet birdwatcher. With a flourish, he whipped out his smartphone and opened his favourite bird song identification app. Pointing it skyward, he confidently announced 'oystercatcher', followed by 'purple sandpiper'.

'What's that one over there?' I asked.

'It's a gull, Stephen,' he replied, as it landed near its companions by the water's edge ten metres away.

'Ah, but what type of gull is it?'

'Well, there are many different types of gulls, you know,' he added, puffing out his chest defensively. 'Herring gulls, lesser black-backed gulls, great black-backed gulls.'

I nodded, questioningly, as if I'd stumped him.

'But that one, my friend, is just a bog-standard, common-or-garden gull. The kind that steals your chips at the seaside,' he retorted.

The peace was absolute, broken only by the sounds of the birds... and the satisfying hiss of a couple more Arctic beers being opened. We sat on rickety chairs, nibbled some peanuts and bashed the beer cans together.

'*Skål!*', I said. '*Slàinte,*' came the reply.

It was well past nine, and the sun still hung high in the sky. We strolled around the campsite and headland, hoping to work off some of the calorific spagbol we'd served up for supper. Our *hytte*, charming in its simplicity, felt positively rustic compared to the striking glass-fronted cabins set precariously on stilts along the cliff edge. These modern marvels seemed to strain towards the outer reaches of the fjord, their gaze fixed on the distant, snow-capped Høgtuvbreen, 1,294 metres above sea level. Its peak protruded from the centre of a large and shrinking glacier area, which may not even exist come the end of this century.

From our terrace we watched small boats bobbing in the harbour as a father–daughter duo launched their sea kayak for a post-dinner paddle. The waters, fed by the glacier as well as the sea, would be barely above freezing.

We spread our maps out on the table and plotted the next day's route.

Our journey to the Lofoten Islands was taking us far from the most direct path. But first we needed to reach Bodø and tackle our longest ferry crossing yet. I reflected on the structured nature of this trip and how it differed from my spontaneous approach in Spain. This time we were more intentional. Norway's coastline was a labyrinth of possibilities, offering countless routes to our next destination, so careful planning was essential. Some routes were clearly too long and demanding, others too linear and potentially monotonous. The challenge was to create an itinerary that maximised enjoyment and interest while limiting our riding time to a comfortable six or seven hours per day.

The following day we would cross into the Arctic Circle, a significant milestone in our northward progress. Gothenburg, our overnight stop a week ago, felt like a distant memory. We were now further north than Iceland, further than most of Alaska. Incredibly, our goal of Nordkapp still lay 1,200 kilometres away, assuming we took no detours. At approximately 25,000 kilometres long Norway has the second longest coastline in the world; only Canada beats it.

13

Football and Fish
Bodø–Lofoten Islands

Yttervik to Bodø

Next morning I threw open the curtains to find a squabble of gulls again, this time ganged up on our motorbikes. Fortunately they hadn't left their trademark calling cards and flew off at the sight of me, naked, peering out the window. Charming. Our incredible streak of good weather seemed destined to end, as YR, the excellent Norwegian Meteorological Institute app, forecasted heavy rain later that day. Exactly what you don't want when you're about to cross the Arctic Circle.

Ralph and I decided to forgo a leisurely breakfast on our fjord-view terrace, opting instead for a quick coffee and skyr. We packed our bags and hit the road, leaving Yttervik with a tinge of sadness. It had been a wonderful overnight stay. I'll cherish for a long time the memory of our tranquil and balmy evening's birdwatching by the fjord.

The road wound north towards Mo i Rana, an industrial town with a defunct steelworks. As we climbed into the hills, moorland transitioned into arctic tundra, with rugged rocks lining the road. We were enjoying superb, dry riding on the undulating, bendy roads. The light traffic made it an absolute pleasure. After an hour and a quarter, we arrived at the Arctic Circle Centre, marked by a large stone topped with the metal globe at 66° 33' N. The year 1990 was inscribed on the globe because that was the last time its position was correct. The Arctic Circle's exact position depends on the earth's axial tilt, which fluctuates by more than two degrees over 41,000 years. The line moves forty-eight feet annually, so I've scheduled a return visit in AD 42990 when it's in the right place again.

The Arctic Circle's real significance is that it marks the southernmost latitude where, on the shortest day of the year, the sun never rises, and conversely never sets on the summer solstice. We were truly in the Land of the Midnight Sun.

The car park was full of campervans making their own pilgrimage to Nordkapp. Among them we spotted a group of Spanish-registered BMW bikes with "Tarifa to Nordkapp" stickers. As they prepared to leave, I chatted with Miguel, who had started his journey in Jerez, near Tarifa, and had stayed in the parador in Arcos. We swapped stories of our travels from the bottom of Europe. Chatting with fellow bikers is one of the great rituals of motorcycle travel and we exchanged good wishes for our respective journeys.

'*Deja el lado brillante para arriba.*' (Stay shiny side up). And we both meant it.

Ralph and I wandered around the large dome of the visitor's centre, trudging through snow, slush and mud to examine the various memorials.

'It's a wee bit like Glenshee, don't you think,' Ralph pondered.

The place had a slightly desolate air, reminiscent of the small Scottish ski resort out of season but with added reindeer. Some of them were stuffed, like the little fella who greeted us mournfully inside the main entrance. No doubt the Arctic Circle Centre gets busloads of tourists and there was certainly no shortage of souvenirs in the shop. I resisted the temptation to buy a reindeer hide and settled for a postcard with the Arctic stamp and a sticker to add to the growing collection plastered over the bike.

The promised rain hadn't yet appeared, so after a coffee pitstop we continued up the E6 in a happy mood. The road straightened out, the morning's bends disappearing as we hit the high tundra. We followed closely the course of a river, the waters crashing over rocks a few metres to our right. The trees were stunted in this harsh environment, and the sun had disappeared behind the greying clouds.

'Yup, it really does feel like the Cairngorms now. I've ridden all this way and I'm back home in Scotland again.'

I watched Ralph's head swivelling from side to side, taking in the views, no doubt dreaming of bagpipes, whisky and haggis.

In the distance the mountains wore their eternal winter vests. This is the land of permafrost, but it's thawing at an alarming rate due to climate change. *Taliks* (areas of unfrozen ground) and *thermokarst* (ground subsidence) are signs of the ground's emergence from the deep freezer, so my touring geologist told me. It was almost mid summer, and though we were leaving behind the exceptionally warm weather of Oslo, it was still around 15 degrees; ominously, almost 50% warmer than the average here for June.

Soon the Nordland railway, a 729-kilometre route between Trondheim and Bodø, the longest in the country, emerged out of the moorland alongside the road. The first stage opened in 1882 but it wasn't completed until 1962. Much of it was built by the Wehrmacht during WW2, or rather by their POWs, several thousand of whom died during its construction. It wasn't hard to imagine the harsh wintry conditions they had to endure. At the Arctic Circle Centre, we had paused in front of the memorial commemorating the forced labourers from the Soviet Union and Yugoslavia who had died here.

With ever greyer skies obscuring the sun and featureless moorland, the only splashes of colour were the yellow lines down the middle of the road. The road was occasionally crisscrossed by complex Meccano-like bridges that carried the railroad.] There was no traffic around, yet despite the temptation we stuck doggedly to the speed limits. The Honda's cruise control was a godsend, not least in relieving the cramp in my wrists from hours on the handlebars.

At Kistrand, a tiny settlement opposite the islet of Skjaeret, we pulled into a lay-by for a chocolate bar and a drink. Directly opposite was a large pole topped with a speed camera, its lenses staring menacingly onto the road. Nobody triggered it. Fines of a percentage of your annual income plus a minimum eighteen-day jail sentence for excessive speed are good reasons to avoid the flash. £94,000 is the current record fine in Norway.

We rolled into Bodø mid afternoon, having covered 253 kms through spectacularly big scenery. The town itself, however, is an architecturally challenged place, having been flattened by the Luftwaffe during the Second World War. Functional would be a generous description of its subsequent rebuilding.

'It's not pretty is it?' I shouted to Ralph over the noise of a roadmender's pneumatic drill.

Extensive roadworks in the town centre added to the challenge as Ralph and I circled repeatedly like teenagers cruising on a Saturday night, trying to find our Smarthotel. We both managed to miss the sign on the side of the building as we were concentrating on dodging the potholes.

Ralph had a narrow escape again. We'd pulled up to consult the map when his foot slipped on a loose bit of tarmac thrown up from a rut. I could hear him grunting and cursing as he struggled to keep his Beemer upright. It had been a day or two since we'd had a cock-up, so we were due one. He must have been eating his spinach, though, as he grappled it back to vertical and the drama was averted.

We parked the bikes in a concrete bunker next door, two for the price of one since we squeezed them into a single space, conspicuously shackled against unwanted attention and with a note for any nosy parking warden.

Lugging our luggage into the hotel rooms was exhausting, and by the time we'd dumped it, we were both ready for a beer or three. On cue, as we headed to the Piccadilly pub, the rain did its worst. I'd learned an expression in Norwegian: *Utepilsvær*. It's used any time it's not raining. It loosely translates as pub garden weather. It certainly wasn't *Utepilsvær* now. Within minutes we were soaked through, more so than at any point on the entire trip. This was apparently quite normal for a June day in Bodø.

The Piccadilly, established in 1985, had the charm of a much older establishment, with dark wood interiors, period lamps and sepia prints on the wall. It oozed character and stocked a wide range of beers, both Norwegian and international. This being cruise-ship territory, the Brooklyn lager was likely for the American visitors. The place was nearly empty—perhaps the rain was too heavy even for the locals—so we fell into a relaxed conversation with Morten, the bartender. His girlfriend was studying at St Andrew's University, so his English was flawless and he was knowledgeable about beer and alcohol duty rates, subjects with which Ralph and I were also somewhat familiar.

'So, Morten,' Ralph enquired, 'What's the most popular beer here?'

'Well,' he replied, 'Nordlands Pils is always a good choice, but if you're feeling adventurous, you could try a Saison Lagret På Hvitvinstønner. It's a bit of a tongue-twister, though.'

We decided to sample both, but at £9 for 400ml of standard strength beer, we weren't planning on making a night of it. After enjoying our selections, we bade Morten '*Snakkes*' (See ya) and ventured back out into the deluge.

With Bodø's restaurants either closed or too far to swim to in the downpour, we dripped into the nearby Scandic Hotel. From the top floor restaurant in Northern Norway's tallest building, we enjoyed a great view of the harbour and our moored-up ferry that would take us to the fabled Lofoten Islands. As we tucked into reindeer burgers, our thoughts turned to the weather. Had our luck run out or was this downpour merely the opening salvo in a meteorological battle we were destined to fight from now on?

'Ralph,' I said, reflectively, 'there are times when I wish I were back in southern Spain, you know.'

'The forecast's better for tomorrow,' he replied optimistically.

A pool of water was spreading from underneath our table towards our neighbours.

I smiled wanly, shaking my head. 'I admire your ability to look on the bright side, you know. But seriously, if this is a taste of the Arctic summer, I'll have to upgrade my rain gear for the rest of the trip.'

'It's a wee bit dreich oot there, I'll grant you that,' Ralph conceded.

'Think of the stories we'll have to tell back home... "Remember that time we braved the Arctic monsoon on our motorbikes?"'

'The things we go through for our audience, eh,' I joked, raising my glass of aquavit.

'To adventure!'

Ralph clinked his glass against mine. 'And may our waterproofs not spring a leak.'

I told you he is a glass half full kind of guy.

Bodø to the Lofoten Islands

If the fjords are the string section of Norway's orchestra, providing beautiful, silvery and seductive melodic themes for this magical country, then the Lofoten Islands are where the percussion players get to join in, their crashing cymbals and thunderous timpani representing the thrilling and awe-inspiring natural features of these islands.

It's a place I'd longed to visit. In summer, the crystal clear light of the north bathes this archipelago with a breathtaking sharpness, the mountains jagged and the dark red *rorbuer* standing in artistic relief against the rocks and grass. It's a landscape that stirs the soul and inspires poets.

Islands rise
as ancient shards
sharks' teeth that split the lip
of the greatest wave,
daggers to the belly
of the snarling wind
that's on the prowl
to snatch your children
snatch your mind
and carry it far away
into the freezer of northern skies.
                                        Lea Knowles, 2020

Our four-hour ferry crossing from Bodø to Moskenes in the Lofoten Islands was mercifully calm, a relief after the torrential rain in Bodø. We were glad to have our motorbikes securely lashed down on the car deck, as this long, open sea crossing can get rough. By now, we were practically experts at securing our bikes with straps and ratchet ties, otherwise we might have been scooping up shattered, scattered parts upon arrival.

As we approached Moskenes, faint glimmers of sun and blue sky began peeking through the clouds. I stood on the stern deck and watched the dark mountains rise dramatically from the sea, their flanks still flecked with winter snow. The rugged coastline was dotted with small houses, some ruddy-brown, others glaringly white. We sailed past the red and white lighthouse atop the bouldered harbour wall and into the harbour.

There was a scramble to disembark. We were only a short hop away from Å, a village at the southern tip of the Lofoten Islands, renowned for its be-stilted wooden buildings. Lofoten offered a wealth of sights, so we soon headed north, passing through the beautiful harbour town of Reine. The road was superb, new tarmac winding alongside the fjord and over a series of bridges to the islands of Andøya and Sakrisøya. It was like playing hopscotch over water, one skerry following another, linked seamlessly by elegant bridges.

Still relatively early in the season, the islands were quiet, and the traffic was light. The Lofoten Islands are home to only 24,500 people, yet over a million visitors flocked there in 2023 drawn by the spectacular scenery and its movie backdrops (including Disney's *Frozen*).

Our tyres rolled to a halt on the rubbly parking area outside Anita's Sjømat. Hunger had set in. The enormous array of vacantly staring cod heads hanging on drying racks outside the deli/seafood restaurant wasn't exactly an appetiser, but inside, the aromas of fish soup and other seafood delights were overwhelmingly enticing. Pick 'n mix baskets of dried fish lined the entrance and fishing nets and tackle dangled everywhere in the bright, airy wooden hut. Even the huge hanging lamps were made of dried codfish.

We settled for the fiskesuppe at 259kr (£19). It was delicious and beautifully presented, but at that price it needed to be. The tables were busy, so the high prices weren't deterring anyone. Then again, given the remoteness of Lofoten, you're essentially a captive market.

We continued the afternoon's ride, taking it easy to soak in the spectacular mountain views. I have spent plenty of time in the Alps, Picos and Pyrenees, but the Lofoten hills had a unique charm. They're not particularly high (the tallest, Higravtindan on Austvågøy, is a mere 1,161 metres above sea level), but their character, enhanced by the dramatic seascapes, is undeniable. It's reminiscent of the west coast of the Scottish Highlands around Knoydart and Kintail, but without the midges.

We pulled into a lay-by to take a breather and enjoy the views. A dark green SUV pulled up right beside us, and a stern female voice said, 'You cannot stop here. This is a passing place. You must move on. You will obstruct the traffic.'

As she moved off, unsmiling, we saw a sign on her tailgate "Lofoten Ranger" and the large letter M on a pole she had obscured. M stands for *Møteplass* or passing place. The fact we were the only traffic for miles didn't influence her determination to see the law upheld. Suitably chastised, we continued to Kabelvåg and our accommodation for the next couple of nights, a *rorbu*.

These small huts, often floating on wooden poles above the water, were where fishermen traditionally rested and stored equipment. The deep browny-red colour originated from a time when cod liver oil paint was plentiful and cheap. We approached ours through the hamlet of Nyvågar, with its tiny, white-planked chapel. A long wooden pier led to a row of two-storey *rorbuer*, linked together and facing a long inlet with small boats moored in front. Clouds scudded across the jagged peaks of the nearby mountains. The photos on its website could never hope to capture the beauty of the scene. It was a bargain, too, costing only 4.8 fish soups per person per night, including breakfast. Our newly adopted universal currency measure (*fiskesuppe*) was to disguise the true cost of living here.

We left the bikes in what must be one of the most scenic parking spots imaginable. Inside our *rorbu*, we had basic but comfortable accommodation: a small kitchen, two bedrooms and a bathroom. A fisherman, or two slightly damp bikers, could want for little else. We lacked only fishing rods. Staring at the sea wouldn't magically bring fish to our laps, we decided, so we headed to the nearby Restaurant Nyvågar. It was another characterful place, with an old boat dominating the entrance hall. A couple of Hansa beers barely touched the sides, and two enormous flounders in hollandaise sauce on a vegetable mash were devoured with gusto.

We'd been on the go nonstop for twelve days, so we planned to take some time off to do some proper sightseeing and exploring in the Lofoten Islands. Driving from end to end would only take two hours, but that would be like rushing straight through the National Gallery and out through the gift shop—what would be the point? The extra days here also served as a buffer, in case any problems had delayed us earlier in the trip. Since we'd settled into a well-rehearsed routine and hadn't had any mishaps for several days, Ralph and I hoped the rest of the trip would go smoothly.

The question was, which plan to follow? After dinner we wandered up a small hill overlooking the Lofoten Aquarium a few hundred metres away (no wonder the flounder was so fresh). Our goal, post-Lofoten, was Tromsø.

'You do realise it's 421 kilometres from here to Tromsø?' Ralph asked, a hint of concern in his voice.

'That's a long way,' I agreed, my mind racing through the possibilities and stating the bleeding obvious.

'And the weather's supposed to change,' he added, a touch of foreboding in his tone.

'Like Bodø?' I asked, remembering the downpour.

'Like Bodø,' Ralph confirmed with a sigh, his earlier meteorological optimism having evaporated as quickly as an ice cube in a cooker.

That settled it. We decided, with regret, to cut our stay in the *rorbu* short by a day to break up the long journey to the world's most northerly city. We'd stop in Senja, Norway's second largest island on the way. At reception, we informed them of our change of plans. 'No refund,' the receptionist stated matter-of-factly. Fair enough. Suddenly our accommodation here was costing us 7.08 fish soups. Thank Cod for credit cards.

The next day promised a bit of sunny weather before it all broke. We had plenty to explore: museums, art galleries, the flounder-less aquarium, a salmon fishery information centre and the world's most spectacular football stadium.

Lofoten Islands

Back in Bodø we had planned to visit the reputedly excellent Norsk Luftfartsmuseum. As a pilot, I'm a fan of anything to do with aviation, so it would have been an appealing landing spot for me. Unfortunately it didn't open until late morning and we had a ferry to catch. The cathedral (more reminiscent of something out of a 1960s council estate than Trondheim's medieval masterpiece) was also closed, as it was Monday. So we were delighted to discover that not only were Kabelvåg's cultural attractions open, but we were staying right next door to them.

But first, to breakfast a short distance away. The clinker boat in the hotel had been transformed into a buffet table with an enormous pane of glass laid over it. A true smørgasbord was spread across its length. Here is a small sample of the epicurean delights that awaited:

- brunost (brown cheese)
- grøt (porridge)
- laks og eggerøre (smoked salmon and eggs)
- nøkkelost (cumin and clove cheese)

There were also the usual cold meats and toothsome artisan breads. Lurking among the various cured salmon, mackerel, trout and cod were slices of *Hvalbiff* (whale steak). They were dark black and square, about the size of an After Eight mint. Rich, smoky, salty, slightly chewy, and like a gamey tuna, *Hval* (whale meat) is still commercially harvested in Norway. The only other countries to flout the

1986 international commercial whaling ban are Iceland and Japan. In the interest of research I tried an After Eight and can confirm that I prefer the chocolate ones.

The Lofotenmuseet museum was only a couple of whale spouts away, and it was a pleasure to wander around in civilian clothes rather than the cumbersome biking gear. The cod fishing industry has traditionally been of immense importance to Norway, and the Lofoten Islands in particular. From January to March, millions of cod from the Barents Sea migrate to the Norwegian coast to breed, with most coming to Lofoten, where they're caught. Drying the fish by cold air and wind was, and still is, the traditional way to preserve it. The wooden racks on which the stockfish (unsalted fish, especially cod) are hung are called *hjell*. It's important not to confuse stockfish with *klippfisk*, which is the same, but salted. Since the early 1700s Norwegians have exported both types to Europe. The Catholic Church's practice of abstaining from meat on Fridays was a boon for Lofoten fishermen, and their preserved cod found its way onto tables in Madrid and Lisbon, where it's now known as *bacalao*.

I bet you're glad you asked.

The museum housed an extensive array of fishing boats, equipment, engines, and a couple of reconstructed *rorbuer*, showcasing the harsh lifestyle of the area's fishermen. We had a guided tour, led by a local primary school teacher who happened to be waiting for her students to arrive. She explained that, as in many lucrative industries, there was a Mr Big involved—in this case, the local squire who owned the cabins, the fishing grounds and the *hjeller*. The fishermen had to sell their catch to him, at his prices, not theirs.

She paused, a twinkle in her eye. 'But the most interesting thing about cod, in my opinion, is their barbel. It's that little whisker-like thing hanging from their chin. It's a sensory organ, like a cat's whiskers, that helps them find food in the dark depths of the ocean. Imagine having a built-in food detector.'

I nodded in agreement, rubbing my nose. 'I've got one, it can smell a bacon sarnie from a hundred yards.'

The squire's manor house was on site. It must have been galling for the fishermen to peep through the windows at the elaborately laid table with its crystal glasses, chandeliers and a large grandfather clock. The aroma of fresh bread from his bakery and the scent of fermenting beer from his brewery must have been tantalisingly close yet out of reach. The squire, Caspar Lorch, went bankrupt in 1901, which left the fishermen to find new markets, boats, fishing grounds, and places to live. Some things never change.

The Lofoten Aquarium and Salmon Industry Information Centre was on our visit list, but for a break between fish courses we popped into the grass-covered Gallery Espolin. I confess I hadn't heard of Kaare Espolin Johnson before. Ralph and I shelled out half a fish soup to see the art of a colour-blind man with cataracts. Despite his visual challenges, Espolin produced a prodigious body of work, mainly in black and white, often using soot as a medium. Fans of Scandi-noir TV and films would feel at home in the gallery. Norway's dark Arctic seas, brooding hills and forests lend themselves, as in Lillehammer's art museum, to subjects and depictions with a malevolent, often grimly threatening tone. You can understand why they suffer from SAD, seasonal affective disorder, during the polar night.

'Which one was your favourite?' I asked Ralph, as we emerged blinking into the daylight.

'The Shrek-like figures of his *Juksafiskere (1956)*, paying homage to the raw character of the Lofoten fishermen. That one was good,' was his studied verdict.

Next up was the Lofoten Aquarium. I'm not usually a fan of seals and otters being kept in captivity, but this environment was more open and spacious than most. The keeper had a massive bucket of fish from which to feed them. It must have been terribly frustrating for the inmates to glimpse their free cousins a few wiggles away in the wild. The capacious interior aquarium housed a comprehensive selection of weird and wonderful sea creatures. Ralph and I debated which most resembled me.

'On balance, I'd say the Atlantic wolffish.'

'Because it's got a long, sleek body and a fearsome reputation?' I suggested.

'No, because it's got prominent teeth and is plug-ugly.'

'Ha!'

By now, we were nearly fished out, but one more call remained: the Salmon Industry Information Centre, which was located on a floating pontoon round the back of the hotel.

The Norwegians seem to have a knack for being in the right place at the right time. North Sea oil and gas, hydroelectric power, electric vehicles and now aquaculture, given the trend away from red meats. Riding our bikes around the coastline, it was impossible to ignore the enormous fish pens and specialised boats and equipment in the fjords. Fifty years ago the first pen began operation and now Norwegian salmon has gone from playing second fiddle to cod to being the world's most popular fish, sold in over 100 countries.

Ralph and I headed back to our *rorbu* to gear up for the short ride to the world's most spectacular football pitch.

'A freebie salmon would have been nice,' I grumbled, pulling on my helmet.

'Yeah,' Ralph said, 'it would have smoked nicely on the exhaust pipe.'

Down the road from Kabelvåg was Henningsvaer, a village hanging precariously on a series of interconnecting rocks. What made it even more remarkable was its football stadium. Forget Old Trafford, Bernabeu or the Nou Camp. This was international football at its most basic.

'You ever seen a ground like this before, Stephen?' Ralph asked, eyes wide with astonishment as we rolled up.

'Never,' I replied, 'This is something else.'

Viewers of Amazon's *Grand Tour* might recall the pitch as the gathering point for Clarkson, May and Hammond in their rally cars before their Scandinavian high jinks in *A Scandi Flick*.

This sea-moated pitch is surrounded by lots of *hjeller* racks, a unique way of preventing a miskicked ball from disappearing into the Norwegian Sea. We parked, walked down the player's tunnel (a scree path) and onto the hallowed turf (astro). Ralph, a Nottingham Forest fan and myself,a Stoke City supporter, fantasised about being transferred (free) to Henningsvaer FC. We found a ball lurking by a rubbish bin. I passed it to Ralph, who dribbled around an imaginary defender and unleashed a powerful half volley which sailed high over the net. The crowd of several thousand... drying codfish... remained eerily silent.

'It bobbled just before I kicked it,' Ralph exclaimed, disappointed at missing his chance of glory.

'Better luck next time,' I laughed, and went to retrieve the ball that was lodged between two unimpressed cod.

After the excitement of the world's most spectacular and unique football stadium, we headed into Henningsvaer itself. A tidy, arty fishing village full of charming shops and restaurants, it was a place to relax, enjoy a leisurely *fika* and simply watch the world go by. We borrowed a couple of chairs on the boardwalk by the harbour and did precisely that.

We bumped into a group of bikers, mainly from Finland. Most were on Moto Guzzis or Ducatis, a refreshing change from the ubiquitous BMW GS. We also met a young Swedish couple. She dwarfed him, a gentle giantess on a tiny, fully loaded 1970s Yamaha RD350. He, a mere hobbit in comparison, clung to her back like a tenacious squirrel. Their bike was packed with an outdoor shop's worth of camping gear. The risk of exceeding the speed limits probably wouldn't have bothered them, though how long the suspension would last was anyone's guess.

That evening we headed to Kabelvåg for dinner, having made a reservation earlier. It seemed a bit unnecessary now, as the enormous Brygga restaurant and bar was practically empty. Burgers and beers dispatched, it was time for the serious business of route planning. Our destination for the next day was the island of Senja, and we had multiple options for getting there. We'd already dismissed going directly to Tromsø, so we wanted to make the most of this extra day.

Just as we were deep in discussion, a waitress approached.

'Would you like anything else?' she asked politely. 'Only, we are about to close.'

It was only nine o'clock.

'*Nei takk. Bare regningen, takk.*'

If they were going to kick us out, at least I wanted to practice the few words of Norwegian I'd learned for 'Bill, please'.

I quickly folded the maps. The route planning would have to wait until breakfast.

14

The Far, Far North
Tromsø–Alta, Nordkapp

Lofoten Islands to Mefjord

It was with a touch of sadness that we packed up our kit at Nyvågar, leaving the idyllic *rorbu* that had been our home for the past couple of days. Lofoten had charmed us with its fishy allure. We had adjusted our plans to avoid an otherwise long ride to Tromsø. As much as I enjoy a long day in the saddle, Norway is best consumed in smaller bites, not wolfed down like an all-you-can-eat buffet. We'd even considered taking the ferry from Harstad to Tromsø directly, but since we were returning by sea we wanted to stay on dry land if possible. Anyway, it was academic: the ferry was for foot passengers only.

It was good to be back on the bikes with a clear destination in mind. Ralph and I easily fell back into our usual routine: he'd lead, I'd overtake while filming dramatically with the GoPro, then he'd zoom past as I tried to make him look like a racer. It was good fun, especially with the 50 mph speed limit requiring creative camera angles. Our ride was punctuated by our usual stream of bad gags, somehow managing to dredge up new material after fourteen days together. I'm sure he'd hidden a joke book somewhere or was reading Viz under the bedcovers.

We were heading to the northernmost tip of Lofoten, the harbour town of Andenes, on the island of Andøya. Our island hopping had started at Å, so we hadn't made much progress down the alphabet. The roads were superb: twisty but not too challenging, dry and free of loose stones or potholes. Around us were mountains and inlets, strewn with small boats at anchor, awaiting their weekend release.

We continued north, island hopping from Austvågøya over two spectacular bridges that spanned Risøysundet. They're not solely utilitarian concrete slabs, but soaring, slender arches that disguise their size and reach with elegant grace. The many ships that pass beneath, including large vessels like Hurtigruten ferries and cruise ships, require ample clearance. Riding over these bridges with windsocks billowing is an intimidating yet exhilarating experience. It's a long way down and you get blown about a lot. Imagine riding a windy rollercoaster on a motorbike and you get the idea.

The mountains flattened as we left the heart of Lofoten behind. The breeze picked up, and soon we were both leaning into the wind, our bikes listing precariously to starboard to maintain a straight course. We pulled into the hamlet of Dverberg for a rest and a drink. The boats taking shelter in the small anchorage bobbed around like children in a schoolyard, full of energy but going nowhere. Across the sound, the steep mountains of Grytøya, a large, sparsely populated island (42 sq. m.; population 433), rose sharply from the sea, their grey peaks glowering like a pod of distant killer whales.

To stretch our legs before continuing to Andenes, we wandered around the hamlet: harbour, Co-Op, hairdressers, a few houses and—astonishingly—a motorcycle museum. The Andøy MC Museum (prop. Bjørn) was housed in a red wooden shack, with an ancient and rusty spoked rear wheel dangling outside like a pub sign. Our hopes soared that we might learn more about Tempo, the legendary (according to the poster on the wall) Norwegian motorbike manufactured between 1931 and 1994. The Scandinavians have a penchant for quirky little museums, many dedicated to motorbikes, as we discovered on the trip. However, their opening hours remained a mystery, as few had fixed schedules.

I rang the phone number posted on the door, hoping to convince the owner to open the doors exclusively for us. It went straight to voicemail. I left a message.

'Hei! Bjørn? We're two English bikers. We've come thousands of kilometres and would love to see your vintage Norwegian motorcycles. Any chance you could open up for us?'

We hung around for a few minutes to see if he rang back. But alas, no answer. Maybe he was busy getting his hair done or perhaps he had been blown off his bike into the sea.

Disappointed, Ralph and I swung a leg over the saddles again and set sail for Andenes. The incessant winds whipped across the water, picking up sand and seaweed from the beach and battering us mercilessly. It was a relief to finally arrive in the relative shelter of the town and to scrape off the strands of wind-blown kelp that now clung to my handlebars and panniers.

After the sublime scenery of the rest of Lofoten, Andenes was a bit of a let down. Lacking any discernible aesthetic appeal it was a relentless expanse of gloomy drabness. The guidebook aptly described it as having a "lonely, end-of-road feel". It wouldn't have surprised me to find out it was twinned with the equally down-at-heel North Wales port of Holyhead. No offence to Andenes.

On the plus side, Andenes is Norway's principal centre for whale watching. We had a ferry to catch, but with a few hours to kill, I set off in search of the Tourist Information Office. The signs led me to a 1970s office block. I opened the door and was greeted by several people in white coats milling around behind a reception desk.

'Is this the Tourist Office?' I enquired, peering through the doorway.

One of the white-coated figures glanced up, a hint of amusement in her eyes. 'No, sir, this is a dental surgery.'

'Oh,' I replied, feeling a bit foolish.

'Do you happen to know where the Tourist Office is?'

'It was here,' another figure chimed in, 'but it's closed down now.'

'Ah, I see,' I mumbled, thwarted for the second time in an hour.

'Since you're here, though,' the first figure offered with a smile, 'would you like any dental treatment?'

It's a quiet place, Andenes.

I politely declined their kind offer and set off to find somewhere for lunch. A group of touring motorbikes parked outside a place off the main drag caught my eye and we entered a surprisingly stylish and welcoming restaurant called Arresten. Despite the odd name, the food was anything but prison grub, and we eagerly tucked into freshly caught cod and chips.

By the time we finished our meal, the ferry queue had grown considerably. Neither of us wanted to leave our bikes exposed to the wind, so we hovered nearby, ready to catch them if a gust knocked them over. An imposing figure ambled towards us. Klaus, a 6' 4" Dutchman, also on a motorbike, was as loud and larger-than-life as they come. He had the look of a man who was familiar with the boxing ring. He wasn't concerned about his battered bike being blown over, so we became a captive audience for his rants.

'Fucking weather,' he boomed, his voice echoing across the harbour.

'Fucking place. Fucking mountains. Fucking sea.'

'You're not enjoying the trip, Klaus?' Ralph asked rhetorically, a hint of amusement in his voice.

Klaus, seemingly oblivious to the sarcasm, grumbled, 'Wouldn't bother going to Nordkapp. Same shit as fucking here.'

Klaus's worldview was, to say the least, a tad different from ours. His gloom was almost comical. Ralph made the mistake of explaining why we were hovering by our bikes instead of sheltering like most sensible people were. Klaus promptly grabbed hold of Ralph's BMW and began shaking it violently, as if to demonstrate its stability. My mate's eyes widened in horror as he lunged to rescue his beloved machine from the Dutchman's clutches before any damage could be done.

'Klaus, haud aff the bike! Drop it.' Ralph exclaimed, physically wrestling his bike away from Klaus, who ambled away, clearly confused that a Scotsman didn't trust him with his pride and joy.

It did occur to me that 'drop it' may not have been the most helpful phrase in the circumstances.

Our ferry crossing to Gryllefjord on the lovely island of Senja was a rough one. So rough, in fact, that I found myself mesmerised by a picture hanging on the wall, swinging through a ninety-degree arc. At least it provided a reference point for my woozy stomach and kept our fish suppers intact.

The turbulent journey even inspired a bit of verse:

The waves did churn, the boat did heave,

My lunch wanted out, I begged reprieve.

With pallid face, I sought land's embrace,

A crueller crossing? Hard to conceive.

Ralph thought I should stick to the day job. I reminded him that I was basically doing nothing these days.

'That's what I mean.'

The skies remained heavy with low, grey clouds as we landed in the picturesque village of Gryllefjord. Klaus had already disembarked, pulling over into a lay-by. Ralph and I briefly debated whether to stop and check on him, but a quick glance at each other was enough. We twisted the throttles and sped off, leaving Klaus to harass someone else that evening.

Our target for the night was Mefjord Brygge and the hour was already getting late. We were keen to arrive before our hotel's kitchen closed; on the plus side, the threatened rain hadn't materialised, so far. We wound our way along the rugged coastline, over bridges and precarious hillside roads that plunged deep into the fjords. At Straumsbotn the road veered inland and the Fyklesvei 862 led back into the mountain range that stood between us and Mefjord.

High in the hills, past the still-frozen Krokelvvatnet lake, a large, unmissable yellow sign appeared: 'Stopp. Vent på ledebil.'

I could understand *Stopp* but the rest was beyond me. I feared that continued progress was, like our evening meal, likely off the menu, especially as a barrier blocked the entire road. The only other souls around were four attractive girls in a Finnish-registered Volvo. Things were looking up, especially after our encounter with Klaus. They spoke English but not Norwegian and had no clue what was going on even though they'd already been waiting for twenty minutes. We debated whether to send an advance party to investigate.

'Fear not, my fine Finnish friends!' I rose to the challenge with the bravado of a knight in slightly tarnished armour. 'I shall venture forth and solve this mystery!'

Ralph, clearly captivated by the blonde bombshells, practically shoved me towards the barrier, eager to get back to whatever tall tale he was weaving for his new audience. I suspected it involved a talking moose and a set of bagpipes.

I carefully manoeuvred my bike past the barrier and ventured onward. A kilometre later, a series of explosions answered my question. A guide car, parked haphazardly across the road, blocked the entrance to the newly bored Skaland tunnel. Its driver, a peeved-looking teenager with a pockmarked face like the moon's surface, clearly wasn't thrilled by my intrusion. He waved me back down the road with a two-fingered gesture, which I chose to interpret as a two-minute wait.

'Looks like we're not going anywhere for a bit,' I reported back to the group, thinking that my chances of dinner were disappearing without trace.

'At least we're not alone in this,' one of the Finnish girls said with a shrug. 'Maybe we use the time to practise more our English?'

Ralph and I exchanged glances. The evening was starting to look up. Maybe this roadblock wasn't such a bad thing.

'So, as I was saying, this is how you pronounce *gneiss* ...'

Ralph was mid-flow when, twenty minutes later, Mr Lunarsurface reappeared, less peeved and more polite.

'Okay you guys, be quick. We blast again in ten minutes. Go, go, go.'

We jumped on board, flashed a jaunty goodbye to our new Finnish friends and scooted off pronto. Ralph and I raced through the barrier and soon we were engulfed in the fumes of cordite rather than the fresh mountain air. We rode through the tunnel and had the chance to marvel at the engineering that was burrowing through the solid rock. As we rolled up to our hotel in Mefjord Brygge, weary from our lengthiest day on the road yet (as measured by hours in the saddle), we were relieved we hadn't attempted to reach Tromsø in one go. The prospect of a warm meal, assuming the cook hadn't already packed up, and a comfortable bed was more appealing than pushing ourselves further. We parked our bikes on a wooden landing stage next to the water, breathing a collective sigh of relief at Klaus's absence.

'You know,' I confessed, 'I'm starting to think we wouldn't have been the best travel companions for him anyway.'

Ralph chuckled. 'We're clearly not adventurous enough. He probably thinks we're a couple of boring old farts.'

'Well,' I countered, 'at least we're boring old farts who haven't accidentally pushed their bikes into a fjord.'

'What if he comes back later?' Ralph muttered, anxiously.

We looked at each other quizzically. 'Better shift them in that case'.

Mefjord to Tromsø

'Remember the McWhirter brothers on *Record Breakers*?' I asked Ralph as we packed our gear in the pouring rain the following morning

'Tromsø, as the world's most northerly city, must have been featured at some point.'

'Absolutely.' Ralph exclaimed, a nostalgic gleam in his eye.

'Compulsory viewing in the early seventies, along with *Jackanory*, *Blue Peter* and *Top of the Pops*.'

We prepared to leave our cosy overnight stay at Mefjord Brygge and journey towards the record-breaking city. Ever since our camping gear was pilfered in Bremen, we'd adopted the habit of lugging everything into our rooms, a laborious but necessary precaution.

'I feel like a pack mule,' Ralph grumbled, hauling his panniers through the door and down some slippery wooden steps.

'Think of it as strength training. You need the exercise, anyway,' I quipped back, earning a playful kick in the shins.

As veterans of the crackly black-and-white TV era, Ralph and I were looking forward to reaching this last bastion of civilisation before our final push to Nordkapp. Besides, Tromsø was reported to have a great brewery, and we were both eager for a taste of their brews.

The hotel's car park was packed with Polish-registered vans belonging to builders and plumbers, clearly working on a major local project. Norway seemed to be a popular destination for European tradespeople post-Brexit. I carefully flat-footed my bike past Krzysztof Hydraulik's (Krakow) well-travelled Ford Transit, its back door plastered with stickers from its time in London.

'That reminds me, I need to get a dripping tap fixed at home,' I remarked to Ralph, as we set off into a sodden grey day once again. The clouds were rolling down the hills where, even in mid June, snow still clung to the gullies and cols.

We were looking forward to a shorter day on the bikes, not least because the temperature had plummeted and we risked a cold soaking. I dug out my electric jacket and plugged it into the Honda, cranking up the heated grips and the jacket for a toasty, if slightly damp and steamy ride. Our route took us along the coast, past rows of red-brown holiday cottages and dainty landing stages jutting into the grey Norwegian Sea. The verge, a few metres to our left, offered no barrier between us and a dramatic plunge into the icy depths. Rusty diggers, piles of wood, the occasional abandoned boat, and numerous battered corrugated iron barns lined the route.

Meandering along, enjoying the scenery through a rain-spotted visor, I was suddenly hefted skywards from my saddle by an enormous, unmarked speed hump, nearly invisible against the black tarmac. Somehow I kept hold of the handlebars and steered straight as I landed back abruptly on the pillion seat. Miraculously the bike remained upright and on course. The otherwise lovely road was marred by these tarmac terrors for miles. It seemed the boy racers, whose daredevilish handiwork we'd seen in the form of doughnutty tyre marks earlier in the trip, had been here too, prompting such drastic measures by the authorities.

The rain intensified the briny tang of the sea, each gust carrying a wave of salty air and decaying seaweed. It was a pungent, antiseptic smell, mingling with the sweet scent of damp moss and wildflowers that clung to the cliffsides. The cool spray of the ocean occasionally found its way through my visor, a chilly contrast to the warmth generated by the electric jacket. Riding, I reflected again, was a gallimaufry of sensations: the revolutions of the engine vibrating through my body, the noise of the slipstream and the rumble of the exhaust setting my eardrums a-tremble, the wind whipping at my face, the smell of the sea filling my lungs, the proprioception of fine movements and changes in balance, the clamminess of the raindrops trickling down my neck and the constantly changing vistas flashing before my eyes. I'm sure I would have tasted something too, were it not for the lingering flavour of the breakfast kippers.

It's impossible to travel from Mefjord to Tromsø without crossing the sea somewhere. We reached the *fergekai* (ferry terminal) at Botnhamn in time for the early sailing. With only four crossings a day, we'd sacrificed a coffee stop to make it on time. Still, we were on board and could finally relax a little.

Ralph muttered to himself, immersed in his Kindle.

'Listen to this, Stephen,' he said, his voice slightly muffled by the din on board.

'"Oh, wad some power the giftie gie us to see oursel's as ithers see us."'

'Know who wrote that?'

'Your hero, I guess, Rabbie Burns.'

'Exactly. D'you think Klaus sees himself as a grumpy bugger?' he asked, recalling the Dutchman's invective.

I grinned. 'Dunno. But you must have done something to wind him up. He really wasn't in a great mood.'

I paused, scanned the room over Ralph's shoulder, and whispered, 'Quick, duck.'

Ralph hoicked his jacket up over his head, looking anxiously at me.

'Is it him?'

I giggled.

'Awa', ya bampot.'

Once off the ferry an hour later in Brensholmen, we'd only gone a few kilometres when the traffic came to a standstill. We carefully filtered past the queue—one of the great perks of riding a motorbike. As we approached the lead vehicle, a bearded driver rolled down his window.

'The way is shut,' he announced matter-of-factly. We were getting used to the direct manner of the Nordics.

The large red and yellow barriers blocking the road and the sign reading "*Vegen Stengt*" confirmed his statement. We weren't going to risk sneaking past this time.

A woman emerged from a nearby house, her voice carrying over the idling engines.

'Every fifteen minutes, they open the road. You will see.'

As we waited, the rain, which usually sailed harmlessly over my windscreen and helmet, found a sneaky way under my electric jacket. I was starting to steam. Either I was going to be poached or fried alive. I hurriedly switched off the jacket as a road worker appeared to open the barrier, right on time. Norwegian efficiency at its finest.

The road wound on and the rain intensified, drumming against my helmet and blurring the scenery. I was deeply grateful for the brand new Michelin Road 6 GT tyres I'd fitted before leaving the UK. The surface was slick with rainwater, so straining against all my instincts, I relaxed my hold on the handlebars. I needed to feel every twitch and a death-grip wouldn't help.

Moose, elk and reindeer ambled alongside the road in places, munching on grass and shrubs, completely oblivious to traffic, like overgrown, dim-witted pheasants with fur and antlers. Ralph and I treated Donner and Blitzen with the utmost caution.

We'd barely crossed the Sandnessund bridge onto the island of Tromsøya, passing the airport's perimeter fence, when we were plunged underground into a tunnel that burrowed beneath the entire city of Tromsø. The Langnestunnelen was an engineering spectacle, connected to other tunnels by a series of underground roundabouts bathed in eerie blue neon lights. It felt more like a scene from a sci-fi movie than a bustling city thoroughfare. Ralph and I, our satnav rendered useless underground, became hopelessly disoriented by the confusing signs. We looped around the subterranean roundabouts like bewildered moles before finally emerging near the city centre then onto the Tromsø Bridge, which soared majestically over the strait and back onto the mainland.

'Well, that was an adventure,' I remarked to Ralph.

'Didn't know we signed up for the caving tour of Tromsø,' he replied.

Directly in front of us at the end of the bridge stood the striking Arctic Cathedral (*Ishavskatedralen*), its striking silhouette resembling a giant white Toblerone adorned with stained glass. It's one of the most distinctive buildings north of the Arctic Circle—or anywhere, for that matter.

'Did you know,' I said to Ralph, 'that it is in fact a parish church, not a cathedral.'

'That's a cool place to pray, if ever I saw one,' he replied.

Our home for the night was the Tromsø Lodge, conveniently located around the corner from what we believed was The World's Most Northerly (TWMN) top-flight football club, Tromsø FC. Our imaginary *Record Breakers* I-Spy book declared this a 10-point find (cathedral/parish church 15, underground roundabouts 25), so we settled into our cosy cabin and set off for the TUIL Arena.

'Look at that pitch,' Ralph exclaimed. 'A little patchy, but that's the price you pay for being the northernmost top-flight team.' It was being dug up at the end of the season.

We admired the quaint stadium, only later realising our blunder. This was Tromsdalen FC's ground, which was the equivalent of visiting Accrington Stanley instead of Arsenal. Oops.

With our football fantasy dashed, we turned our attention to a more reliable source of enjoyment: beer. Mack's, the TWMN Brewery, was must-see. Our I-Spy book awarded 5 points per beer, so a few rounds seemed like a good way to boost our score.

We hopped on a bus, crossed the bridge back into the city, ticking off the TWMN Library and University Botanical Garden along the way. Tromsø is a pedestrian-friendly city, and the brewery was conveniently located in the centre, where good breweries should be. We followed our noses to the brewery tap, Ølhallen, a popular tourist attraction and the oldest pub in the city.

'Wonder how these will match up against those brews we dreamed up in the lab back in Wolverhampton, eh Ralph?' I asked.

As beer and pub aficionados, Ralph and I took a professional interest in the offerings. The beers, seventy-two on draught, were creative and varied; the décor and ambiance were traditional and well suited to the target market; the prices were... well, breathtaking.

Each beer had three prices chalked up: 0.17 litres for the impecunious sipper; 0.33 litres for the thirsty; and 0.5 litres for the reckless. A middle-of-the-road Mack Nordlys (4.5% abv) was almost £9, and more exotic options like 'Procrastinator' (8% abv) were £13. Hence the name, presumably. Our points gathering exercise suddenly seemed rather costly, so we opted for a more measured pace, savouring rather than guzzling.

'Remember those *trade visits* we used to do?' I asked Ralph, a smile tugging at the corner of my lips.

'Back when our biggest concern was whether the cask ale had been properly conditioned?'

Ralph chuckled at the memory of nights spent in smoky boozers in Dudley.

'People call them pub crawls, Stephen.'

'Pub crawl or not this is a pilgrimage, the tap-room at the brewery on top of the world.'

A momentary silence settled between us, the memories of those long ago days swirling in the hoppy haze of the bar.

'You know,' Ralph said, his voice taking on a reflective tone, 'I never imagined I'd find myself drinking ales with you in the Arctic. Life takes you in unexpected directions.'

'It certainly does,' I agreed, gazing absentmindedly at the comely barmaid, who had twin blonde plaits that reached to her embonpoint.

We decided to call Derek, our old pub business friend and colleague, to tell him where he'd been missing a trick all those years ago. I dialled Derek's number, a mischievous grin spreading across my face.

'At home, Derek, old pal?' I chirped as he answered our video call. I'd recognise that chintz anywhere. Ralph took the phone from me.

'Stephen and Ralph here, live from the world's northernmost brewery in Tromsø, Norway. You wouldn't believe the prices they're charging for a pint up here. Absolute goldmine, mate.'

'Has Ralph opened his wallet yet, Noz?'

Derek's taciturn sense of humour was as sharp as ever. His nickname for me was because I resembled Norris, a bald, stumpy *Coronation Street* character. He also couldn't resist a passing jibe at Ralph's alleged parsimony.

'Enjoy t' brewery, lads,' Derek's Oldham accent hadn't been dimmed by years of living in the Midlands. 'I hope someone else is organising the piss-up in the brewery for you, because you two couldn't.'

Ralph laughed out loud and handed the phone back.

'Cheers, Derek. We'll bring you back a bottle of one their special brews, if there's anything left in his wallet after this round,' I suggested.

Tomorrow we'd have a chance to explore Tromsø before continuing northwards to Alta and our last overnight stay before the final push to Nordkapp.

We raised our glasses in a hearty 'Skål' to another successful day's riding, then headed out into the chill late air of a northern Norwegian summer to walk back to camp.

Tromsø to Alta

In Tromsø it's impossible to forget you're so far north. Situated 400 kms above the Arctic Circle, the city exudes a polar atmosphere even in midsummer. Buildings and streets are designed for harsh winters and outdoor shops sell thick Nordic jumpers and woolly socks year-round. From mid May to mid July, the sun never sets, turning nightlife into daylife. Tromsø boasts more bars per capita than any other Norwegian city and with a peppy university scene, the streets were teeming with young people enjoying the late summer evening. It's a city brimming with culture, music and museums.

Naturally Ralph and I were drawn to the Polar Museum. Tromsø has been the base for countless Arctic and North Pole expeditions. There can be no better place to learn about Roald Amundsen, the first to reach the Pole. The long and controversial history of whale and seal hunting by generations of Norwegians was on gory display. Whatever one feels about whale hunting it's been historically important to Norwegians, though I found the diorama about the cudgelling of baby seals not a pretty sight.

On our way back to the lodge we popped into a shop for some snacks. Where a typical UK corner shop might offer Marmite crisps as the most exotic flavour, Vikingsnacks came in elk, whale and reindeer varieties. I couldn't see cuddly baby seal ones.

We left Tromsø, vowing to return and explore this captivating city at a more leisurely pace. From November to January, when the sun never rises, it might be a different experience altogether. We'd need those winter woollies then.

To avoid a series of lengthy detours around the fjords that slice into the coastline, we planned to hop on a couple of ferries. First, the Breivikeidet–Svensby crossing, then, after navigating the Lyngen Alps, we'd aim for the longer Lynseidet–Olderdalen ferry. Ferries were such a staple of our journey that I'd researched them thoroughly while planning the itinerary months ago. I learned that, with a few exceptions like the Bodø to Lofoten route, booking in advance wasn't necessary or even possible. Generally, the timetables were frequent and the ferries ran like clockwork. The longer ones, like our two planned today, would be chargeable, but at 43 NOK (£3.25) for Svensby and 156 NOK (£12) for Olderdalen, they weren't exactly bank-breakers.

As we waited in the first ferry queue of the day, shivering in the early morning chill, a delightful Swiss couple took pity on us and invited us into their cosy campervan for coffee, biscuits and a chat. Our stories of the trip grew increasingly ornate as we thawed out. There were times when we envied the shelter of a car or a van and this was one of them.

'You don't fancy giving us a lift, do you?' Ralph joked. 'It's lovely and warm in here.'

'But what will you do with your bikes?' asked Christoph.

'Won't they fit on the back?' I asked.

Christoph looked at us quizzically, not sure if we were serious.

The ferry's horn blared, snapping us back to reality.

'Right, we're on, let's tog up,' I said to Ralph, as he retrieved his gloves from under the table.

We thanked Christoph and Stephanie for their kindness, jammed our helmets loosely onto our heads and headed back into the cold and the queue of vehicles boarding the ferry, ready for the next leg of our journey.

'Lovely people,' he commented, 'I hope we didn't scoff all their biscuits.'

Once across the Svensby crossing, we joined a steady convoy of traffic along the fourteen miles of Ullsfjord, which nearly bisects the Lyngen Alps at Kjosen. These majestic peaks, rising almost 2,000 metres above sea level, stand out dramatically even in this land of awe-inspiring scenery. The Lyngen Alps boast over 140 glaciers, and despite being a Protected Area, they remain one of Norway's most popular climbing and hiking destinations.

The campervans, cars and us (the lone motorcyclists) were bound for the same ferry at Lynseidet. With no rush, we could enjoy a leisurely pace and soak in the surroundings. It was a rare moment of tranquility; even Ralph and I refrained from our usual banter. Instead, a deep, staccato melody began to boom from his intercom: 'Da De De Da Da/Da De De Da Da....'

'*The Ride of the Valkyries,*' I realised, with a smile. 'Never took you for a Wagner fan.'

'These views stir warm trouser feelings, *mein Freund,*' he sang back operatically.

'You're sure it's not last night's curry that prompted your Ring Cycle?' I countered.

I guess even hardened bikers have a soft spot for a bit of opera when the mood strikes. Who knew?

Rolling on to the ferry, we were directed to the "hat rack", the narrow flying side decks overlooking the car deck. It was a steep climb up and down but it kept us out of the way of larger vehicles. The ramp was always a nerve-wracking experience, as the surfaces could be notoriously slippery. With over a week having passed since our last mishap, neither of us wanted to tempt fate. As the ferry crossed the fjord, the temperature dropped to a chilly six degrees, and the surrounding mountains seemed even more blanketed in snow than before. Was this a harbinger of the journey to come? A shiver ran down my spine, not only from the cold air.

Several hours later we arrived in the salmon fishing town of Alta—closer to the North Pole than to Oslo—the high mountains fading in our rearview mirrors. We were now in the land of the Sami, the indigenous people of northern Scandinavia and Russia. Some 45,000 Sami live in the Arctic tundra of Norway and they represent one of the world's oldest cultures, traditionally making their living from reindeer herding.

To say Alta is a salmon fishing town is a bit like saying Wembley is a football pitch. The Alta River is renowned as one of the world's best for salmon fishing. While a limited number of local licenses are issued annually, the real money comes from a handful of out-of-town permits, each costing hundreds of thousands of kroner. Ralph and I checked our pockets, finding a few crumpled banknotes, a used earplug and a lint-covered mint. So, salmon was off the menu tonight, sadly. It seemed Donner or Blitzen would be making the ultimate sacrifice instead.

Our charming log cabin at Alta River Camping was a short hop from the Sami Siida Restaurant, a modern interpretation of a traditional Sami village. The Lavvo pub, essentially a giant tepee, was closed for the evening. We peeked inside. It was lined with with horns and fur skins that covered every surface while a smoky fireplace dominated the centre. Without crowds quaffing beers the place felt a bit melancholy, much like the young reindeer who had approached us outside, his antlers still covered in velvet.

We entered the restaurant, famished after a long day fuelled only by Red Bull. The menu was predictably focused on reindeer: steak, stew, schnitzel, smoked and burger varieties. Sunná, our charming waitress, dressed in traditional Sami Gákti costume, recommended the schnitzel. Served with lingonberry sauce (familiar to any IKEA meatball enthusiast) and mashed potatoes, it was a delicious, if slightly guilt-inducing meal. Ralph and I slinked past the now forlorn reindeer on our way back to camp. We'd go vegan tomorrow, honest.

Tomorrow, if all went well, would see us reach Nordkapp, 150 miles away. We were already over 4,000 kilometres and sixteen days from home in the Midlands, which now felt a long time ago.

'How are feeling, Stephen? I mean, this has been long in the planning. This is the evening before the push, eh.'

'It's a bit like I felt as a kid on Christmas Eve,' I replied, rising to the reindeer theme. 'You know, full of anticipation, hoping that Santa's going to arrive.'

As I lay in bed that night, the sun still piercing the thin curtains, I pondered this quest. I'm a list-ticker by nature. It's what spurred me on to climb Scotland's 283 Munros, as well as every 3000-foot mountain in England, Wales and Ireland. On the bike, Scotland's North Coast 500, Ireland's Wild Atlantic Way, the length of Italy to Sicily and back – they've been goals too. I think I'll always want to achieve something, though Spain taught me the joy of just bumbling around, not aimlessly, but letting chance and serendipity take over. But how would I feel once I reached Nordkapp? Would it be an anti-climax?

Then I remembered Robert Louis Stephenson's words: "I travel not to go anywhere, but to go. I travel for travel's sake. The great affair is to move."

Alta to Nordkapp

At 0727 hours Ralph issued the command to begin our final stage from Alta to Nordkapp.

'The sherpas are briefed, the oxygen tanks are in place, the heavy lifting's been done. I think we can head off. Start engines.'

It wasn't quite up there with *I am just going outside and may be some time*, but it was an attempt at a motivational speech. Ralph was clearly feeling inspired this morning, fired up perhaps by the first decent kip we'd had in days.

Looking suitably rugged with over two weeks' worth of beard sprouting from under his white helmet, he sported a dazzling yellow, oil and mud-encrusted jacket. He sat poised and ready for action on his burbling Beemer parked directly outside the veranda of our wooden camping hut. We were eager at the prospect of a great riding day. The gravel skittered as Ralph moved off. He'd gone a couple of metres when he stopped abruptly, the front wheel slipping on the loose surface.

'Bugger. Left my gloves on the table.'

For once, there wasn't much of a navigation decision to make. Our options were limited to one road, the E6, all the way to Olderfjord, where we'd hang a left directly northwards. From that point onwards it would be an out-and-back road along the Porsangerfjord, which empties out into the Barents Sea. We had 236 kms of riding ahead of us before doubling back and heading south for the first time on the trip, to our overnight stop in Lakselv.

The weather gods were smiling upon us, and the day started brightly. This northern edge of Europe is notorious for sea mists that can roll in at any time of year, so we were delighted by the promise of sunshine, even if the temperatures were cool.

On Saturday, June 17th 2023, a few days shy of the summer solstice, we ambled through moody moorland scenery, through valleys and past mountain ranges that dwarfed the Cairngorms. Yet there was little traffic, apart from fellow pilgrims on motorbikes, some of whom we recognised from earlier encounters. A few were in cars or campervans and even more impressively, some were on bicycles. North of Olderfjord everyone seemed to be on a mission, the Norwegian contingent converging with those who'd taken the Sweden–Finland route, in a race to the (almost) Pole.

The riding was relaxed, ever mindful of the speed cameras. We passed through small towns and hamlets, pondering the question that always arose in these remote corners: What on earth do they do here in the depths of winter, when darkness reigns supreme? Telegraph poles with endless wires and fast-flowing streams accompanied us on our journey; streaks of snow bordered the road and we rode through cuttings and over simple steel bridges that crossed boulder-strewn rivers, their brown, peaty waters flecked with foam.

We pulled into a petrol station for the first of several fill-ups that day. This was no place to run out of fuel, even with our emergency spare can tucked away. The garage forecourt? Forget car dealerships; this was snowmobile territory. Row upon row of them awaited eager buyers and the inevitable return of winter.

Trees were scarce here, and those that did grow remained small, gnarled and bent against the wind. We plunged into a long, newish and noisy tunnel, emerging on the other side to find a fjord stretching out to our right. The air was still heavy with salt and the occasional whiff of kelp. The road clung to the coastal contours, as if following invisible rails. As the morning wore on, the wispy clouds that had hung low at dawn burned off, revealing an azure sky and a sea mirroring its rich hue. The temperature climbed, not quite Mediterranean, but certainly not typical for North Cape. We stopped at a remote café-cum-gift shop and met a silversmith who claimed such conditions graced this region on only ten days a year, if that. We were fortunate indeed.

'Last week,' the silversmith remarked, 'two motorcyclists were blown clean off the road and campervans overturned. It was that windy.'

We exchanged grateful glances. We were indeed blessed.

The landscape had shifted to an uncompromising tundra, a prodigious expanse of brown moss and grass dotted with small lakes, devoid of any trees. Suddenly we plunged into another immense tunnel, the Nordkapptunnelen, which led to Magerøya, the island technically connected to the mainland and home to Nordkapp. Nearly seven kilometres long and reaching almost 700 feet below sea level, the tunnel was an impressive feat of engineering.

We pulled off the road for a rest, eager to savour the day. We had all the time in the world. We wandered across the hard, brown-and-green tundra, with its sedges, mosses and lichens, following a meandering path towards a large cabin by the fjord. It was an idyllic spot, a haven of solitude in this rugged landscape.

The road became hillier as we neared Honningsvåg, the tiny town serving Nordkapp, through which all visitors must pass, including the cruise ship throngs. The road wound upwards gracefully, an irresistible impulse propelling us forward. Huge vistas opened up over the sea. Surely that was the Barents Sea and Nordkapp in the distance, a mere speck now, but those buildings must be it. Excitement mounted. Steep cliffs plunged away on the right. Then, around a bend, two kiosks appeared. We screeched to a halt.

We had reached Nordkapp. Or at least, the commercial entrance to it. Unless you waited until late in the evening, entry was by ticket only: 310 NOK. Who would travel this far and turn back? We paid, received our official yellow sticky label badges and slithered our way onto the parking lot, joining a diverse collection of motorcycles, campervans, cars and pushbikes from various nations, their pilgrimages complete—for now, at least.

We wandered up to the headland plateau where a globe perches on the very edge of the 307-metre-high cliffs that plunge dramatically into the churning ocean. Next stop, Arctic ice and the North Pole. Even though we were at 71°10′21″N 25°47′04″E (further east than Istanbul and St Petersburg), we were still a mind boggling 2,102 kms from the North Pole. But this was the end of the line for our northward journey. It was downhill, er, southwards, from here.

Ralph and I embraced, the culmination of months of planning and thousands of miles of riding. He had a speech prepared:

"*Rydym wedi cyrraedd ym Nordkapp. Mae wedi bod yn daith hir, yn daith anodd, ond rydym yn hapus i fod yma.*"

Did I mention he speaks Welsh too? It was a poetic tribute to our journey's roots in the UK.

Roughly translated, he said it meant, 'We have reached Nordkapp. It has been a long, arduous journey, but we are happy to be here.'

I'll take his word for it.

Not to be outdone I mumbled something I'd prepared earlier in Norwegian.

'*Vi har verden for våre føtter.*'

'What's that mean?', he asked.

'We have the world at our feet.'

We stood quietly, contemplating the moment.

'We certainly have Europe at our feet. Just think, we are further north than anyone else right now. I've never been norther than this,' he added, smiling.

For a fleeting moment I recalled how a hotel yard in Oslo nearly ended our adventure prematurely, if not for a stroke of luck. And of how, even earlier, a slippery roundabout in Andalucía had almost brought my own long quest to a crashing end. A wave of gratitude washed over me as I realised how fortunate we were to have embarked on this journey. We had the means, both time and money, and we rode incredible machines. Nor could we forget the unwavering support of our wives, who had given us their blessing to chase our dreams. I was glad we'd made the trip together. It would have been a bittersweet moment to be here without someone I liked to share it with. This remote place would have felt lonelier, despite the crowds, and the thought of the more return journey? More daunting.

Ralph and I eagerly waited for our turn to pose under the globe. The large, elegant metal structure represented the culmination of a long journey for many travellers, a place to reflect on the vastness of the world and your place within it. There was much swapping of cameras and phones to snap celebratory selfies with the help of some fellow pilgrims. It was a pity we couldn't photograph the bikes under it. We'd have to wait until much later when the place was officially closed to sneak them past the barriers and we'd not enough time to hang around.

We wandered around the headland, taking in the *Children of the World* sculpture and the artistic *Mother and Child* statues. We reflected on the incredible places we'd visited and the diverse people we had met. It had been, we agreed, a truly challenging outing, well worth the effort.

'I'm glad we didn't listen to Klaus and turn back at Andenes,' I exclaimed.

'That was never going to happen. It was Nordkapp or bust for us, Stephen.'

After soaking in the fresh northern air, basking in the unexpected sunshine and stretching our bike-weary legs, it was time to gather some souvenirs. We couldn't resist the coveted pannier stickers, a badge of honour for those who'd made it this far. We grabbed a snack for the long ride ahead, before casting lingering glances back at the much-photographed globe and then reluctantly returning to our dirt-strewn bikes.

'Ready to turn our wheels southward, my friend?' I asked, a hint of wistfulness in my voice.

'Indeed,' he replied, smiling widely. 'But let's not forget, the journey is far from over. We've still got plenty to discover on our way home.'

With a renewed sense of purpose and hearts full of memories, we mounted our bikes and set off on the next chapter, leaving Nordkapp behind, but carrying its spirit with us always.

15

Turning Round
Lakselv–Kirkenes

Seventeen days after leaving Derbyshire we had finally achieved our goal. It felt like a triumph: 5,068 kilometres. But now the homeward journey called. I had devised a cunning plan to avoid retracing our steps by embarking on a new adventure down the Norwegian coast. We were going to sail on the Hurtigruten ship *MS Richard With* from its terminus at Kirkenes—seven kilometres from the Russian border—to Bergen in southern Norway.

You may recall that this plan stemmed from a desire to salvage a hefty deposit I'd paid for a winter coastal cruise with my wife. She, disliking ships, cold and darkness in equal measure, had made it abundantly clear that my surprise present wasn't exactly floating her boat.

We could have stayed near Nordkapp at Honningsvåg and caught the ship the following morning on its return journey. In fact, this was our Plan B in case we ran into trouble reaching Kirkenes. However, I wanted to push our travels as far as possible, to where the barriers to progress were literally impenetrable steel. That meant the Norway–Russia border at Storskog, where Finnmark meets Murmansk Oblast. Even though we'd already had a long day reaching

Nordkapp, we still had 190 kilometres to ride, mostly retracing our earlier steps to reach our overnight stop in Lakselv. Ralph and I had decided over a few beers earlier in the trip that riding 528 kms from Nordkapp to Kirkenes in one day was simply too much. We needed to find somewhere to stay en route.

As we rode south along the slender, picturesque Porsangerfjord, this time with the water on our left, we drank in the wonderful scenery and gloried in the winding roads. We knew that soon we'd be turning inland, leaving the sea behind for over a week and the salty breeze that had become our constant companion on two wheels would be a distant memory.

Herds of white reindeer, some with calves trailing behind, ambled across the road and over the heather-strewn rocks lining the route. We pulled into a lay-by for an energy drink and watched them gambol along, aware of but unfazed by our presence. A few even posed for photos, as though they knew they were unofficial mascots of the region.

The sky remained a clear deep blue and the fjord's surface was only lightly ruffled with whitecaps. The fjord accompanied us to Lakselv where we, like countless others, stopped for petrol and a routine check of the bike's vital fluids. The machines were wearing a thick coat of dust and grime by now, as were we. Our guidebook summed up the small settlement of Lakselv: "Most travellers fill up with petrol and then drive right on by."

As it happened, we were not driving by as we'd opted to stop here overnight.

The Lakselv Hotel was a sprawling, somewhat ramshackle collection of red-brown buildings that vaguely resembled an army barracks, but with decidedly softer sheets. Of course, since I was hauling my bike gear and inner pannier bags, I was assigned the furthest room in the furthest building, down a flight of stairs. Given the hotel's sparse occupancy, I could only surmise that the reception staff possessed a sadistic streak, or perhaps they simply thought I needed the exercise.

The few guests present seemed to consist mainly of a small group of British helicopter engineers working on the new chopper base at Lakselv Banak Airport, primarily a search and rescue facility. The proximity to Russia, a nation with a resurgent military presence in the Arctic, explained NATO's renewed interest in bolstering its defences in the region. Just as the engineers were about to crack under our relentless interrogation, a steaming plate of salmon and frites arrived, saving them from spilling any classified beans. I guess we could have been taken for spies, though dishevelled Ralph was no Bond, nor was I Q.

We settled in with a post-prandial selection of beers and aquavit, the local firewater, to toast our successful Nordkapp mission and record our podcast notes. This had become an enjoyable way to recap our daily escapades.

'When we set off,' Ralph mused, 'I really didn't have a clue what I'd let myself in for. I knew it was a long way, of course, but it's been one surprising day after another, not knowing what's around the corner. I suppose that's been part of the thrill, the not knowing what's around the next bend, over the next mountain pass.'

'I agree,' I said, raising my glass in a toast. 'To the unexpected, the unplanned and the utterly unforgettable. And Ralph—' I paused, a genuine warmth filling my voice, 'thanks for taking the time out to come and share this trip with me.'

Ralph looked at me with surprise, then a broad smile spread across his face. 'Honestly, Stephen, I wouldn't have missed it for the world. It's been an absolute blast, wouldn't you say?'

I nodded. Neither of us had known how it would pan out. Being work colleagues and casual friends is a different proposition to the close, trusting partnership that being riding buddies demands. But it had worked. It had been great.

'Absolutely. And hey, who knows? Maybe we'll tackle another challenging journey together someday.'

'Now you're talking,' Ralph exclaimed, raising his glass once more. 'To future exploits, wherever they may lead us.'

We clinked glasses again, sealing the unspoken bond of friendship forged on countless miles of open road, through rain and shine, laughter and mishaps. It was a moment of pure connection, a reminder that the true magic of travel lies not only in the places we visit, but in the people we share it with.

Karasjok to Kirkenes

The morning was sunny and hot as we threw all our bags on board for another long day in the saddle but not before completing a crucial task: applying our Nordkapp stickers to the bikes. The panniers were covered in souvenirs of places we'd visited, but we'd left a prime position for these, the most prized of all.

At Karasjok we pulled into a Circle K service station (the Canadian giant dominates the Norwegian market), filled our tanks in anticipation of a long stretch without fuel and grabbed a coffee and cinnamon bun to enjoy in the sunshine. An elderly Italian solo motorcyclist on a BMW, covering 700 kms a day, and a young couple on heavily laden pushbikes, managing seventy, both enquired about our tips for their respective routes to Nordkapp. Their experiences would be quite different, I mused. It was hard to offer any meaningful advice beyond 'watch out for the cross-winds' and 'keep going and enjoy it.'

Within a few kilometres of the town, we crossed the Finnish border, which lies in the middle of the River Teno. In winter it is possible to walk across the ice between the two countries. We stopped in the middle of the bridge, the

"Suomi" sign plastered with stickers from past travellers. Our front wheels were in Finland but our rears touched Norwegian tarmac.

Of the 265 kms from Karasjok to Kirkenes, practically every one was arrow straight. Where Norway had been a lilting melody full of twists and turns, Finland was a monotonous drone; where Norway had offered hilly vistas, Finland was pancake flat; where Norway had been drop-dead beautiful, Finland was, well, let's say it lacked a certain *je ne sais quoi*.

To stave off boredom we amused ourselves by overtaking each other, always within the speed limits of course (though we may have occasionally strayed over the double yellows, allegedly). The occasional bridge provided a brief thrill, but mostly we were met with an endless landscape of short pine trees and fleeting glimpses of the countless lakes. There weren't even potholes to dodge. As we were both on the verge of nodding off, a pair of elk ambled across the road in front of us—a much-needed wake-up call. In the middle of nowhere, we stumbled upon a small wooden hut selling a random assortment of cervidae parts: deer skins, elk skulls and unidentifiable moose bits. On aerodynamic grounds alone, I had to talk Ralph out of buying a set of antlers for his top box, though he insisted on posing next to a giant wooden statue of a bear salmon-fishing. It was hard to tell which was the grizzlier specimen.

By mid afternoon the heat was scorching, so we stopped at Sevettijarvi. No facilities, of course, only a large car park next to a lake. We wandered off into the woods to answer nature's call. Ralph emerged a few minutes later, flailing his arms in a frantic St Vitus dance.

'Mozzies! Mozzies!' he shrieked, his voice rising an octave with each syllable. 'They're a' ower me! Waur than the midgies in Skye!'

And they were. Millions of the little blighters had descended upon us the moment we'd stopped. I had a secret weapon: my fold-away midge helmet. Not exactly a fashion statement, but it proved to be a lifesaver in that moment. The route from Karasjok through northern Finland eventually popped out again into Norway west of Neiden or, as the Finns call it, Näätämö. They do like an umlaut or two. On we rode, past countless forests and lakes, covering a total of 381 kms for the day. By late afternoon we reached Kirkenes, the most far-flung outpost of Norway and the West; as far east as Cairo and a stone's throw from the Russian border. We swiftly dumped our gear in our rooms at the Scandic Hotel and headed out. Both of us were eager to go to the Russian frontier.

It took only a few minutes to hit the road east again. Our exhaust notes echoed loudly in the new tunnel by the Storskog–Borisoglebsk border crossing. It was well-lit and eerily empty. Had the border been open we would be only a three-hour drive from Murmansk, the nuclear submarine base of the formidable Russian Northern Fleet. We had arrived on the doorstep of the Russian Bear.

As I gazed across a small lake towards the gently rolling hills in the distance, a shiver ran down my spine. That was Russia over there. It was a chilling reminder that the border was not just a line on a map, but a dividing line between two distinctly different worlds.

We rolled up to the border gates, firmly locked with a sturdy chain. No sign of life stirred in no man's land beyond, though I was certain we were being watched on CCTV. Since the war in Ukraine, the gates had been closed to ordinary Russians wanting to enter Norway, and only a handful of fishermen with dual nationality were allowed to cross into the Schengen zone.

Reaching the easternmost point of our journey, we paused to take photos by the border fence. This was it, we could venture no further east. It was time to turn around and begin the long journey back to the UK.

The closure of the border with Russia had clearly had a significant impact on the Kirkenes economy, which had been heavily reliant on Russian shoppers. Street signs in both Cyrillic and Norwegian were a stark reminder of the town's close ties with Russia and why the shops used to be filled with items difficult to obtain across the border, such as baby milk, nappies, coffee and soap. Now, with the Russian shoppers gone, a sense of unease lingered beneath the town's quieter façade. This was compounded by the fact that roughly 10% of the residents are Russians.

The strength of local feeling against the Putin regime was palpable. Outside the restaurant, a bright blue and yellow van, echoing the Ukrainian flag, patrolled the streets. "Stop War, Stop Putin" was emblazoned across its sides, a clear message of solidarity and resistance.

Desperate for a drink, we beelined towards the hotel bar and mingled with an international gathering of travellers who had made their own journeys to the end of the road. It was a mini United Nations. I had a momentary vision of the cantina scene in Star Wars, as the bar buzzed with a mix of languages and accents. We squeezed onto a pair of battered chrome stools at the bar. The Scots bartender slammed another round of drinks on the counter.

'Another one for the road, warriors?' he chuckled. 'Coz you look like you've seen a few miles in those leathers, friends,' he added, eyeing our attire.

'We've finished a ride up from the UK,' Ralph replied, beaming with scarcely suppressed delight. 'All the way to Nordkapp.'

Two very attractive middle-aged ladies from Minnesota perked up sitting next to us at hearing this.

'You rode the whole way up there?' one of them exclaimed. 'That's awesome.'

'We did,' I chimed in, 'we're Knights of the Road, Two-wheeled Adventurers, Asphalt Cowboys.'

I figured our chiselled appearances might add credibility to my claims. In truth they probably just thought we were a bit, well, scruffy.

An older German couple, who had been quietly nursing their drinks, turned to us out of curiosity.

'I used to ride a Harley, I vos younger,' the man said, gesturing towards his wife with a twinkle in his eye.

'She vud sit on ze back, her arms wrapped around my vaist, ze vind in her hairs.'

He paused, a nostalgic smile playing on his lips.

'Those vere good times, ja? Ze open road, ze thrill of ze riding. A *Fräulein* on ze back seat. It's a feeling you two must know vell.'

Ralph and I looked at each other bemused. We shared his feelings, but had missed out on ze *Fräuleins* somehow.

The Minnesotan ladies were curious to hear about our journey, peppering us with questions about the challenges of riding these northerly landscapes. We wondered if they might like to ride pillion with us. We could probably make room.

'Thanks, but we're headed to Gothenburg to see Bruce Springsteen,' one of them replied.

'So. You're Born to be Wild?' I suggested to our American friends, cheekily.

'No, that was Steppenwolf,' came the innocent reply. 'Bye, cowboys.'

Kirkenes to Hurtigruten

We had a morning to explore Kirkenes. A visit to the *Grenselandmuseet* (Borderland Museum) appealed. It was a poignant reminder of the region's turbulent past, particularly during World War II, when Kirkenes, along with Bodø and Narvik, became a focal point of conflict due to their valuable iron ore deposits. Kirkenes endured relentless bombing raids by Soviet forces because of its strategic location and occupation by German troops. The town was almost completely destroyed. Only thirteen buildings out of 300 survived the onslaught.

The museum vividly captured the struggles of the local population during this terrible period. Stories of families seeking refuge in the mines at Bjørnevatn to escape the aerial bombardment, the town's eventual liberation by the Red Army, and the subsequent challenges of rebuilding their lives in the aftermath of destruction were both heart-wrenching and inspiring.

The museum also explored the complex relationship between Norway and its eastern neighbour. The border, a constant presence in the lives of the people of Sør-Varanger, has been both a source of cooperation and tension throughout history. In recent times, it witnessed a peculiar phenomenon: the influx in 2015 of over 5,000 Syrian refugees on bicycles. This mass migration was fuelled by both the weaponisation of illegal immigration by Putin and a border agreement that barred people from crossing on foot or in vehicles without valid documents. A loophole allowed cyclists to enter Norway and the Schengen area. Cheap Russian bikes were provided by Moscow for the purpose. Many of these bikes remain on display in the museum, a witness to the ingenuity and desperation of those seeking a new life. The Russian border was not only a geographical line, it was an entity that shaped the lives of those in its shadow. Borders had been a feature of our trip; our own travels had taken us across seven of them, peacefully and without drama.

16

Coastal Express
Kirkenes–Bergen

Hurtigruten from Kirkenes to Bergen

We were the lone motorcyclists to board the *MS Richard With* at Kirkenes, Hurtigruten's northernmost stop. While most passengers opted for the twelve-day cruise package, Ralph and I chose this unique way to retrace part of our journey. The Hurtigruten experience wasn't cheap, but compared to the cost of fuel, hotels and meals on the return trip, it made sense.

For the next six days we settled into the delightfully lazy ship routine. My smelly boots were finally confined to my cabin and we quickly adapted to the ship's schedule, which centred mainly on food, which was fishy and fabulous. The ship made regular stops on its gentle voyage back to Bergen, so at least we got a chance to burn off some calories and get some much-needed exercise.

As we sailed southward, familiar places we had visited on our bikes appeared. We also saw charming towns we'd missed on the way up, like Molde and Ålesund, tempting us with the prospect of a return trip. Sailing was a welcome change of pace, a chance to unwind and reflect after weeks on the road. I wrote and read and slept. I thought of my dad, with whom I'd had that early adventure in Germany. He'd have loved this rugged coastline and its wild, raw nature. Sadly we never did get to make a trip to Norway together and now it's too late. He never knew that there is Norwegian DNA in the family. Not a lot, just 4%, but it was on his side; perhaps that explained why I felt so at peace in this wonderful country. I realised perhaps more than ever that our time is limited and we must make the most of each opportunity to enjoy it as best we can. I drank a small aquavit toast to him, my cheeks moist and cold with tears in the deck breeze.

It was midsummer, so the sun never dipped below the horizon. As midnight on the solstice approached Ralph and I were to be found quaffing the rest of the bottle of firewater in one of the two hot tubs on the stern deck.

'You might spot a whale while you're soaking,' he joked.

I laughed, shaking my head. 'Not likely. We'd be lucky to see a dolphin out here.'

But as we settled into the soothing warmth of the tub, a sight emerged from the starboard side that made us gasp in unison. A whale surfaced about 250 metres away, its signature spout shooting into the air like a steamy geyser. I reached for my camera to capture the magnificent creature but it disappeared as quickly as it had appeared, leaving us breathless and awestruck.

'Stunning, simply stunning,' was Ralph's verdict, and for once that was an understatement.

He had picked up his notebook again on board and passed the time by scribbling observations in his journal. Of the solstice he wrote:

"A flat sea, roads, bridges, and birds. It's the longest day today, the shortest night. A concept that has no meaning in the land of the midnight sun, where the sun doesn't sink below the horizon but subsides slowly to a place where it still shines, where you can still feel its warmth, before moving slowly from the west to the east.

The weather on this solstice day is beautiful. The sky is iridescent blue, the sea is flat calm, a looking glass to the clarity of the air and the sky. The mountains are jagged, fearsome, and snow-capped still. By the side of the fjord, a road runs, a narrow river with little traffic, and the little there is moves slowly from somewhere to who knows where, with nobody in any hurry.

The islands are sometimes connected by bridges and sometimes by tunnels, and sometimes not at all, and a ferry takes the cars who are not in a hurry to another island where they can continue to not be in a hurry.

And this is the north of Norway, on Lofoten."

As we continued south, the weather turned a bit dreich, but we still managed to step ashore whenever the itinerary allowed. Hammerfest, allegedly the most northerly town in the world, was brutalist and utilitarian. It lacked airs and graces but had a motorcycle club, appropriately named MC Hammerfest. In Trollfjord we watched sea eagles swoop to pick up writhing salmon the size of my arm from the cold waters. Our route took us back to Svolvaer and the Lofoten Islands; we were overjoyed to be back there. We spent some time in the local War Memorial Museum, where Norway's cruel suffering in WW2 was documented in unsparing detail. Geographically the centre of the Norwegian coastline, Brønnøysund was a beautiful little town and we stumbled upon a delightful music concert in a church, while we sheltered from the rain. It was all most agreeable and were it not for the ship's siren we might have lingered longer.

The Hurtigruten provided a relaxing alternative way of seeing Norway. It was like the pepper sauce on a deliciously cooked steak, not the main course, but an enhancement that added depth and flavour to the overall experience. It also saved thousands of kilometres of riding down the far less interesting inland eastern route, if we had wanted to avoid retracing much of our route. As we approached Bergen's bustling port, and disembarkation, the sun re-emerged and the temperature soared. I was sweating profusely even before donning my heavy riding gear, which had been neglected for days. The cargo area became a makeshift sauna as we awaited the signal to disembark. We left our sea legs behind and became landlubbers once more.

In Bergen

But first, a challenge. Finding a parking space in this labyrinthine city was proving to be an uphill battle. Not for nothing is it known as the city of seven mountains. And as we navigated the steep and narrow cobbled streets to our prized parking place high above the harbour, I had a growing suspicion that Bergen held more surprises. Down below us vessels jostled for mooring spots while sleek yachts were tethered cheek-by-jowl with weathered fishing boats in the harbour. The bustling fish market, Torget, at the water's edge, was brimming with glistening slabs of fish and crustaceans, some still wriggling like stranded sunbathers.

We locked up the bikes carefully. Although it's a very safe city Bergen no doubt has its share of opportunist thieves and we were nervous. We flung our gear into the hotel and made a quick getaway into town. In the summer heat, the local women, blessed with fair hair and Nordic beauty, embraced the sunshine, their short skirts and breezy blouses adding a touch of carefree elegance to the scene. They strolled along the waterfront, admired by handsome Nordic men sporting designer stubble and gym-honed physiques.

In front of the Metz Bar sat two grizzly bikers, beers in hand, wearing tatty tee-shirts, piratical headgear and shades to hide the bags under their eyes. A casual observer might have assumed we were also talent spotting. We were. But bikes as well as the girls had caught our eye.

'Bellagio,' Ralph exclaimed, pointing excitedly towards the harbourside. 'You know, I'm sure that's a Bellagio.'

I squinted into the afternoon sun. 'You mean the one that's riding past us right now?'

'No, the one parked on the edge of the pavement,' Ralph clarified, enthusiastically. 'With the twin pipes. It's a cracking Guzzi, quite rare.'

The good burghers of Bergen, we discovered, had a delightful custom of holding an impromptu bike fest most evenings by the harbour wall on Bryggen, with its beautiful, brightly coloured wooden buildings. Good weather brought out a cornucopia of motorcycles, from a pristine Triumph T120 Bonneville, its black paint gleaming like a sergeant-major's boots, to a battered Beemer adorned with more stickers and random bits than any bike I'd ever seen. An old fish crate, repurposed as a top box, added a touch of quirky charm.

'Look at that beauty,' Ralph exclaimed, pointing to a vintage Norton Commando. 'Wouldn't mind taking that for a spin.'

'Well, if you can find its owner, I'm sure he or she would be delighted to let a random Scotsman simply ride off into the sunset on their pride and joy,' I said, forgetting there was no sunset.

We finished our beers and wandered over to chat with the riders, eager to swap stories and rubberneck their machines. The atmosphere was relaxed and convivial, a shared passion for motorcycles bridging any language barriers.

We were tempted to join the party with our own bikes. Perhaps, just perhaps, we could become honorary members of this exclusive club, if only for an evening. But they were securely locked away in a secret location and we didn't fancy risking a hefty parking bill. Besides, as Ralph pointed out,

'We wouldn't want to upstage the locals, would we?' We didn't see a single Nordkapp sticker anywhere.

Our modest hotel was around the corner from the action, a stone's throw from the spectacular funicular railway. The rooms were so compact that I had to shuffle sideways from the bed to the shower, which doubled as my laundry. Traveling so light had meant regular scrubbing sessions with pants in the sink (not while wearing them, obviously). The TV served as a makeshift drying rack, a sight that must have puzzled the cleaner.

'You know,' Ralph mused as he came to compare our bijou rooms, 'I'm starting to think our bikes have more spacious accommodation than we do.'

'I'm sure they'd also appreciate a good wash after the miles we've put on them,' I replied, tossing a pair of damp socks onto the telly.

Despite the cramped quarters, the hotel's location couldn't be beaten. We were within walking distance of everything, from the bustling fish market to the historic Bryggen area. And with the impromptu bike fest a stroll away, we were ideally situated to soak up Bergen's lively atmosphere. And that, we agreed, was worth a little bit of spatial compromise.

I confess, this wasn't Plan A. We should have been luxuriating in roomy accommodation at the Bergen Børs hotel around the corner. However, I had miscalculated the number of nights on the Hurtigruten, thinking it was six instead of five. As a result, I'd only budgeted for one night in Bergen, not two. Our downgrade to the Harbour Hotel was a happy accident, granting us an extra day to explore Bergen, a buffer in case of any bike troubles and the opportunity to chat with the charming bartender in the hotel bar.

Anastasia, a beautiful young woman in her early twenties, was born in Norway to Greek parents and spoke English with a London twang. She was fluent in Greek, of course, but also had Norwegian, Swedish, Spanish, French and German up her linguistic sleeve. Impressive, although Ralph did deduct points for her lack of Welsh.

'So, Anastasia,' he enquired, leaning nonchalantly against the bar, 'how does a young woman with such a diverse linguistic background end up pulling pints in Bergen?'

He has an unconventional store of chat-up lines.

Anastasia laughed, her eyes sparkling. 'I've always loved languages,' she replied, expertly topping off a pint of Mack, 'and after university, I wanted to travel and immerse myself in different cultures. Bergen has the right vibes: beautiful scenery, cool people and a chance to improve my Norwegian. Plus, I met a local guy who completely swept me off my feet.' She winked playfully. 'He's the reason I decided to stay.'

We decided to take the funicular up to Fløyen. The views from the summit were spectacular, panoramic vistas of Bergen and its surroundings stretching out before us. However, as I stood there taking in the sights, a potent musky odour wafted by. I glanced at Ralph, who was also wrinkling his nose. This wasn't his usual aftershave; this was distinctly *Eau de Chèvre*.

'I think we've found the source of that pungent perfume,' Ralph said, pointing towards a herd of goats meandering about the summit.

Dozens of them roamed freely, but these were high-tech goats equipped with solar-powered transponders. If they strayed too close to the fence at the edge of the precipice, their necks received a mild electric shock, like a caprine version of the buzz wire game.

'Clever,' I mused. 'Pity they haven't extended the system to suicidal reindeer and kamikaze moose on the roads.'

The top of Fløyen was a haven for families, with countless trails and impressive playgrounds. Ralph and I, not for the first time on the trip, embraced our inner kid and scrambled across rope ladders, conquered challenging climbing towers, and then whizzed down the slides. Not even a grumpy park warden in sight to dampen our fun.

An hour or so later we talked animatedly as we made our way back down the hill, marvelling at the quirky charm of Bergen and its eclectic mix of attractions. The Culture Vulture Bikers had been dormant for a few days, so we set off to replenish our cultural quotient by exploring some of Bergen's renowned museums.

Our first stop was Fantoft to see another stave church (*Stavkirke*). Sadly, although the first church was built on the site in 1150, an arsonist destroyed Fantoft and several other magnificent *Stavkirken* in 1992. The current church is a replica, but still impressive.

Next stop, a little out of town, was the Edvard Grieg Museum in Troldhaugen. It and the composer's former home were in a sublime setting, overlooking Lake Nordås, where he and his wife Nina spent twenty-two summers. Their shared grave is also on site, though tucked away in a cliff face, requiring rope and climbing skills to read the inscriptions. They wouldn't let us play *Chopsticks* on his piano. Can't think why.

The light railway (free with the Bergen Card) whisked us back to the city centre in style. We'd missed lunch and my good intentions of waiting until dinner evaporated the moment I spotted the scruffy red and yellow wooden shack that is the celebrated Trekroneren Pølsekiosk. This fast food stand is the crème de la crème of sausages. They offer artisan bangers made from wild game, reindeer, lamb, pork and beef. The aroma wafting from the rows of sausages sizzling on the griddle was as irresistible as the scent of a chip shop after a chilly winter's football practice. Faced with dozens of sauce choices, I couldn't resist diving into a Bratwurst mit Currysoße. I'd learned to love these meaty morsels when I was working in Bavaria all those years ago, and could never resist them even now.

Earlier in the day, we'd visited the *Norge Fiskerimuseum* (Norwegian Fisheries Museum). After our deep dives into the fishing industry in Lofoten and on the Hurtigruten, we reckoned we were at GCSE level in fish knowledge. So when the ruddy cheeked receptionist at the museum started quizzing us about klippfisk, we were quicker to answer than sharks in a salmon net.

'What's the difference between stockfish and klippfisk?' she asked, her grin clearly not expecting much response.

'Easy peasy,' Ralph replied confidently. 'Stockfish is unsalted, klippfisk is salted.'

'And what's the significance of the Catholic Church's meat-free Fridays?' she continued, raising an eyebrow.

'Boosted the demand for preserved cod,' I chimed in, 'sending Norwegian exports soaring across Europe.'

The receptionist nodded approvingly. 'You two are quite the experts,' she congratulated us, probably thinking *smartarses*.

Walking back into town, we passed by smart office buildings where many employees seemed to be sporting swimming gear and taking refreshing dips in the harbour during their coffee breaks.

'Now that's what I call a perk,' Ralph remarked with a sigh. 'Imagine being able to swap teleconferences for trunks or briefcases for bikinis.'

'Yeah, especially those,' I chipped in.

Bergen truly was a treasure trove of noteworthy sights and experiences. I was grateful for the unexpected extra day, allowing us to fully immerse ourselves in this seductive city. At the Bryggens Museum on the waterfront, we learned about the tumultuous history of Bergen's many fires and examined the numerous runes unearthed during various archaeological digs. Most bore inscriptions, some professing undying love, others seemingly invitations to meet Ingrid behind the boat shed.

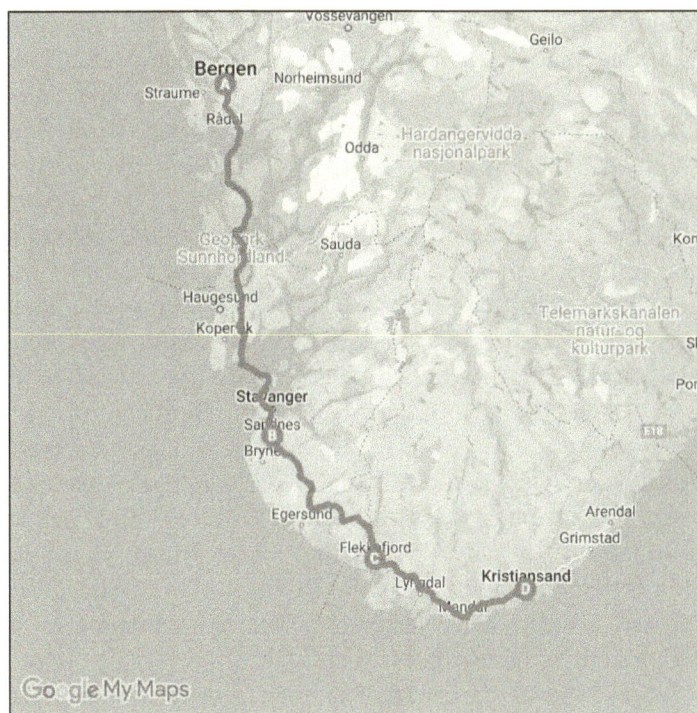

Bergen to Sandnes

It was time to hit the road again. We geared up for the final legs of our journey. The routine felt familiar and comforting, though never completely relaxing. There's always something to think about, too many minor mishaps that could derail the day. We retrieved our bikes from their secure spot. The car park operators had an open-door policy which we took full advantage of, avoiding the exorbitant fees.

Bergen's challenging roads greeted us within minutes of setting off in the first rain for days. We battled greasy, cambered cobblestones—thighs tense, grips tight and forearms rigid. In due course, the downpour eased, the cobbles smoothed out into tarmac, and long tunnels guided us south toward Sandnes. I regained my flow, feeling at ease

with the bike's quarter-ton weight as I coaxed it through the
sweeping bends of the E39 towards the Halhjem–Våga ferry.
The coastal route from Bergen to Stavanger would be a
marathon by road alone; the direct route utilised islands like
steppingstones, with ferries again an integral part of the
network.

In the thousands of kilometres I'd ridden, I had never
encountered another Honda NT1100 rider, despite its
popularity as the top-selling touring bike in Europe. Perhaps
they all headed south, leaving the Germans and their
ubiquitous BMW GS1250s to dominate the north (and
everywhere else). Yet, in the queue for the Halhjem ferry, an
alter ego appeared: 38 ELF, an identical Honda, ridden by
Jukka Kainulainen from Finland. Over coffee on board we
swapped touring stories about Norway and other
destinations. Jukka's bike sported stickers from Romania
(the Transalpina route), and the Balkans, where he'd visited
Mostar, which was a destination that was creeping onto
Ralph's and my future travel wishlist.

From Sandvik to Leirvik, the road hugged the striking
coastline, hopping over Hebridean-like bridges and islets
before coming to a halt at a metal barrier in Arsvågen. The
second major ferry of the day would carry us across the
Boknafjorden to Mortavika, followed by a series of island-
hopping bridges leading to Stavanger. This oil city, twinned,
unsurprisingly, with Aberdeen, was a bit of a letdown after
Bergen's charm. However, the waterfront and clapboard
houses were undeniably pretty and bustling with
preparations for a food and drink festival. Our hopes for
delicious street food were dashed, though, as we were a day
early. Typical. We settled for sandwiches on the breezy
promenade. In an already pricey country, Stavanger had a
reputation for being the most expensive, which is why our
billet was in nearby Sandnes.

Stepping into the Kronen Gaard Hotel was like stepping
back in time. Built in 1898, the historic building seemed

untouched by the modern world and exuded an air of charming antiquity. It felt like we were sleeping in a well-loved antique shop, surrounded by history and whispers of the past. However, the few staff members were young and energetic. Jolina, a young Serbian from Croatia, seemed to be the hotel manager, bartender, waitress and probably gardener rolled into one. With few other guests to keep her busy, we found ourselves discussing Balkan politics over dinner.

'I'm planning to return home eventually,' Jolina revealed, 'but I know it won't be easy to find work with my background and surname.'

The lingering effects of ethnic cleansing following the breakup of Yugoslavia in the early 1990s were still painfully evident. Discrimination was rife. It was yet another reminder of Europe's fractured history and the ongoing struggles for reconciliation.

'This trip has been eye-opening,' I remarked, swirling the wine in my glass. 'I learned how tough the Norwegians had it in the war. The place is steeped in its history. But so many divisions still shape Europe today.'

Jolina nodded sombrely. 'I hope one day in my country we can learn from the past and build a better future together,' she said ruefully.

Sandnes to Kristiansand

The following day, after a hearty Norwegian breakfast shared with a group of cheerful cycling retirees, Ralph and I parted ways for only the second time during our journey. He, eager to experience the contrasting scenery and pace of the main highway and to steer away from some of the hairier hairpin bends, opted for the more conventional E39. I was drawn by the allure of the Nordsjøveien coastal road, one I'd seen on YouTube.

We pulled up at the exit from the car park. I'd go left and Ralph, right. I turned to him and we fist-bumped.

'Well,' I said, 'enjoy the ride. See you in Flekkefjord for a well-deserved coffee and cake.'

A grin spread across his face. 'Last yin there's buyin', Stephen!'

I patted my pockets to check my wallet was there. I was going to need it.

The coastal route proved to be a sensory delight, with the scent of seaweed filling my helmet for miles as the flat highway hugged the stony beach. It was a traffic-free ride, the wind whistling past my ears, and the rhythmic sound of the waves crashing against the shore for miles my only companion.

At Hauge, with the heat of the day building under a relentless sun, the scent of freshly laid tarmac replaced the briny smell of seaweed as I waited at the roadworks traffic lights with a couple of studded-leather bikers on Harleys. When the light turned green, they roared off, their engines shattering the tranquil air. I, however, was sipping the route like a fine wine. The bends were beautifully engineered, predictable yet demanding exactly the right amount of skill, an optimal blend of line, pace, lean angle and torque.

I came onto the crux of the Nordsjøveien. It was a thrilling ride along the challenging R44 and through the precipitous hairpin bends above Jøssingfjord. I felt almost suspended in time, with ever changing views of lakes and forests, mountains and fjords that unfolded around each corner. A long, low concrete wall on my right was the only barrier between the road and the fjord, hundreds of feet below. The rock face on my left suddenly jutted out over the road and I was swallowed by a dark tunnel carved into the cliff. Moments later I was spat out the other side, directly into a final sharp hairpin turn that descended steeply towards Jøssingfjord, a place etched in history by the *Altmark* incident.

The so named German tanker, carrying British prisoners of war, was attacked by the Royal Navy in neutral waters, an event that some historians argue provided Hitler with the pretext he needed to invade Norway. The fjord, silent witness to that dramatic event, now lay before me, its tranquil waters belying its tumultuous past.

This superb stretch of road deserves to be better known. It's scenic, historic and challenging—the Trollstigen of the South.

As I rolled into Flekkefjord, I spotted two familiar figures; one was Ralph, who'd enjoyed his alternative route, the other, waiting by a sleek grey bike, was Erling Larsen, a retired oil guy with a passion for his Honda NT1100. We had arranged to meet him here via Facebook, on which he was the administrator for the Norway Honda NT1100 group. He'd been a helpful source of information for the trip and we wanted to swap tales.

'Stephen!' Erling exclaimed, a broad smile on his face as I pulled up beside him.

'*Hjertelig velkommen til Flekkefjord*! Welcome to Flekkefjord. How was the ride on the Nordsjøveien?'

'Absolutely superb,' I replied, removing my helmet. 'What a fabulous stretch of road. I loved it. Twisty, scenic, Wow factor big time. How was your route?'

Erling beamed. 'Not as challenging as yours. Glad you enjoyed it. I had a dentist's appointment in town this morning. I only live a short way from here, bit of a commute really.'

As we walked together to a nearby coffee shop, he shared a hair-raising tale of an encounter the previous year with a reindeer that nearly injured him and which almost totalled the Honda. Fortunately, he emerged unscathed, unlike the reindeer.

'It was like something out of a bad cartoon,' Erling said 'One moment I'm cruising along, sticking to the speed limit, enjoying the scenery, the next, this massive deer comes out of the woods. I swear, I could see its nostrils flaring as it charged towards me.'

The dead reindeer probably provided plenty of sausage later... but the £7,000 dent in his machine and his wallet showed that the strict *fartsgrensen* are lifesavers. A few kilometres an hour faster and he'd have been toast. His story reminded us that even experienced riders aren't immune to the unexpected hazards of the road.

After lunch spent talking about the tough Norwegian winters and how, when spring comes, he pulls his bike out of hibernation and sets off on solo adventures, Erling sped off towards Lyngdal, a distant, cheery wave his farewell. We followed at a more leisurely pace, even more mindful of the fearsome speed cameras as we made our way steadily to Kristiansand.

Before we'd set off on this Nordic jaunt the return journey to England posed a logistical puzzle which had occupied me for a while, until I landed on a solution. Retracing our steps through Sweden and Denmark would add considerable distance to an already lengthy voyage and much of the route would be familiar, unless we went far out of our way. The shorter ferry from southern Norway to Hirsthals in northern Denmark, followed by a cross-country trip through Germany, was an attractive option. I was about to book tickets, when I stumbled upon the Holland–Norway Line's new overnight service to Emden, Germany. Cabins on these cruise-ferries fill up quickly, so I booked it without hesitation. I'd spent restless nights on ferry seats and floors before; those were experiences I didn't want to repeat.

A couple of hours after leaving Flekkefjord, Ralph and I lined up to board the *MS Romantika*, which looked more like a cruise ship than a hardworking ferry. We chatted to fellow bikers in the queue. There was a middle-aged Norwegian couple en route to the south of France. She, petite, blonde, a newbie rider, rode a heavily laden, brand-new GS, almost as tall as she was. They planned to tackle dirt tracks on their route. An accident waiting to happen, we feared.

For many years there have been no direct crossings from Norway to Britain, other than for freight. Another rider, Gary, on a Royal Enfield, was heading back to Aberdeen from Helsinki. He was frustrated knowing that home was a mere 350 miles away westwards across the North Sea. When we landed in Emden he faced a further 1,500-mile journey by road. We think of the USA as being the country of big distances, but Europe offers mammoth trips too, as we had found out.

Bill from Ipswich sat astride a neon-green Kawasaki, returning from his annual pilgrimage to meet fellow enthusiasts near Oslo. He had a whole collection of Kawasakis at home. His passion verged on obsession from which we were rescued by the tannoy announcement to start boarding. We skipped back to the bikes and started engines for our last few metres on Norwegian soil. There was a magic to Norway that had brought these adventurers together on this ship, united by our love of motorcycle touring.

We leant on the stern deck rail as the ship left Kristiansand and Norway faded into the distance.

'You know what, Ralph, I feel sad at leaving; it's been simply wonderful, this trip,' I sighed.

There was a pause. I wondered if he'd heard. Then came a familiar Scottish voice: 'Still o'er these scenes my mem'ry wakes, And fondly broods with miser care; Time but the impression stronger makes, As streams their channels deeper wear.'

'Yeah, it's been pure dead brilliant, so it has.'

I should have guessed that at this moment Ralph would have sought inspiration in Burns.

The wind picked up, turning playful gusts into a full-blown gale. Chairs on the stern deck took flight, joining a growing

pile by the railings. The ship's singer valiantly battled both
the elements and a rapidly dwindling audience, but even his
most ardent fans eventually retreated indoors, seeking
refuge from the coming storm.

Emden – Rotterdam – Hull – Midlands

Emden, the next morning, was shrouded in a dull mist and
drizzle, an uninviting start for the long trek to Rotterdam.
This leg proved to be the most challenging of the entire
journey, which made us appreciate the luck we'd had with
the weather for most of the way. Grey clouds mirrored our
glum mood as we battled kamikaze Dutch lorry drivers, who
seemed determined to overtake us despite our best efforts to
stay out of their way, as the tarmac grew wetter and spray
enveloped us from all sides.

Near Amsterdam, the motorway ballooned to a dizzying
twelve lanes, six in each direction, with spurs branching off

haphazardly. More than once, the deafening blast of an air horn warned us of an impending artic about to thunder past and then swerve across our path. Ralph and I kept up a nervous running commentary, trying to predict the next bandit's approach. It was exhausting.

We took refuge in a McDonald's to regain our composure and dry out. Over greasy burgers and lukewarm coffee, Ralph and I agreed that Klaus could keep his Holland. It was a relief to finally roll onto the P&O ferry *Pride of Rotterdam* for the overnight journey back to Hull. We were grateful to be in one piece after 385 extraordinarily difficult kilometres, the scariest I had ever ridden.

Our spirits were revived when we discovered cask Marston's Pedigree in the ship's bar, a treat we'd missed on the way over. Having worked at the brewery for many years, downing a few pints of it felt like a fitting way to toast our Nordkapp triumph.

'To Nordkapp, Ralph.' I raised my glass, a nostalgic smile on my face.

'To Nordkapp, and to surviving the Dutch motorways,' Ralph added with a hearty laugh.

We clinked glasses, the familiar taste of home a comforting reminder that our adventure was coming full circle.

The next morning, around 7.30 a.m., we rode off the ship to fill up with fuel and embark on the last stretch of our journey. Ralph and I rode together to a pub near my home in Derbyshire, for a final coffee and a chance to reflect on our incredible adventure. We sat in comfortable silence, the warmth of the coffee cup a soothing contrast to the cool morning air. Our eyes met across the table, a silent acknowledgment of the bond we'd forged over thousands of miles.

'I'll miss those endless Norwegian roads,' Ralph remarked, a hint of melancholy in his voice.

'And the reindeer sausages?' I added with a chuckle.

We laughed, the sound echoing through the quiet pub. It was nostalgic, knowing that our road trip had come to an end. But the memories we had created would last a lifetime.

'It's been a hell of a ride, Stephen,' Ralph said, raising his mug in a toast. 'To Nordkapp, to adventure, and to friendship.'

'One for the record books, that's for sure; nearly 4,000 miles since we left home twenty-nine days ago.'

'So, fancy doing another one next year?' I asked.

He raised an eyebrow, which I took as a yes.

I waved Ralph off on the short journey home, to catch up with family, laundry and his emails. We were both changed from the journey, in different ways. It had been the trip of a lifetime for us both, an extraordinary opportunity to do something special, to see places we might never see again, to travel with open minds and glad hearts. For Ralph, the trip was an escape from his busy work schedule and a chance to chill. For me it was the thrill of adventure and exploration while I still could.

My motorcycle had taken me the length of Europe. No further south or north could I travel. That box was ticked, and I began to think of what future exploits we might have.

I had one more call to make before I went back home. I'd not seen my mum for a long while. It was she who'd encouraged me to learn languages. In her younger days she had worked as a translator. Old and frailer now, she lived in a care home.

I walked into her small room, carrying my crash helmet and still wearing the gear I'd had on for a month.

'Oh, Stevie, it's you. Hang on a minute, I'm just finishing the crossword. Then you can tell me all about your adventures.'

Hurtigruten Coastal Express route
(reproduced by kind permission)

Acknowledgements

This book and indeed my adventures in the first place would not have been possible without the support and love of my wife, Judith. She has put up with my absences and with the long hours spent writing, without complaint, and has always encouraged me to follow my dreams, whether in the Scottish hills, flying over the green fields of the Peak District, or on two wheels. My family and friends have been great supporters and, when the occasion demanded it, constructive critics.

I was delighted that Ralph could join me for Nordkapp. We've known each other for years but this was the trip that changed us from being ex-colleagues to proper mates. His Zen-like calm, sense of humour and diligent research were huge assets on our journey. I look forward to many more days and weeks out on two wheels together.

My daughter, Nicola, made a great contribution to the book's cover design.

I am grateful to my sister, Julie, for her close attention to detail in an early version of the manuscript.

My thanks go to Alan Whelan, my editor. Alan is a far more adventurous motorcycle rider than I ever will be. Indeed, it was reading his own stories in Africa that inspired me to push my own boundaries. He was unfailingly patient and helpful in getting my first book to publication.

My friend Chris Stretton, whose dodgy Vespa I bought, fired up my enthusiasm for two wheels again.

Mark Minion of Bob Minion Motorcycles in Derby. Mark encouraged me onto a Honda motorbike for the first time and has always been a source of practical advice.

Lea Knowles' poem *Lofoten* appears by permission of Allpoetry.com.

Finally, I'm ever in debt to those I have met on the way, who have provided me with the material to write about, many of whom have subscribed to my Honda Wanderlust blog: https://substack.com/@stephenoliver

The Author

At seventeen, armed with a schoolboy's German and a thirst for adventure, I embarked on my first trip to Europe. It was a journey that would change my life, igniting a passion for exploring the world, immersing myself in different cultures and collecting languages like some gather stamps.

That summer I navigated the bustling streets of Cologne with my dad in tow, where we promptly lost our car. It was a baptism by fire—or rather, by misplaced vehicle. We stumbled through conversations with amused locals, backtracked through the city's dodgy alleyways and marvelled at the grandeur of Cologne Cathedral until eventually the local police helped us find our car, where we'd left it, on *Einbahnstrasse* (one-way street).

This misadventure sparked a lifelong passion for exploring the world, a passion further fuelled by my time at Oxford, where I honed my language skills and even caught the attention of MI6 (an offer I politely declined, preferring beer to Bond). My love of beer led to a career in brewing, which took me across the globe, from the beer gardens of Bavaria to the breweries in Beijing.

Years later, newly retired and with rusty languages to polish, I found myself drawn back to the open road, this time on a motorcycle. I was ready to rediscover the freedom of exploration, to embrace the unexpected, and to delve deeper into the heart of Europe, one country, one language, one beer at a time.